BMW 2500, 2800, 3.0, 3.3, Barv
1968-1977 Autobook

BMW 2500 1968-77
BMW 2800 1968-71
BMW 2800 CS, CA 1968-71
BMW 3.0 S, SA, SI 1971-77
BMW 3.0 CS, CSA, CSI, CSL 1971-75
BMW 3.0 LA 1975-77
BMW 3.3 L, LA, LIA 1974-77
BMW Bavaria 1972-74

The Autobooks series of Owners Workshop Manuals is republished by VelocePress
(www.VelocePress.com) in cooperation with Brooklands Books, Ltd.

For a complete list of the Autobooks series of Owners Workshop Manuals republished by VelocePress please visit our web site at www.VelocePress.com

Contents

Publication Information

© 2010 Veloce Enterprises Inc., San Antonio, Texas 78230
Reprinted in cooperation with Brooklands Books, Ltd., Surrey, England

The previous edition was issued as:

ISBN 0 85147 943 X

First Edition   1977
Second Edition, fully revised   1979

Information on the Use of this Publication

This series of manuals is an invaluable resource for the classic car enthusiast and a "must have" for owners interested in performing their own maintenance. These manuals include detailed repair and service data and comprehensive step-by-step instructions and illustrations on dismantling, overhauling, and re-assembly. There are many time saving hints and tips included and there is an easy to follow fault diagnosis at the end of each chapter. Certain assemblies require the use of expensive special tools and although repair information is included it is recommended that these repairs be performed by factory authorized service centers.

In today's information age we are constantly subject to changes in common practice, new technology, availability of improved materials and increased awareness of chemical toxicity. As such, it is advised that the user consult with an experienced professional prior to undertaking any procedure described herein. While every care has been taken to ensure correctness of information, it is obviously not possible to guarantee complete freedom from errors or omissions or to accept liability arising from such errors or omissions. Therefore, any individual that uses the information contained within, or elects to perform or participate in do-it-yourself repairs or modifications acknowledges that there is a risk factor involved and that the publisher or its associates cannot be held responsible for personal injury or property damage resulting from the use of the information or the outcome of such procedures.

It is important that the reader recognizes that any instructions may refer to either the right-hand or left-hand sides of the vehicle or the components and that the directions are followed carefully. One final word of advice, this publication is intended to be used as a reference guide, and when in doubt the reader should consult with a qualified technician.

Introduction

As a service to the classic car enthusiast **VelocePress**, in close cooperation with **Brooklands Books Ltd**., has brought this and other repair manuals previously published as part of the Autobook - Autopress Owners Workshop Manual Series back into print. The book you now hold in your hand, while unchanged from the original edition, was printed using the latest state of the art digital technology. The advent of print-on-demand has forever changed the publishing process, never has information been so accessible and it is our hope that this book serves your informational needs for years to come. If this is your first exposure to digital publishing, we hope that you are pleased with the results. Many more titles of interest to the classic automobile and motorcycle enthusiast, collector and restorer are available via our website at **www.VelocePress.com.** We hope that you find this title as interesting as we do.

Note from the publisher

The information presented is true and complete to the best of our knowledge. All recommendations are made without any guarantees on the part of the author or the publisher, who also disclaim all liability incurred with the use of this information.

Trademarks

We recognize that some words, model names and designations, for example, mentioned herein are the property of the trademark holder. We use them for identification purposes only. This is not an official publication.

CHAPTER 1

THE ENGINE

1 : 1 Description

The engine is an in-line, six-cylinder, single overhead camshaft unit with crossflow induction and exhaust. A section through a cylinder and valve gear is shown in **FIG 1 : 1**, a section through the engine timing gear in **FIG 1 : 2**. The camshaft is driven by roller chain from a sprocket on the crankshaft. The valves, set in line along each side of the light alloy cylinder head, operate in pressed-in valve guides. Cast iron valve seat inserts are provided at each valve position in the head. The valves are operated from the camshaft by means of rockers, an eccentric device being provided at each rocker tip to allow for valve clearance adjustment. The camshaft drives the distributor by means of a gear, and is provided with a special eccentric to operate the mechanical fuel pump.

The cylinder block is integral with the upper half of the crankcase, the lower half of which is formed by the oil sump. The light alloy pistons run directly in the crankcase bores, each piston being provided with two compression rings and a single oil control ring.

The counterbalanced crankshaft is a special steel casting. Crankshaft axial play is taken by a thrust bearing. The main and big-end bearings are provided with renewable shell-type inserts.

A rotor (Eaton type) oil pump driven by chain from the crankshaft sprocket draws oil from the sump beneath the engine and supplies it to the system under pressure. A relief valve is fitted to the system to limit the maximum oil pressure when the engine is cold. Pressure oil is fully filtered before being passed to the main oil gallery which runs along the lefthand side of the engine. From this point the oil is routed to the main and big-end bearings and to the camshaft and rocker shaft support bearings. The valve gear is lubricated by jets from an oil pipe and from oil draining from the rocker shaft and camshaft bearings, the pistons and cylinders being lubricated directly by supply jets and indirectly by oil splash from the big-end bearings.

1 : 2 Removing and refitting the engine

The normal operations of decarbonising and servicing the cylinder head can be carried out without the need for engine removal, as can the majority of engine servicing procedures, including the removal of piston and connecting rod assemblies. However, if crankshaft removal is necessary or if attention to the cylinder bores is required, engine removal will be necessary. For some overhaul work, certain special tools are essential and

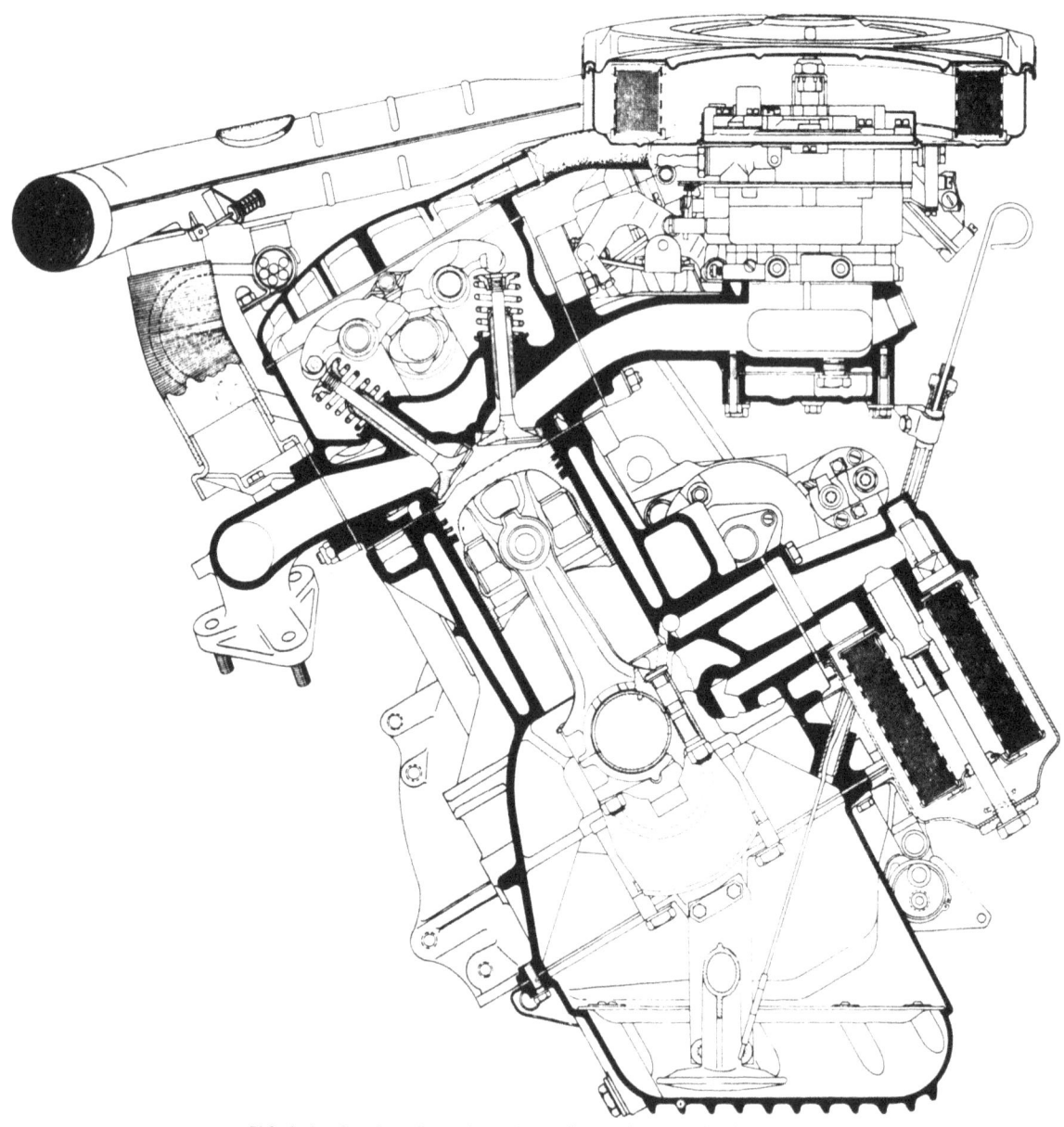

FIG 1:1 Section through engine cylinder, head and valve gear

the owner would be well advised to check on the availability of these factory tools or suitable substitutes before tackling the items involved. If the operator is not a skilled automobile engineer, it is suggested that much useful information will be found in **Hints on Maintenance and Overhaul** at the end of this manual and that it be read before starting work. It must be stressed that the lifting equipment used to remove the engine from the car should be sound, firmly based and not likely to collapse under the weight it will be supporting.

Owners of vehicles fitted with air conditioning (refrigeration) systems should consult a BMW

service station before attempting engine removal procedures, or any servicing procedure which involves the disconnecting or removal of system components or hoses, so that advice can be obtained concerning the discharging of the system. If the pressurised system is opened, liquid refrigerant will escape, immediately evaporating and instantly freezing anything it contacts. Uncontrolled release of the refrigerant will cause severe frostbite or possibly more serious injury if it contacts any part of the body. For this reason, all work involving air conditioning system

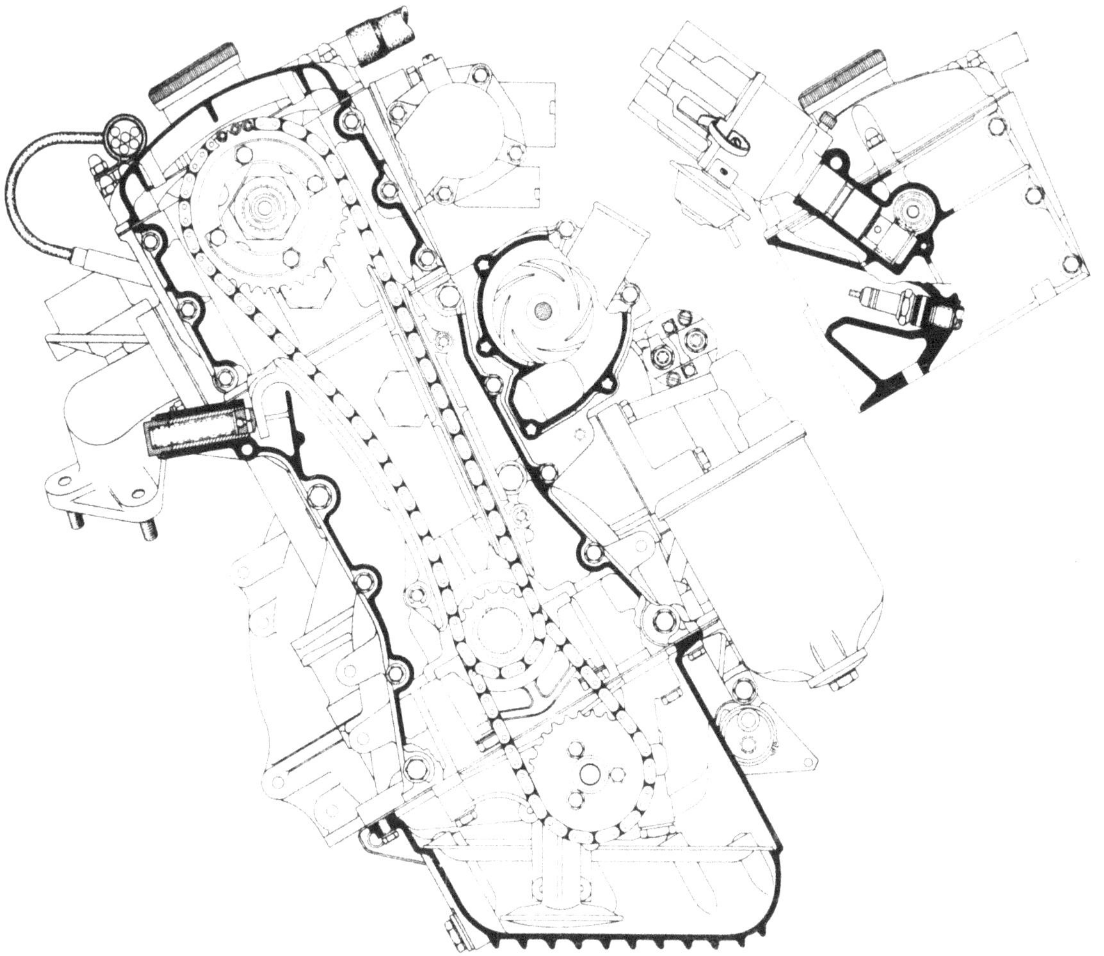

FIG 1:2   Section through engine valve timing gear

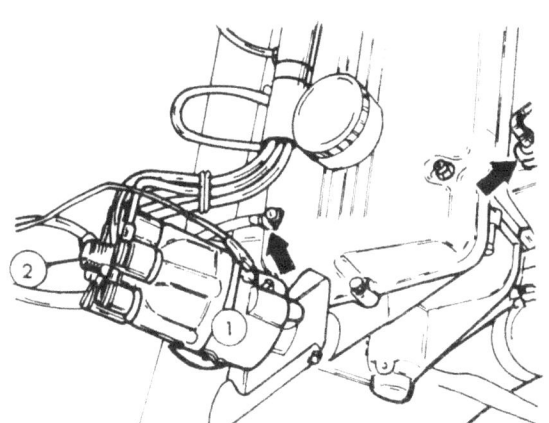

FIG 1:3   Disconnecting wiring and earth lead

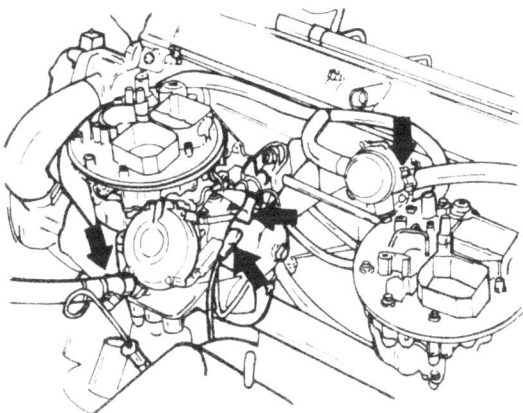

FIG 1:4   Disconnecting hoses and wiring

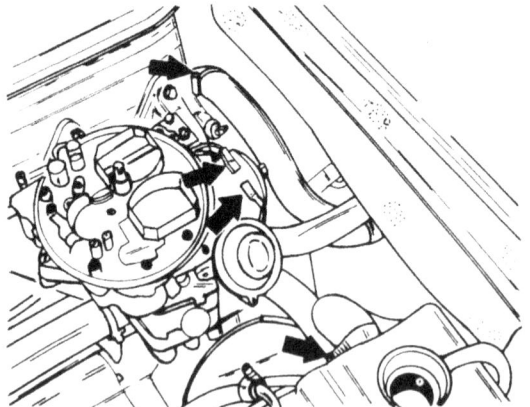

FIG 1:5   Disconnecting hoses and wiring

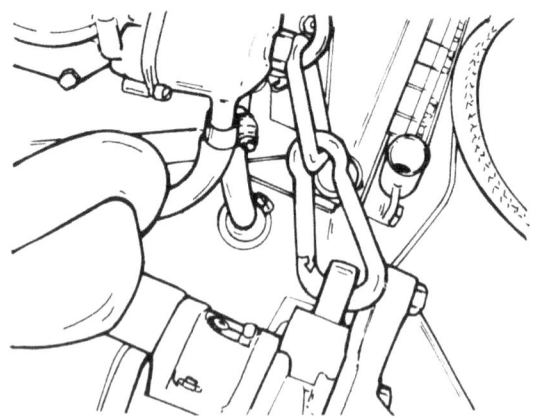

FIG 1:8   Engine rear lifting lug

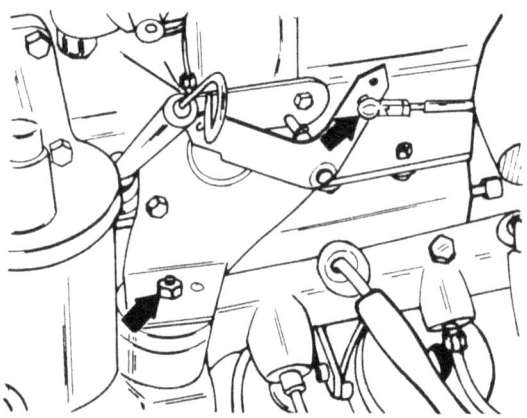

FIG 1:6   Disconnecting accelerator linkage and engine mounting

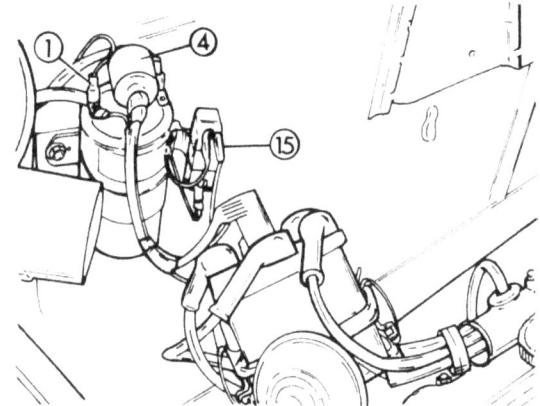

FIG 1:9   Disconnecting cables from coil

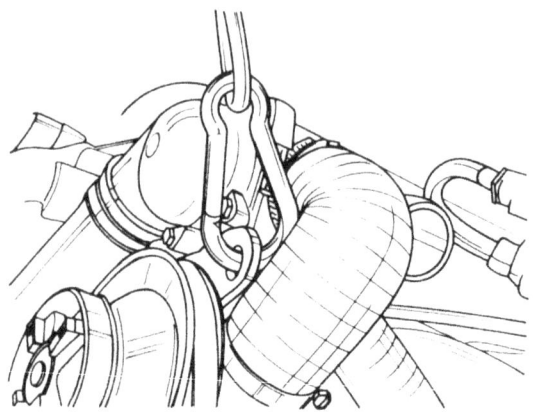

FIG 1:7   Engine front lifting lug

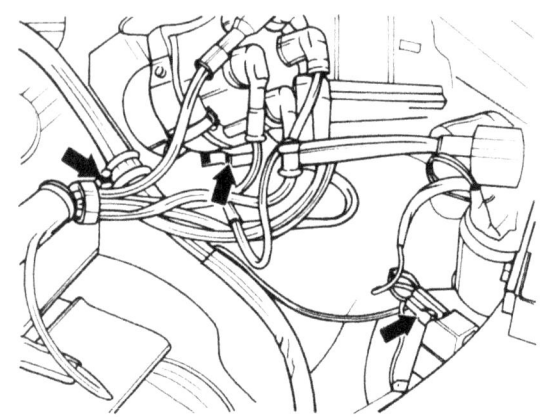

FIG 1:10   Cable plugs and clamp

components, apart from the servicing procedures described in Chapter 13, should be entrusted only to a BMW service station having the necessary special equipment and trained personnel.

Removal, models equipped with carburetters:

Disconnect the battery earth cable. Refer to **Chapter 13** and remove the bonnet, then to **Chapter 4** and remove the radiator. Remove the screenwash reservoir, then refer to **Chapter 2** and remove the air cleaner assembly.

Refer to **FIG 1 : 3** and disconnect cables 1 and 2 and the earth lead (arrowed) from the rocker cover. Refer to **Chapter 4** and remove the cooling fan. Refer to **FIG 1 : 4** and disconnect the vacuum hose, fuel hose and wiring connector (arrowed). Refer to **FIG 1 : 5** and disconnect wiring, earth cable and water hoses arrowed.

Refer to **Chapter 12** and disconnect the wiring from the starter solenoid and the wiring from the rear of the alternator. Refer to **FIG 1 : 6** and disconnect the accelerator linkage. Remove the lower cover panel from beneath the engine compartment, if fitted.

On models fitted with power steering, refer to **Chapter 10** and disconnect the power steering pump from its mountings without disconnecting the hoses. Support the pump by suitable means so that it is held clear of the engine.

Attach the lifting equipment to the lugs at the front and rear of the engine as shown in **FIGS 1 : 7** and **1 : 8**.

Refer to **Chapter 6** or **Chapter 7** and remove the transmission. On models fitted with manual transmission, remove the clutch slave cylinder and the clutch release arm and bearing as described in **Chapter 5**. Remove the reversing light lead and, if fitted, the clutch hydraulic hose from the retaining clips. Remove the nuts securing the lefthand and righthand engine mounting brackets to the mounting rubbers, then carefully lift the engine and swing out to the righthand side to remove.

Refitting:

This is a reversal of the removal procedure, making sure that all component fixings are tightened to the specified torque figures.

Removal models with fuel injection systems:

Remove the bonnet as described in **Chapter 13**. Disconnect the battery earth cable and remove the screenwash reservoir. Remove the air cleaner assembly as described in **Chapter 2** and the radiator as described in **Chapter 4**. Refer to **FIG 1 : 9** and pull cables 1 and 4 from the ignition coil and the white cable 15 from ballast resistor. When disconnecting cables, always pull on the plug connector and not on the cable itself.

Refer to **FIG 1 : 10** and disconnect the cable clamp from rocker cover and cable plug from distributor insert. Refer to **FIG 1 : 11** and disconnect cable 1 from injection valves, 2 from temperature sensor, 3 from throttle switch and 4 from starter valve. Disconnect cable 5 from air collector support and remove protective tube 6 from rocker cover. Remove plug from pressure sensor as shown in **FIG 1 : 12**. Refer to **FIG 1 : 13** and remove connecting plugs from main relay 7 and cold start relay 8. Refer to

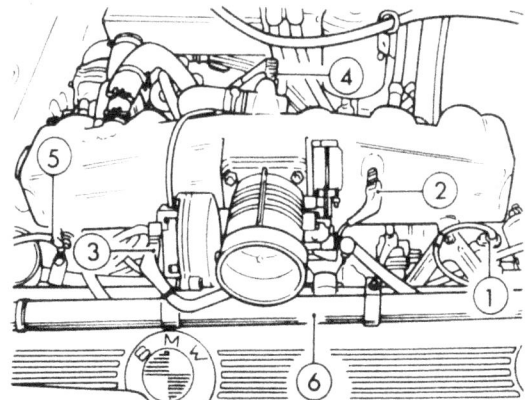

FIG 1 : 11 Cable connections and protective tube

FIG 1 : 12 Cable support and plug

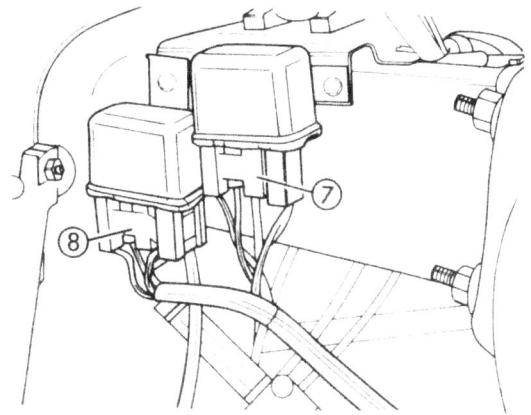

FIG 1 : 13 Relay connector plugs

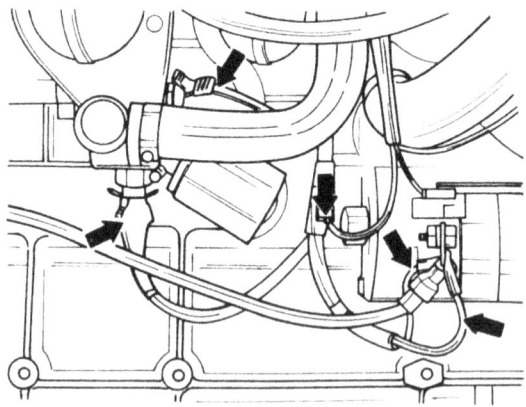

FIG 1 :14   Switch, sensor and starter cable connections

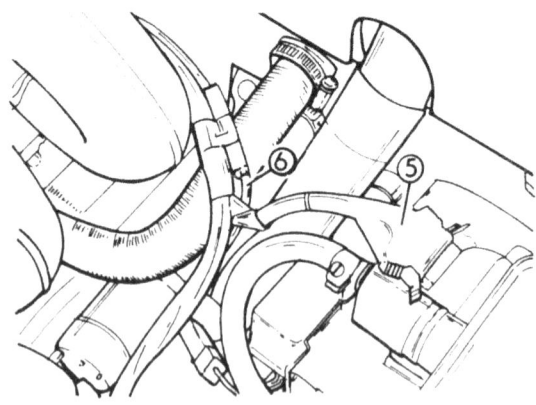

FIG 1 :17   Cable and plug connections

FIG 1 :15   Removing loom plug

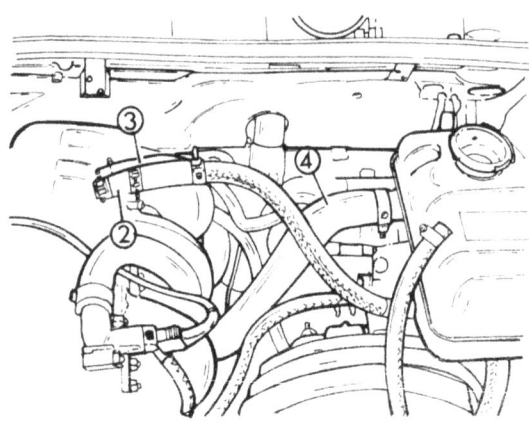

FIG 1 :16   Hose connections

FIG 1 :14 and disconnect cables from water temperature sensor, temperature retard switch and from starter motor connections.

If a loom plug is fitted, it should be removed as shown in **FIG 1 :15**. Inspect rubber seal 1 and renew if damaged or perished. Note that plug connections must be in perfect condition, otherwise operational faults may result.

Refer to **FIG 1 :16** and disconnect hoses 2 and 3 from collector vessel and hose 4 from expansion tank. Refer to **FIG 1 :17** and disconnect plug 5 and connector 6. Disconnect the throttle linkage bars. Refer to **FIG 1 :18** and disconnect heater hoses 9 and 10. When refitting these hoses, note that plate 11 and the hoses must be pressed hard against the splashboard before tightening the clips. Disconnect the earth cable (arrowed) from the splashboard.

Refer to **Chapter 12** and disconnect the alternator wiring. Refer to **FIG 1 :19** and remove fuel hose from regulator and pipes 13 and 14. Pull cable from temperature switch. Refer to **Chapter 4** and remove the cooling fan. Remove the nut from the lefthand engine mounting, which is similar to that shown in **FIG 1 :6**. Remove the cover panel from beneath the engine compartment. If power steering is fitted, refer to **Chapter 10** and remove the pump, supporting it safely so that the hoses are not strained.

On models fitted with automatic transmission, remove the transmission as described in **Chapter 7**. On models with manual transmission, remove the transmission as described in **Chapter 6** and the slave cylinder, clutch release arm and bearing as described in **Chapter 5**. Attach tool 7000 or other suitable lifting equipment to the front and rear lifting lugs as shown in **FIGS 1 :7** and **1 :8**. Make a final check to ensure that all wiring, hoses and control linkages have been disconnected from the engine assembly, then lift the engine and swing it to the right to remove from the engine compartment.

Refitting:

This is a reversal of the removal procedure, making sure that all component fixings are tightened to the specified torque figures.

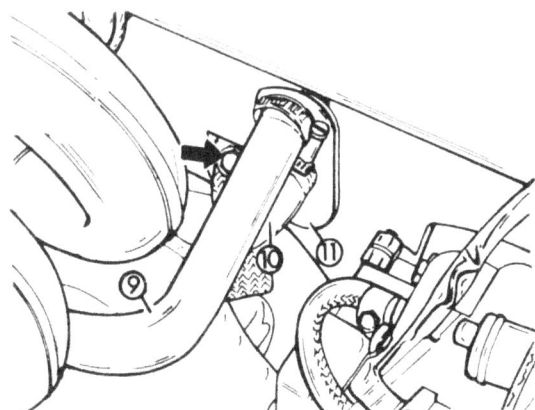

FIG 1:18 Heater hoses and earth cable

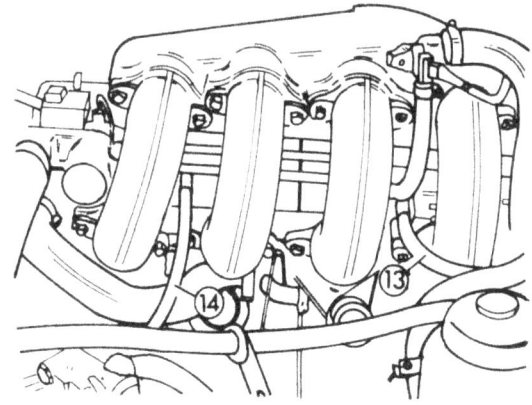

FIG 1:19 Fuel hose and switch cable connections

1:3 Removing and refitting cylinder head

Removal, models with fuel injection systems:

Disconnect the battery earth cable. Refer to **Chapter 4** and drain the cooling system. Loosen the clamp on the throttle butterfly manifold. Remove the air cleaner assembly, pulling the hose from the splashboard at the same time. Remove the screenwash reservoir.

Disconnect the wiring from the engine and associated components in the manner described in **Section 1:2** and as shown in **FIGS 1:10** to **1:14** inclusive.

Disconnect the HT and LT leads from the coil and disconnect the LT connector and vacuum pipe at the distributor. Remove the distributor cap.

Refer to **FIG 1:20**. Detach the HT leads from the sparking plugs and remove the lead protector tube. Pull off the bleed hose. Slacken the rocker cover bolts in the reverse order to that shown in the illustration, then remove the rocker cover and gasket. Refer to **FIG 1:21** and disconnect hoses 5, 6, 7 and 8. Refer to **FIG 1:18** and disconnect heater hoses 9 and 10. Disconnect the heater hose from the expansion tank. Disconnect the oil pressure switch cable at the connector located close to hoses 9 and 10. Note that these hoses, together with plate 11, must be pressed hard against the splashboard when refitting.

Refer to **Chapter 3** and turn the engine to the firing point for No 1 cylinder. Refer to **FIG 1:22** and disconnect hoses by releasing clips 12 and 13, then pull off connector 14 and remove support bracket 15. Refer to **Section 1:6** and detach the camshaft sprocket. **Neither the crankshaft nor camshaft must be turned while the camshaft sprocket is disconnected, unless the head is completely removed, otherwise the valves may contact the pistons and cause serious internal damage.**

Refer to **FIG 1:23** and disconnect the throttle linkage and the intake preheating hose. Remove the clamp from the exhaust support at the gearbox, and loosen the triangular flanges on exhaust silencer. Disconnect the exhaust pipes at the manifold flanges. Note that when refitting the pipes to manifold flanges, new gaskets should be used and the stud threads should be smeared with Molycote paste.

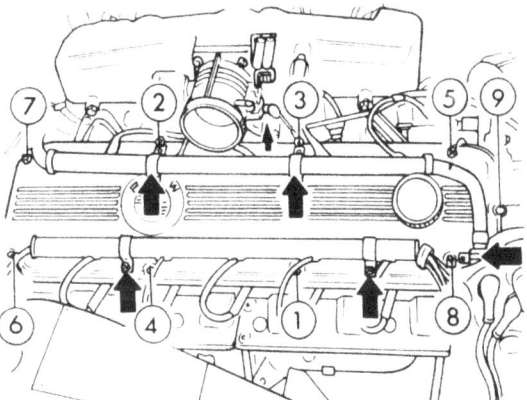

FIG 1:20 Rocker cover bolt tightening sequence. Fuel injection engine shown

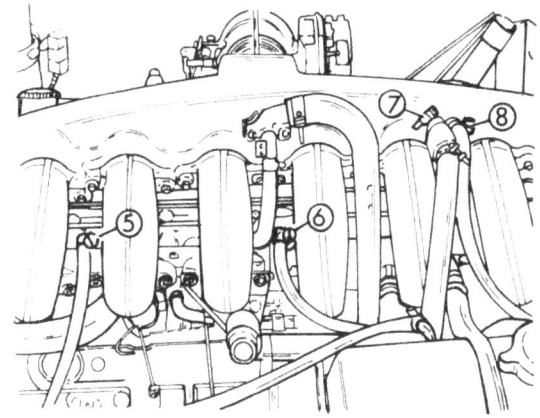

FIG 1:21 Disconnecting hoses

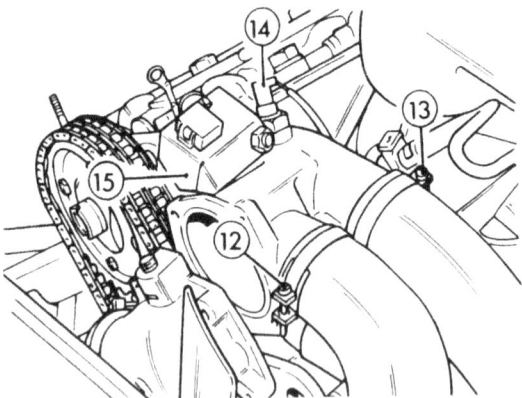

FIG 1:22 Hose clips, cable connector and support bracket

FIG 1:23 Throttle linkage and water hose

FIG 1:24 Cylinder head bolt tightening sequence

FIG 1:25 Installing guide pins

Slacken the cylinder head fixing bolts in the reverse order of that shown in **FIG 1:24**. Remove the bolts from the positions arrowed in **FIG 1:25**, then install suitable guide pins to prevent the rocker shafts from being displaced or distorted. Remove the remaining bolts and carefully lift off the cylinder head. Remove and discard the cylinder head gasket.

Refit the cylinder head as described later in this section.

Removal, models equipped with carburetters:

Disconnect the battery earth cable. Remove the air cleaner assembly. Refer to **Chapter 4** and drain the cooling system. Refer to **FIG 1:26** and remove hose 1 from fuel pump, disconnect throttle linkage rods 2 and pull off cables 3, 4, 5 and 6. Refer to **FIG 1:27** and disconnect the vacuum hose and dipstick support as shown by the arrows. Refer to **FIG 1:28** and disconnect hoses 7, 8, 9 and 10.

Refer to **FIG 1:20**. Disconnect the HT leads from the sparking plugs then remove the lead protector tube. Slacken the fixing bolts in the reverse order of that shown in the illustration then remove the bolts and detach the rocker cover.

Refer to **Chapter 3** and turn the engine to the firing point for No 1 cylinder. Refer to **Section 1:6** and detach the camshaft sprocket. **Neither the crankshaft nor camshaft must be turned while the camshaft sprocket is disconnected, unless the cylinder head is completely removed, otherwise the valves may contact the pistons and cause serious internal damage.**

Remove the exhaust pipe clamp from the gearbox and loosen the triangular flanges on the exhaust silencer. Disconnect the exhaust pipes from the manifolds. Note that, when refitting the pipes to manifold flanges, new gaskets should be used and the stud threads should be smeared with Molycote paste.

Loosen the cylinder head bolts in the reverse order of that shown in **FIG 1:24**, then remove the bolts from the positions arrowed in **FIG 1:25** and insert suitable guide pins to prevent rocker shafts from being displaced or distorted. Remove the remaining bolts and lift off the cylinder head. Remove and discard the head gasket.

16

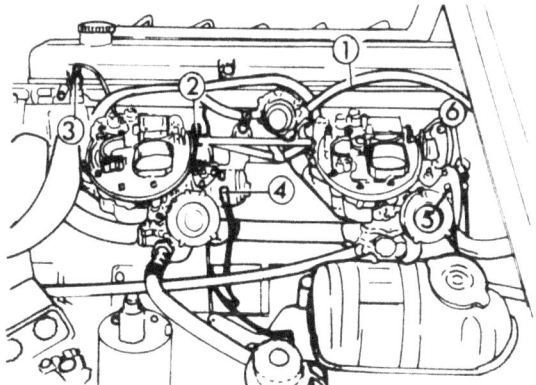

FIG 1:26 Disconnecting hose, linkage and cables

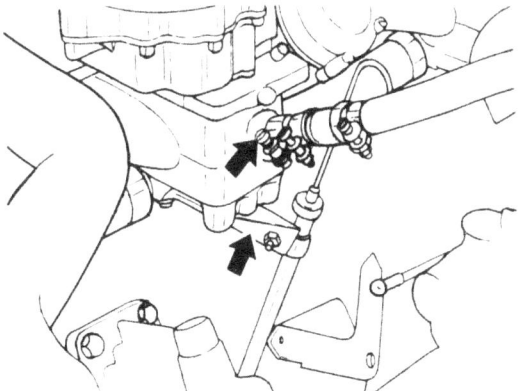

FIG 1:27 Vacuum hose and dipstick support

Refitting, all models:

The instructions concerning the correct alignment of camshaft and crankshaft must be observed, otherwise the valves may contact the pistons and cause serious internal damage.

If the crankshaft position has been disturbed, turn the crankshaft until piston No 1 (front) is at the top of its bore, with the ignition timing marks aligned at TDC as described in **Chapter 3**. Clean the joint faces of cylinder head and block, avoiding the use of sharp tools which would scratch the surfaces.

Make sure that the threaded holes for the cylinder head bolts in the block are clear of oil. If oil is present, the bolts may not exert sufficient pressure to hold the cylinder head down even though the correct torque figure is achieved. It is also possible for pressure on the oil to cause cracking of the cylinder block as the bolts are tightened.

Fit a new head gasket into position on the cylinder block, making sure that the gasket is the correct way up by checking that each hole in the gasket matches the appropriate bore in the block surface. Apply Atmosit or similar sealer to the gasket at the points circled in **FIG 1:29** only.

Before installing cylinder head, make sure that the camshaft is correctly aligned with the cam lobes for No 6 (rear) cylinder in the overlap position as described in **Section 1:4**. Fit the cylinder head carefully into position and install the cylinder head bolts through the vacant holes. Remove the guide pins and fit the remaining bolts. Tighten the bolts in the order shown in **FIG 1:24**, in three successive stages, of 3, 6.8 and 7.2kgm (22, 48 and 52lb ft).

Refit the remaining components in the reverse order of removal, following the instructions given in **Section 1:6** when installing the sprocket and chain assembly to the camshaft. Before installing the rocker cover, set the valve clearances as described in **Section 1:5**. Use a new rocker cover gasket and tighten the cover fixing bolts in the order shown in **FIG 1:20**. On models equipped with fuel injection systems, ensure that the earth cable is connected at point 5 and the loom clamp at point 9. On completion, refill the cooling system as described in **Chapter 4**, set ignition timing as described in **Chapter 3**. and carry out the idle speed adjustments given in **Chapter 2**.

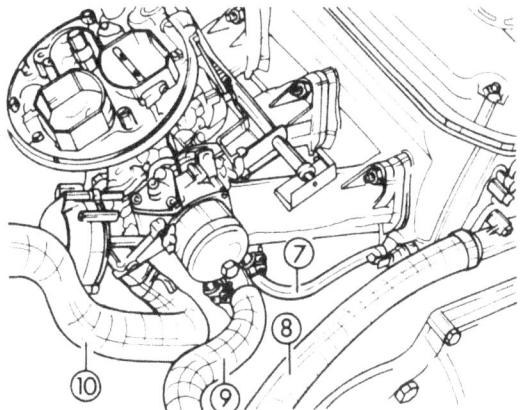

FIG 1:28 Disconnecting hoses

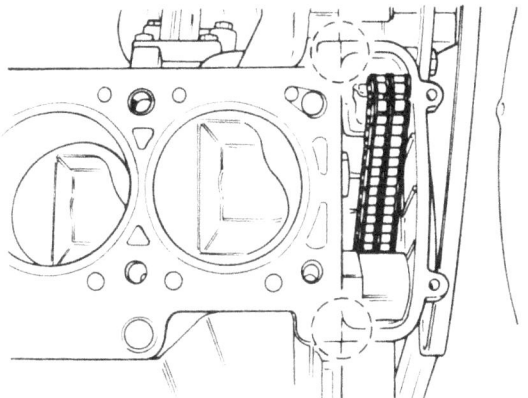

FIG 1:29 Sealant application points at head gasket

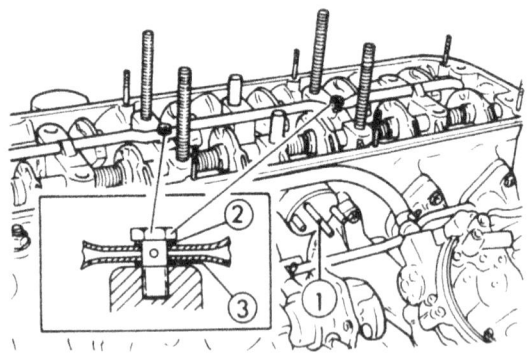

FIG 1:30   Pump pushrod 1 and oil pipe seals 2 and 3

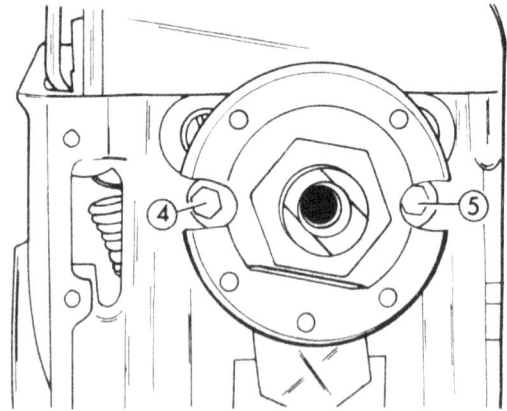

FIG 1:33   Camshaft guide plate screws

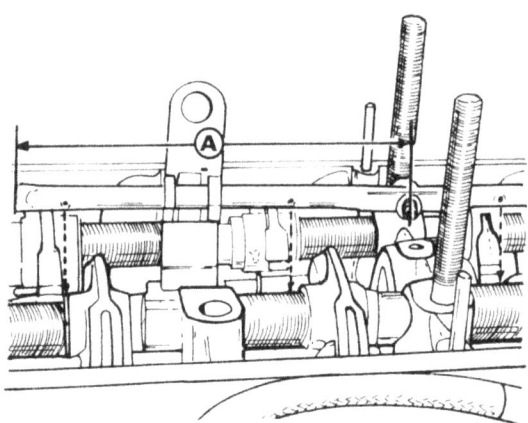

FIG 1:31   Oil pipe installation

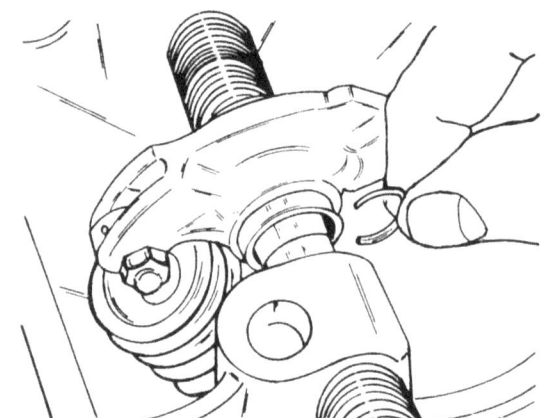

FIG 1:34   Rocker shaft circlip removal

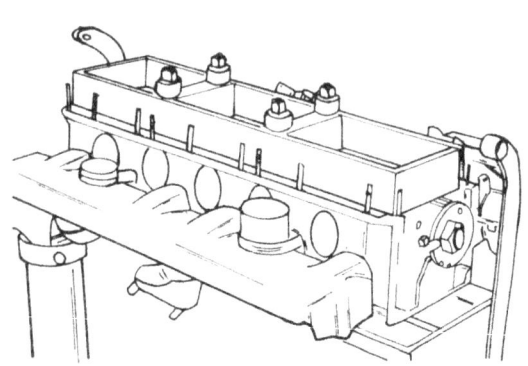

FIG 1:32   Compression frame installation

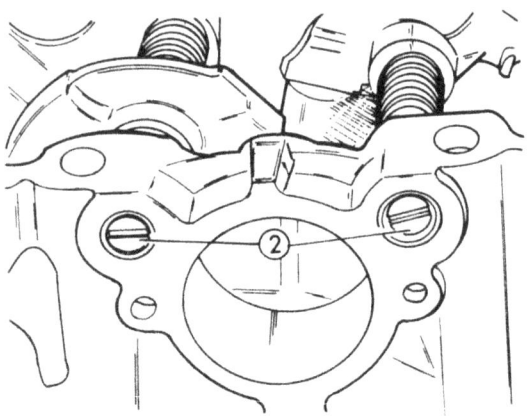

FIG 1:35   Rocker shaft locking bolts

After the engine has been given a trial run, allow it to cool down to approximately 35°C (95°F) then remove the rocker cover and retighten the cylinder head bolts as described previously. After the car has been driven for a distance of approximately 1000km (600 miles), the cylinder head bolts must again be retightened when the engine has cooled to the temperature stated. To do this, slacken each bolt a little before retightening to the specified torque figure, keeping to the correct procedure as described previously. Finally, check and if necessary reset valve clearances as described in **Section 1:5**.

1:4 Servicing head, valves and camshaft

Dismantling:

It is not necessary to remove the inlet or exhaust manifolds unless renewal of the manifolds or gaskets is required, but it is recommended that carburetters be removed from inlet manifolds to prevent damage. Support the head on suitable blocks of wood while work is carried out, to prevent damage to the light alloy surfaces. **Note that all valve gear components must be kept in the correct order for refitting in their original positions if they are not to be renewed.**

Refer to **FIG 1:30** and, on models fitted with mechanical fuel pump, remove the pump and pushrod 1. Remove the oil feed pipe, noting the correct positions of seals 2 and 3 for correct refitting. Note that the pipe must be refitted with the oil holes aligned to spray oil between the camshaft lobes and rocker tips at each valve position (see **FIG 1:31**) and that dimension **A** should be 180 ± 0.5mm (7.087 ± 0.02in), measured in a forward direction. Refer to **Chapter 3** and remove the distributor.

Refer to **Section 1:5** and set all valve clearances to the maximum possible, this being necessary to prevent subsequent damage to the valves. Attach compression frame 7003-1 and evenly tighten the fixings, as shown in **FIG 1:32**. The use of this tool is essential in order to compress the valve springs and relieve rocker pressure on camshaft lobes before removing camshaft and rocker shafts. When the tool is in position, handle the cylinder head carefully to prevent damage to the valves projecting from combustion chambers.

Remove the camshaft guide plate fixing screws shown at 4 and 5 in **FIG 1:33**, then carefully pull the camshaft assembly from the cylinder head.

To remove the rocker shafts, refer to **FIG 1:34**. Push back thrust rings and rocker arms then pull off circlips. Unscrew the locking bolts shown at 2 in **FIG 1:35**. Note that these bolts must be smeared with Loctite No 73 during reassembly. Rocker shafts must be removed using tool 7004 or other suitable slide hammer assembly as shown in **FIG 1:36**. Screw the tool into the rocker shaft and remove the locating pin. Operate the slide hammer to carefully pull the rocker shaft from the cylinder head, collecting springs 3 (see **FIG 1:37**), discs 4, rocker arms 5 and thrust rings 6 as they come free. Note the order of these components for correct reassembly. Remove the rear cover to allow removal of the rear rocker shafts as shown in **FIG 1:38**. Note the position of the seal 1 for correct reassembly and use a new gasket 2 of the correct type if the original is not in perfect condition.

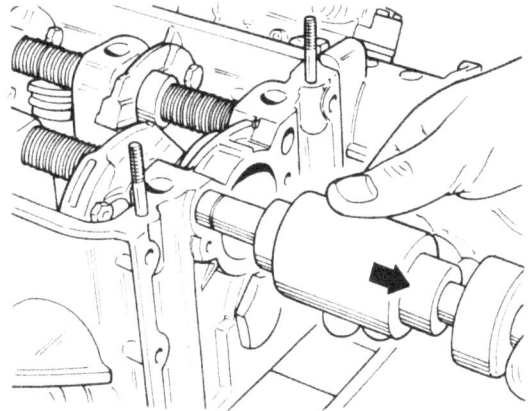

FIG 1:36   Rocker shaft removal

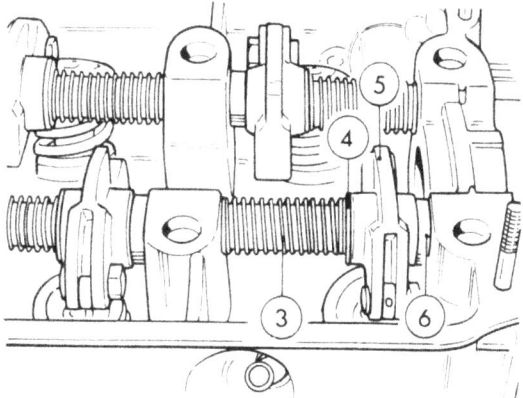

FIG 1:37   Locations of rocker gear components

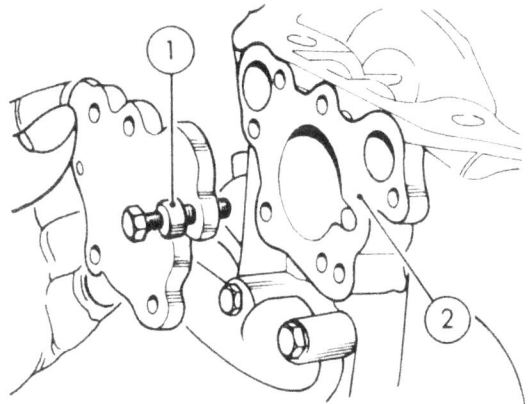

FIG 1:38   Rear rocker shaft cover removal

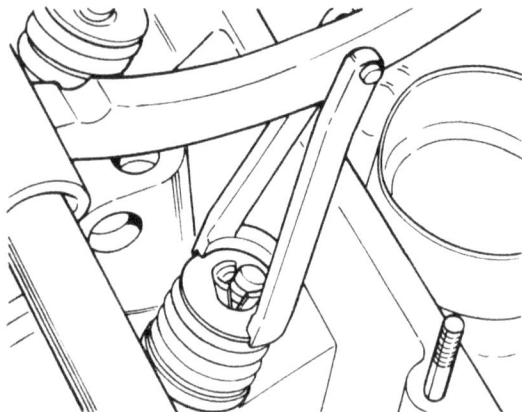

FIG 1:39 Removing valve using spring compressor tool

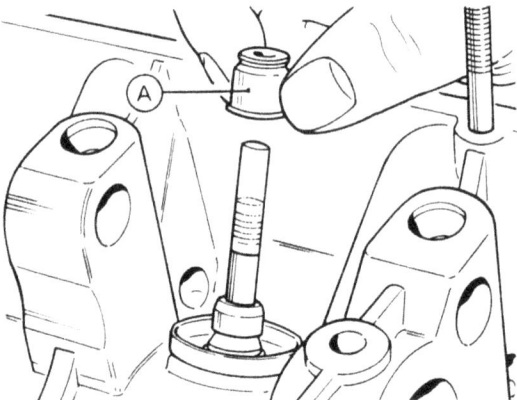

FIG 1:40 Valve stem seal installation

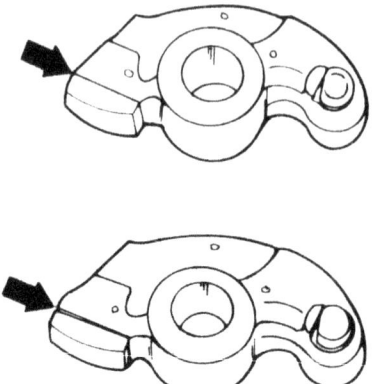

FIG 1:41 Rocker arm cam followers

Remove the compression frame. Use a suitable spring compressor such as that shown in **FIG 1:39** to remove the valve assemblies from the cylinder head. With the spring compressed, remove the split taper collets then remove the compressor tool and remove the valve springs and caps. Remove valve stem seals **A** as shown in **FIG 1:40**. Inspect the seals carefully and renew any found worn or damaged, as faulty seals can be responsible for high oil consumption. Note that the grooves in the valve stem should be covered with adhesive tape as shown in the illustration when installing the seals, to prevent damage. Remove any burrs or ridges from the upper part of the valve stems, then remove the valves from the cylinder head. Unless the valves are being renewed, store them in the correct order so that they may be refitted into the original bores from which they were removed.

Valves:

When the valves have been cleaned of carbon deposits, they must be inspected for serviceability. Valves with bent stems or badly burned heads must be renewed. Valves with pitted seats can be re-cut at a service station, but if they are too far gone for this remedial treatment, new valves will be required. Valves that are in serviceable condition can be ground to their seats as described later.

Valve guides:

Valve guides that are worn or scored must be renewed. As the guides must be pressed into or out of place, reamed, then the valve seat re-cut for concentricity, this work should be carried out by a service station having the necessary special equipment.

Valve seat inserts:

Valve seat inserts that are pitted or burned must be refaced or, if they are too far gone for remedial treatment, renewed. As either operation requires the use of special equipment, the work should be carried out by a service station. If the valve seat inserts are serviceable, they should be ground to the valves as described later.

Valve springs:

Test the valve springs by comparing with the data given in the **Appendix**, or by comparing their efficiency with that of new springs. To compare with a new spring, insert both old and new springs end to end with a metal plate between them into the jaws of a vice. If the old spring is weakened, it will close up first when pressure is applied. Take care that the springs do not fly out of the vice under pressure. Any spring which is distorted, or which is shorter or weaker than standard, should be renewed.

Rockers and shafts:

Check all rocker gear components for excessive wear, scoring or other damage and renew parts as necessary. Check the cam followers on the rocker arms as shown in **FIG 1:41**, renewing any rocker having a damaged or loose follower.

Camshaft and bearings:

Inspect the working surfaces of camshaft lobes and journals for signs of wear, damage or seizure. If the camshaft is to be renewed, refer to **FIG 1:42** and remove nut 1, lockplate 3, sprocket flange 2 and guide plate 4. Transfer parts 1, 2 and 4, together with a new lockplate 3, to the new camshaft.

Cylinder head:

Carefully clean the cylinder head and make sure that all oil and water passages are clear. Check the mating surface for flatness and for nicks or other damage. The mating surface of the head can be refaced at a service station, but if damage or distortion is too serious for this remedial work to be carried out satisfactorily, or if the head is cracked or otherwise damaged, a new cylinder head should be fitted. If the head is resurfaced, the upper timing case cover must also be machined by a similar amount.

Decarbonising and valve grinding:

Avoid the use of sharp tools which could damage the cylinder head or combustion chambers. Remove all traces of carbon deposits from the combustion chambers, inlet and exhaust ports and joint faces. If the pistons have not been removed and cleaned during previous engine dismantling, plug the oilways and waterways in the top surface of the cylinder block with pieces of rag to prevent the entry of dirt, then clean the carbon from the piston crowns, using a blunt instrument to avoid scratching.

To grind-in valves, use medium grade carborundum paste unless the seats are in very good condition, when fine grade paste can be used at once. Always finish with fine grade. A light spring under the valve head will assist in the operation and allow the valve to be lifted from its seat without releasing the grinding tool. Use a suction cup tool and grind with a semi-rotary movement. Allow the valve to rise off its seat occasionally by pressure of the spring under the head, then turn to a new position before resuming the grinding procedure.

Use paste sparingly. When both valve and insert mating seats have a smooth matt grey finish, clean away all traces of grinding compounds from port and valve.

Reassembly:

This is a reversal of the removal procedure, using the compression frame shown in **FIG 1:32** to depress the valve springs before installing rocker shafts and camshaft. Rocker shafts must be installed so that the grooves in the shafts are properly positioned to allow for the fitting of cylinder head bolts. Install the camshaft and secure the guide plate, then check that the camshaft can turn freely. Before releasing the compression frame, turn the camshaft until the cam lobes for cylinder No 6 (rear) are pointing upwards by equal amounts, this being the valve overlap position when the inlet and exhaust valves will be opened equally by the cam lobes. The threaded hole in the camshaft flange must be aligned with the projection on the head as shown in **FIG 1:43**. Check camshaft end play, using feeler gauges between flange and guide plate as shown in **FIG 1:44**. The correct figure is 0.03 to 0.18mm (0.0012 to 0.007in). If the

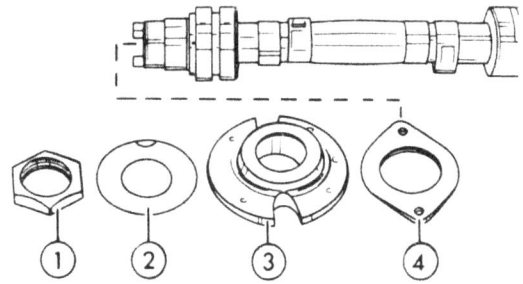

FIG 1:42 Camshaft components

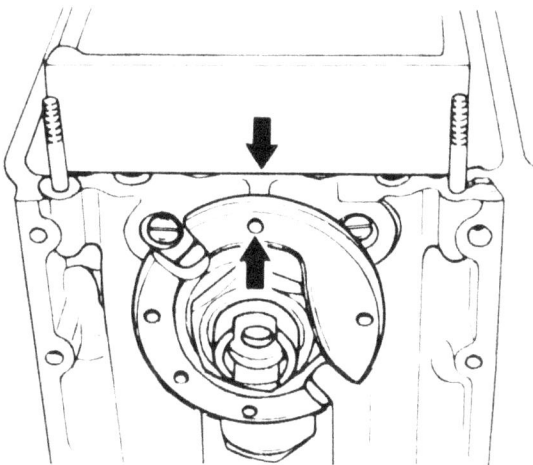

FIG 1:43 Camshaft alignment

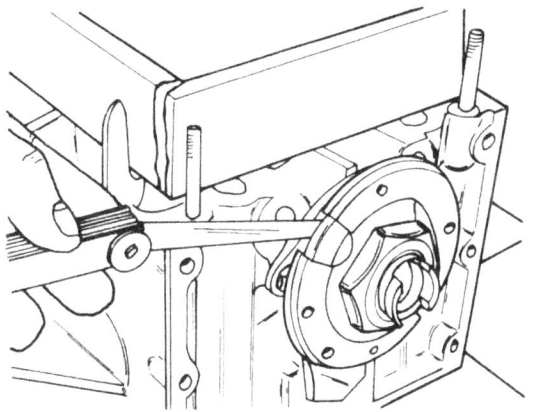

FIG 1:44 Checking camshaft end play

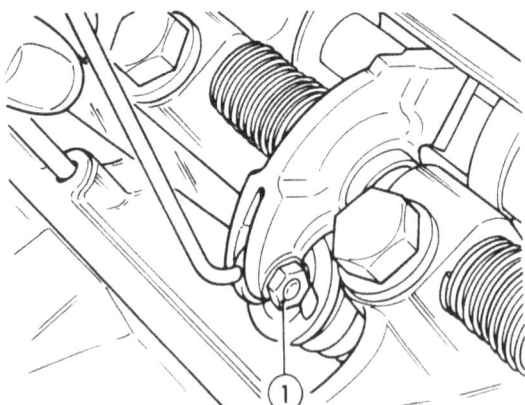

FIG 1:45   Valve clearance adjustment

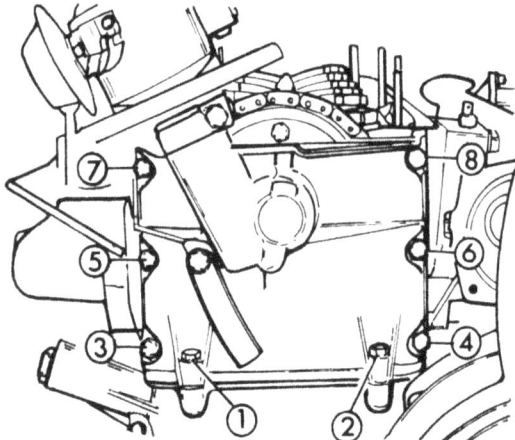

FIG 1:46   Upper timing case cover bolt tightening sequence

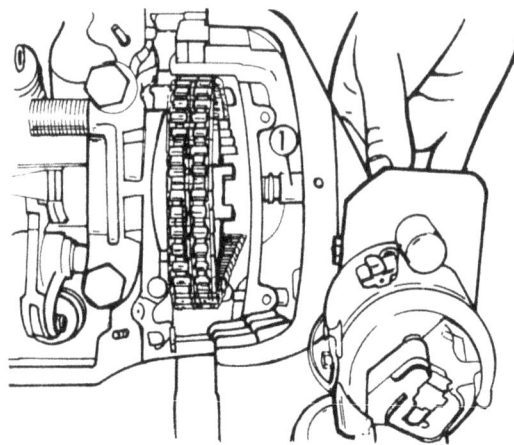

FIG 1:47   Upper timing case cover removal

upper figure is exceeded, a new guide plate should be fitted. Make sure that the camshaft is aligned properly as aligned previously before removing the compression frame.

1:5 Valve clearance adjustment

The correct adjustment of valve clearances is important as they affect engine timing and performance considerably. Excessive clearance will reduce valve lift and opening duration and reduce engine performance, causing excessive wear of the valve gear components and noisy operation. Insufficient or zero clearance will again affect engine timing and in some circumstances can hold the valve clear of its seat. This will result in much reduced performance due to lost compression and the possibility of burned valves and seats. Valve clearances should be checked at the intervals recommended in the manufacturer's service schedule as routine maintenance and, additionally, whenever the cylinder head has been serviced.

Adjustment must be made when the engine is cool, so a warm engine should be allowed to cool to a maximum coolant temperature of 35°C (95°F). Correct clearances under these conditions are 0.25 to 0.30mm (0.010 to 0.012in) for both inlet and exhaust valves.

Refer to **Section 1:3** and remove the rocker cover. The engine can be turned by means of tool 7008-1 which locks onto the timing chain where it passes over the camshaft sprocket, but if such a tool is not available the engine should be turned by pushing the car forwards in top gear (manual transmission), by pulling on the alternator drive belt, or by using a spanner on the crankshaft pulley nut. In all cases, the engine will be easier to turn if the sparking plugs are first removed. Turn the engine until the valves for No 6 (rear) cylinder are on the overlap, this being when both inlet and exhaust valves are equally depressed by the rockers. With the engine in this position, the piston in No 1 (front) cylinder will be at TDC on the compression stroke with the valves for that cylinder in the correct positions for checking and adjusting clearances. The engine should be turned in stages to bring the valves for Nos 6, 2, 4, 1, 5 and 3 to overlap positions in turn, when the valves for cylinders 1, 5, 3, 6, 2 and 4 respectively will be brought to the correct positions for checking and adjustment.

Use feeler gauges to check the clearance between the adjustment mechanism and valve stem as shown in **FIG 1:45**. No adjustment is necessary if the clearance is between the limits stated, but if not it should be reset by slackening locknut 1 and using a rod or other suitable tool to rotate the eccentric as necessary. A feeler of the correct thickness should slide smoothly in the gap, being neither tight nor loose. When clearance is correct, tighten the locknut and recheck. Repeat the adjustment at the opposite valve for the same cylinder before proceeding to the next pair of valves in the sequence stated previously. On completion, refit the rocker cover using a new gasket unless the original is in perfect condition. Tighten the rocker cover fixing bolts in the order shown in **FIG 1:20**.

1:6 Timing gear

It should not normally be necessary to renew the timing chain due to wear until the vehicle has covered approximately 50,000km (30,000 miles), as the tensioner assembly maintains chain tension until the wear limit is reached. If excessive timing chain noise is noticed before this distance has been covered, the chain tensioner should be checked and bled as described later, before checking the chain for wear or damage.

It is necessary to remove both upper and lower timing case covers to remove the chain and lower sprocket. If the camshaft sprocket only is to be detached to allow for cylinder head removal, it is only necessary to remove the chain tensioner then remove the upper timing case cover for access to the sprocket fixing bolts. Note the warning given in **Section 1:3** concerning the correct alignment of camshaft and crankshaft to prevent damage to valves and pistons when the camshaft sprocket is detached.

Timing case cover removal:

Upper cover:

Refer to **Chapter 3** and remove the distributor cap, LT lead and vacuum pipe(s) from the distributor, then turn the engine until it is aligned at the firing point for No 1 cylinder. Refer to **Chapter 4** and detach the thermostat cover and remove the thermostat. Refer to **Section 1:3** and remove the rocker cover.

Slacken the fixing bolts in the order shown in **FIG 1:46**, then remove the bolts and detach the upper timing case cover complete with distributor and drive gear 1 as shown in **FIG 1:47**.

Before refitting the cover, check that the portion of the cylinder head gasket onto which the cover fits, is undamaged. If necessary, the cylinder head must be removed as described in **Section 1:3** and the gasket renewed. Apply Atmosit or similar sealant to the points indicated by the lower arrows in **FIG 1:48**. The engine and distributor must be set at the firing point for No 1 cylinder as described in **Chapter 3** and the distributor drive gear shown at 1 in **FIG 1:47** must be fitted so that it engages the slot in the camshaft without disturbing the settings. Refit the cover securing bolts and tighten bolts 1 and 2 gently (see **FIG 1:46**). Now fully tighten the remaining bolts in the order shown, then finally tighten bolts 1 and 2. Refit the remaining components in the reverse order of removal. On completion, check ignition timing as described in **Chapter 3**.

Lower cover:

Remove the upper timing case cover as described previously, then remove the chain tensioner piston as described later. Refer to **Chapter 4** and remove the alternator drive belt.

Remove the lower cover panel from beneath the engine, if fitted. Unscrew the fixing nut and use a suitable puller to remove the crankshaft pulley and damper assembly, noting the correct position of the locating key shown at 1 in **FIG 1:49**. To lock the engine when unscrewing the nut on manual transmission models, bottom gear should be selected and the handbrake fully applied. Alternatively, remove the cover plate from beneath the rear of the engine and use tool 6069 or similar to lock the flywheel against rotation. On automatic transmission models, the latter method should be employed, using tool 6069-1 or similar. Note that, if the hub of the damper is severely

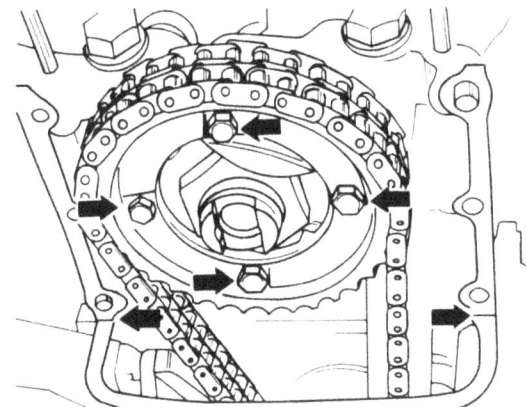

FIG 1:48 Camshaft sprocket bolts and sealant application points

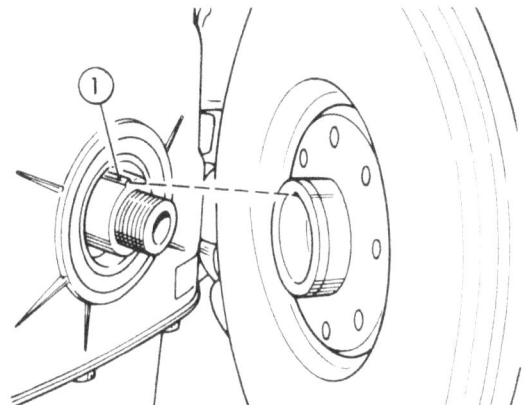

FIG 1:49 Removing crankshaft pulley and damper assembly

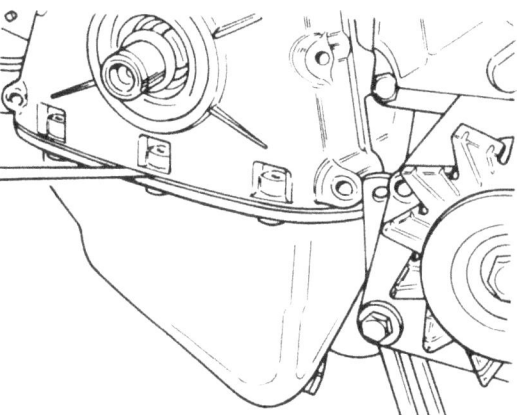

FIG 1:50 Separating lower cover from sump gasket

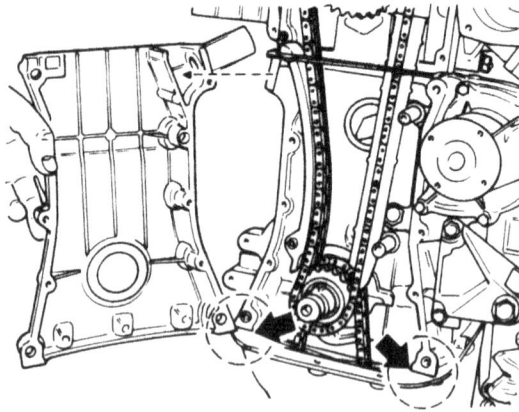

FIG 1:51 Lower timing case cover installation

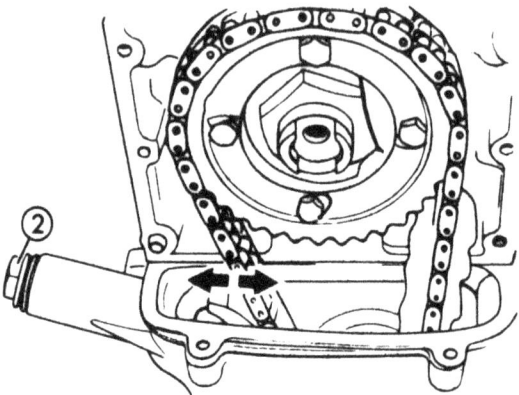

FIG 1:52 Chain tensioner plug 2

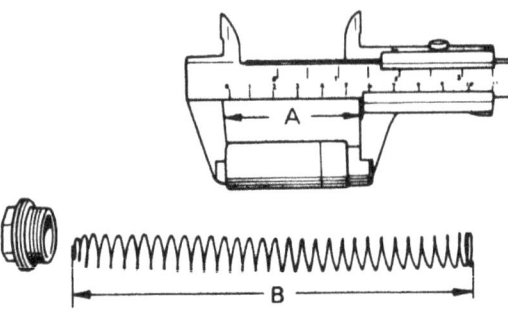

FIG 1:53 Length of piston A and spring B

scored, the seal should be located during reassembly so that the sealing lip makes contact in front of or behind the scored area.

Remove the bolts securing the lower timing case cover to the cylinder block and remove the bolts between cover and front of sump. Slacken but do not remove the remaining sump bolts. Use a thin blade to carefully separate the timing case from the sump gasket at the front, as shown in **FIG 1:50**. Note that, if the sump gasket is damaged, the sump must be removed as described in **Section 1:8** and the gasket renewed. Remove the timing case cover.

When refitting the cover, coat the joint faces between sump and crankcase with Atmosit or similar sealer, as shown by the lower arrows in **FIG 1:51**. Note that the pickup web for the tensioner piston must be located in the oil pocket indicated by the upper arrow. Install the timing cover to cylinder block fixing bolts and tighten gently, then fit the case to sump bolts and tighten these and the remaining sump bolts before finally tightening the timing case to block bolts. Tighten bolts alternately and evenly to avoid distortion. Refit the remaining components in the reverse order of removal.

Chain tensioner assembly:

Removal:

Remove the upper timing case cover as described previously. This is necessary for access to the oil pocket in order to bleed the tensioner when refitted. Unscrew the tensioner and plug shown in **FIG 1:52**, taking care to press it inwards as it comes free to prevent the powerful spring from flying out. Remove the spring and piston from the housing.

Before installing the tensioner assembly, refer to **FIG 1:53** and check dimensions **A** and **B**. On earlier models, installed length **A** for the piston is 57.4mm (2.26in), modified on later models to 62mm (2.441in). Renew the piston if shorter than standard or if worn or damaged. Free length **B** of compression spring should be 155.5mm (6.122in). Renew the spring if significantly shorter than standard or if damaged or distorted. Note that the end of the spring with tapered coils should face towards the end plug. Refer to **FIG 1:54** and use an air line to check that the vent slots 1 are not blocked. If the slots are blocked or have become displaced, press out the valve and clean the slots. When refitting the valve, do not block the slots with the perforated disc.

When refitting the tensioner, fit the piston spring and end plug then tighten the plug a few turns only, so that oil will be able to escape past the threads. Fill the oil pocket in the lower timing case cover with engine oil. Use a screwdriver to move the tensioner rail backwards and forwards as indicated by the arrows in **FIG 1:52**, until oil emerges past the end plug threads. This operation is essential to bleed air from the tensioner assembly. On completion, tighten the end plug fully then refit the remaining components in the reverse order of removal.

Timing chain removal:

Remove the upper and lower timing case covers as described previously. Release the lockplates and remove the four camshaft sprocket securing bolts (see **FIG 1:48**). **Neither the crankshaft nor camshaft must** be turned while the camshaft sprocket is detached, unless the cylinder head is completely removed, otherwise the valves may contact the pistons and cause serious internal damage.

Remove the camshaft sprocket from the chain, then remove the chain from the crankshaft sprocket. Carefully swing the chain from the slide rail to the righthand side. Check the chain and sprockets for wear or damage which would dictate renewal. To remove the crankshaft sprocket, the oil pump sprocket must first be removed as described in **Section 1:9**. Remove the locating key and the 'O' ring seal, then pull the sprocket from the crankshaft using a suitable puller such as tool 7006. There is no need to install the 'O' ring when refitting the sprocket.

The timing chain should be installed in the reverse order of removal, making sure that the oil pump drive chain, if removed, is properly tensioned as described in **Section 1:9**. When installing camshaft sprocket, fit the sprocket to the chain so that locating pin 1 is at the eight o'clock position (see **FIG 1:55**). The hole in the sprocket must be aligned with the threaded hole in the camshaft and the projection on the cylinder head as shown by the upper arrow. Use new lockplates to secure the camshaft sprocket fixing bolts.

1:7 External oil filter

The oil filter is of the renewable cartridge type and should be renewed at the intervals recommended in the manufacturer's service schedule. A section through the filter assembly is shown in **FIG 1:56**. Oil from the pump enters through passage 1, passes through the filter, then is supplied through passage 2 to the engine lubrication points. If the filter should become blocked and restrict oil flow, oil pressure will open relief valve 3 to effectively bypass the filter canister. This ensures that engine lubrication is maintained, albeit with unfiltered oil.

To renew the filter element, place a suitable container beneath the filter to catch oil spillage, then unscrew the central bolt and detach the canister. Remove and discard the filter element, then remove the rubber sealing ring from the mounting and discard. Clean any dirt or sludge from the inside of the canister, then install a new filter element. Fit a new sealing ring to the mounting, making sure that it seats properly in the groove and is not twisted. Refit the canister, making sure that it seats correctly on the seal, then tighten the fixing bolt. Turn the canister slightly while tightening, to ensure a good seal. Start the engine and allow to run for a few minutes while checking for oil leaks at the filter canister, then switch off and top up the engine oil as necessary to compensate for that used to fill the canister.

1:8 Sump removal and refitting

Removal:

Remove the lower cover panel from beneath the engine, if fitted. Drain the engine oil, collecting it in a clean container if it is to be re-used. Refer to **Chapter 9** and remove the anti-roll bar. Refer to **Chapter 4** and slacken the alternator mounting bolts.

If power steering is fitted, refer to **Chapter 10** and detach the power steering pump, leaving the hoses connected. Wire the pump away from the work area so that the hoses are not strained.

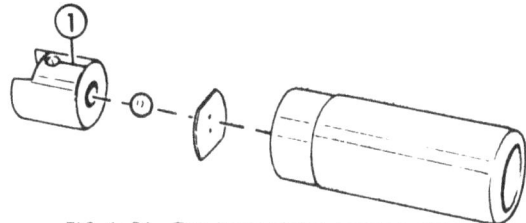

FIG 1:54   Tensioner piston components

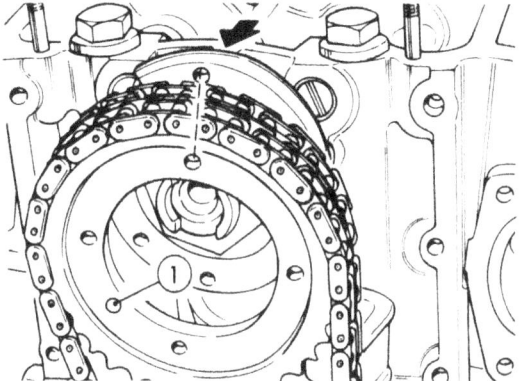

FIG 1:55   Camshaft sprocket alignment

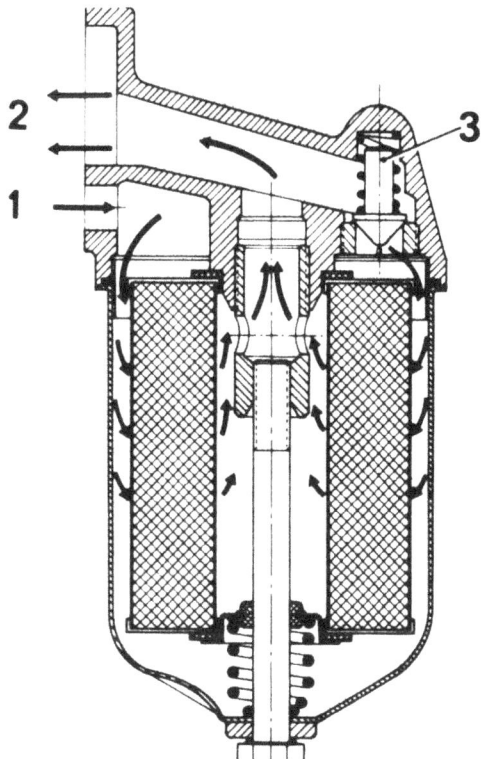

FIG 1:56   Section through oil filter assembly

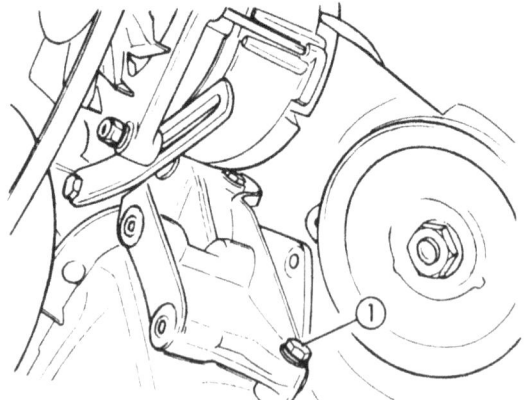

FIG 1:57   Bearing block fixing screw

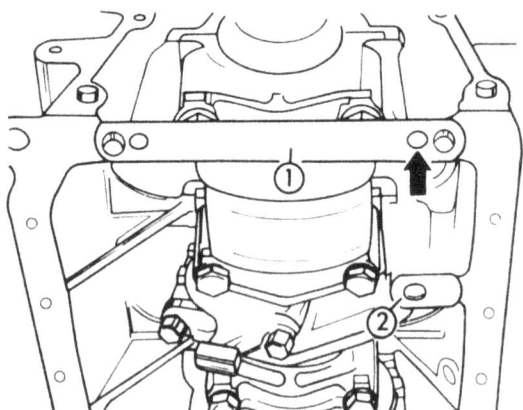

FIG 1:60   Oil pump mounting shims

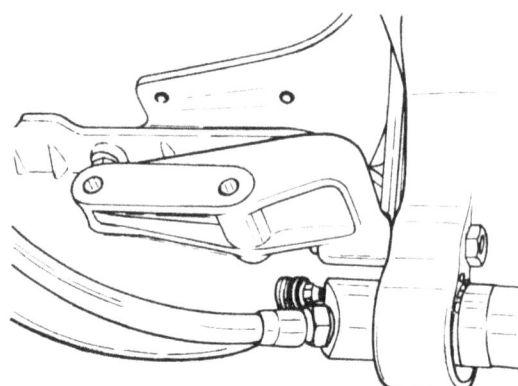

FIG 1:58   Detaching support bracket

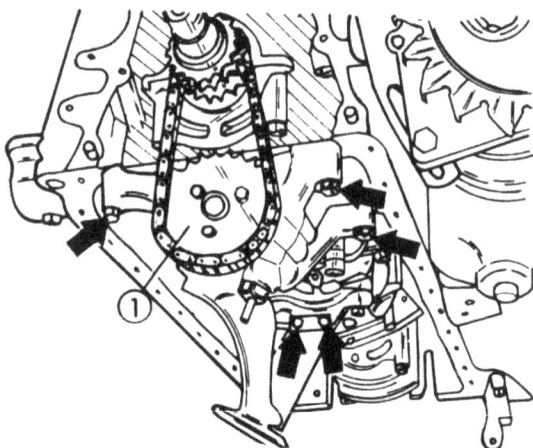

FIG 1:59   Oil pump and strainer removal

Remove the oil level dipstick. Refer to **FIG 1:57** and remove screw 1 from the bearing block. Loosen the bearing block until access to the sump fixing bolts behind it can be gained. Partly detach the support bracket shown in **FIG 1:58** for access to the sump bolts behind the bracket. Remove all sump fixing bolts.

Turn the engine until the connecting rod big-end for No 6 cylinder is above the sump joint line. Lower the front of the sump, then turn the rear towards the support bracket and remove. Remove and discard the sump gasket.

Refitting:

This is a reversal of the removal procedure, using a new sump gasket. Make sure that the mating surfaces of sump and crankcase are clean. Coat the junctions between the timing case cover and crankcase at the front and between crankcase and rear cover at the rear, using Atmosit or other suitable sealant. Tighten the sump fixing bolts alternately and evenly to avoid distortion. Refit the dipstick and refill the sump with engine oil to the correct level. Check that the dipstick guide tube projects from the engine crankcase by 218 ± 0.5mm ($8.583 \pm .020$in). If this dimension is incorrect, a false oil level reading will be obtained when the dipstick is used. Set drive belt tension as described in **Chapter 4**.

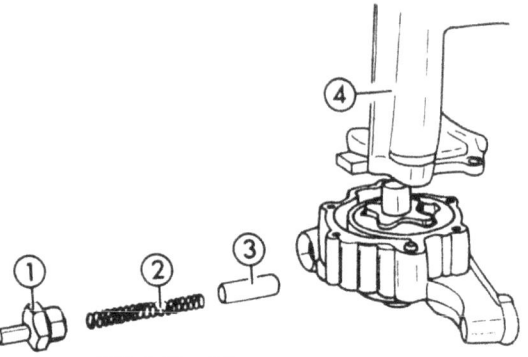

FIG 1:61   Oil pump components

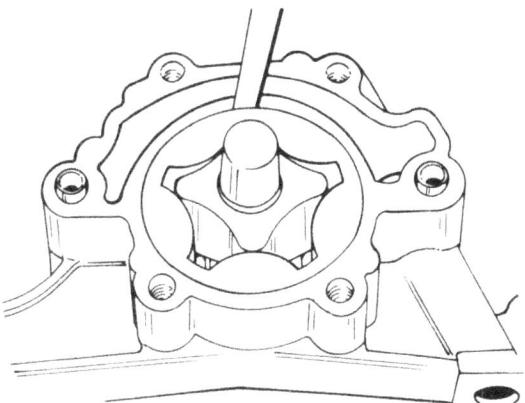

FIG 1:62 Checking clearance between outer rotor and body

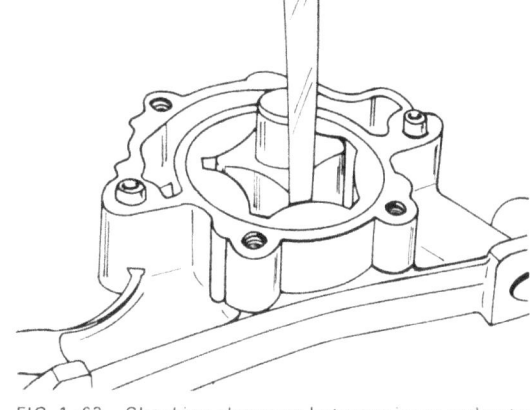

FIG 1:63 Checking clearance between inner and outer rotors

1:9 Oil pump and strainer

Removal:

Remove the sump as described in **Section 1:8**. Refer to **FIG 1:59**. Remove sprocket 1 and detach the pump fixing bolts arrowed, then remove the pump and strainer from the crankcase. Collect the front and rear mounting shims.

Refitting:

This is a reversal of the removal procedure, but chain tension must be correctly adjusted. To do this, front and rear shims 1 and 2 must be installed between pump mounting flanges and crankcase as shown in **FIG 1:60**. Note the correct location of oil hole arrowed in shim 1. Shims must be of equal thickness front and rear and added until the pump drive chain can be pressed inwards slightly with gentle thumb pressure at a point midway between sprockets. When correct, slacken the strainer support plate upper mounting bolts and move the plate up or down as necessary so that the pick-up pipe is not strained, then retighten the bolts. Refit the sump as described in **Section 1:8**

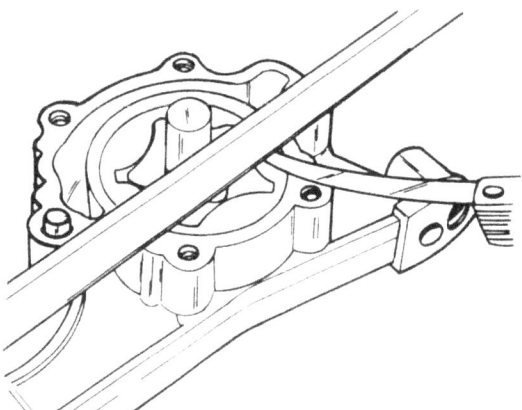

FIG 1:64 Checking clearance between rotors and housing

Oil pump overhaul:

Remove the pump as described previously. Refer to **FIG 1:61** and unscrew threaded union 1. Remove spring 2 and piston 3. Remove pump cover and strainer assembly 4.

Use feeler gauges to check pump internal clearances. Check clearance between outer rotor and body as shown in **FIG 1:62**, which should be 0.1 ± 0.025mm (0.004 ± 0.001in). If maximum permitted clearance is exceeded, renew the pump body. Check clearance between inner and outer rotors as shown in **FIG 1:63**, which should be 0.12 to 0.30mm (0.0047 to 0.0118in). Excessive clearance will dictate renewal of both rotors. Check clearance between top surface of rotors and housing face, using a straightedge as shown in **FIG 1:64**. This should be 0.050 to 0.091mm (0.002 to 0.0036in). If clearance is excessive, renew the pump housing.

To remove the rotors, use a suitable puller to pull off the outer flange. Never attempt to drive or lever off the

FIG 1:65 Checking flange and rotor installation

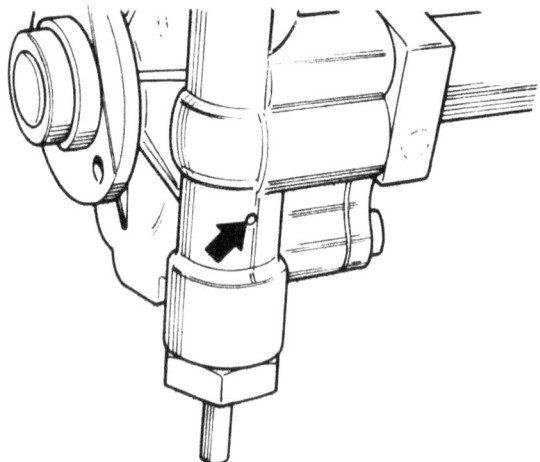

FIG 1 : 66   Oil pump vent hole

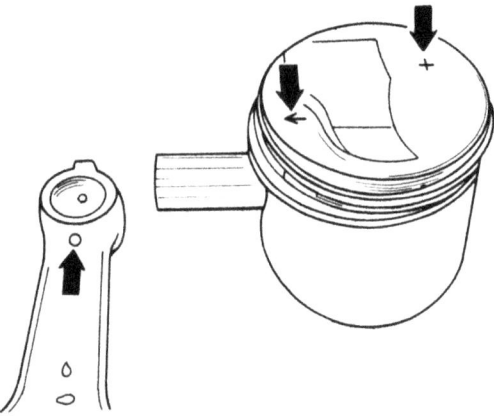

FIG 1 : 67   Piston, gudgeon pin and connecting rod

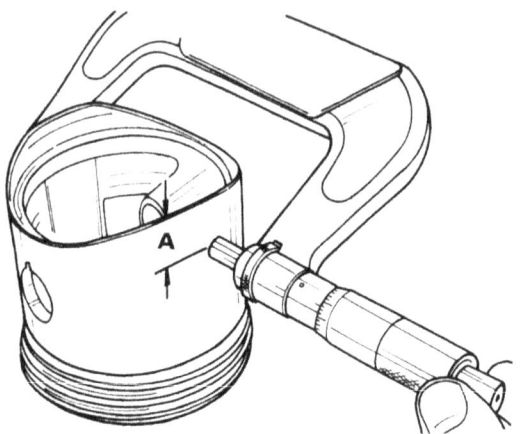

FIG 1 : 68   Measuring piston diameter

flange. When installing, press into position until distance **A** between flange and inner rotor is 44.3 ± 0.1mm (1.744 ± 0.004in) as shown in **FIG 1 : 65**. Some pump units are provided with a vent hole as shown in **FIG 1 : 66**. If so, it is important to ensure that the hole is clear.

On completion, clean the oil pick-up pipe and strainer, then reassemble the oil pump in the reverse order of dismantling. Refit the pump as described previously.

1 : 10 Pistons and connecting rods

Removal:

Remove the cylinder head as described in **Section 1 : 3** and the sump as described in **Section 1 : 8**. If the car is raised for access to the underside, support it safely on floor stands.

The connecting rods and caps are numbered 1 to 6 from the front of the engine. Turn the crankshaft as necessary to bring each connecting rod in turn to the lower position, then remove nuts and detach the caps and shell bearing. Note that all components must be kept in the correct order for refitting in their original positions if they are not to be renewed.

Push the piston and connecting rod assembly upwards and remove through the top of the bore, then remove the upper shell bearing from the connecting rod. Repeat the operation described to remove each assembly in turn. Note that, when refitting the assemblies, a suitable ring compressor should be used when entering rings into cylinder bores, and that pistons and big-end bearing shells should be lubricated with engine oil.

Remove the gudgeon pins to separate pistons from connecting rods. Note that gudgeon pins must be fitted in their original positions as they are matched to the pistons. The oil hole in the small-end of the connecting rod must face towards the front of the engine, together with the arrow on the piston crown (see **FIG 1 : 67**). The other mark on the piston will be either a plus (+) or minus (−) sign which indicates the weight group of the piston. Replacement pistons must be of the same group as the original.

Pistons and rings:

Clean carbon deposits from the piston crowns, then gently ease the rings from their grooves and remove them over the tops of the pistons. Keep all parts in the correct order, if not to be renewed. Clean carbon from the piston ring grooves, for which job a piece broken from an old piston ring ground to a chisel point will prove an ideal tool. Inspect the pistons for score marks or any sign of seizure, which would dictate renewal.

Check the cylinder bores for score marks and remove glaze and carbon deposits. Badly scored or worn surfaces will dictate a rebore to accept new pistons, this being a specialist job.

Check the clearance of each piston in its bore, measuring the outside diameter of the piston at distance **A** from the lower skirt at right angles to the gudgeon pin bore, **FIG 1 : 68**. For Mahle pistons, dimension **A** should be 20.5mm (0.807in) for 2500 models and 15mm (0.591in) for all other models. For KS pistons, **A** should be 26.25mm (1.033in) for 2500 models, 24.05mm (0.947in) for all 2800 and 3.0 models and 14.9mm

(0.587in) for 3.3L models. For Nural pistons, **A** should be 16.2mm (0.638in) for all models. For Alcan pistons, **A** should be 18.5mm (0.728in) for 2800 models, 21.4mm (0.843in) for 3.0S models and 17.5mm (0.689in) for 3.0Si models.

Use an internal measuring gauge to check the maximum diameter of cylinder bores, measuring at top, bottom and centre. Calculate the maximum clearance of each piston in its bore from the measurements taken and compare with the figures given in **Technical Data**. Excessive clearance will dictate the fitting of new pistons of the same size or, possibly, reboring of the cylinders to accept oversize pistons, which is a specialist job.

Fit the piston rings one at a time into the bore from which they were removed, pushing them down into the bore with the correct inverted piston to ensure squareness. Measure the gap between the ends of the ring while it is positioned in the bore, using feeler gauges as shown in **FIG 1 : 69**. This clearance should be within the limits for the appropriate ring given in **Technical Data**. Hold each of the rings in turn in the piston groove from which it was removed as shown in **FIG 1 : 70**, then measure the side clearance in the groove with feeler gauges. This clearance should be within the limits for the appropriate ring given in **Technical Data**. If the clearance measurements in either test are at or near the wear limits, new rings should be fitted. If the fitting of new rings does not cure excessive ring to groove clearance, new pistons also will be required. Excessive ring clearance can be responsible for high oil consumption and poor engine performance.

Check the gudgeon pins for wear, scoring or pitting and renew complete with piston if necessary. Gudgeon pins should be a thumb push fit in the small-end bores. If excessive clearance is caused by wear of the small-end bush, a new bush can be installed and reamed to size. As press equipment is necessary to remove and install bushes, the work should be carried out at a service station.

Carefully fit the piston rings to the pistons as shown in **FIG 1 : 71**, noting that the 'Top' mark on each ring must be uppermost. Space the ring gaps at 180° intervals around the piston.

Connecting rods:

A connecting rod that is damaged in any way should be renewed. Check rods for bending or twisting, any such condition dictating realignment on special equipment at a service station, or renewal if the condition cannot be rectified.

If there has been a big-end bearing failure, the crankpin must be examined for damage and for transfer of metal to its surface. The oilway in the crankshaft must be checked to ensure that there is no obstruction. Big-end bearing clearance can be checked by the use of Plastigage, which is the trade name for a precisely calibrated plastic filament. The filament is laid across the bearing to be measured for working clearance as shown in **FIG 1 : 72**, the bearing cap fitted and the nuts tightened to the specified torque. The bearing is then dismantled and the width of the flattened filament measured with the scale supplied with the material. The figure thus measured is the actual bearing clearance. Both main and big-end bearing clearances are measured in a similar manner.

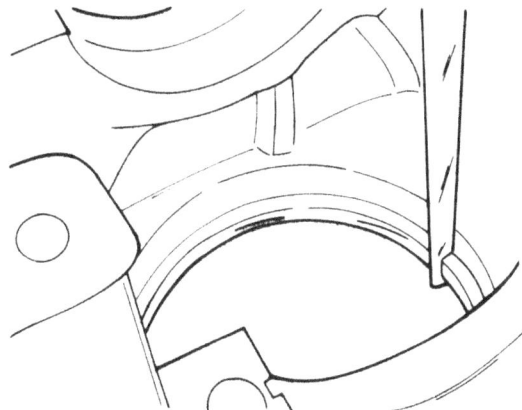

FIG 1 : 69   Checking piston ring end gap

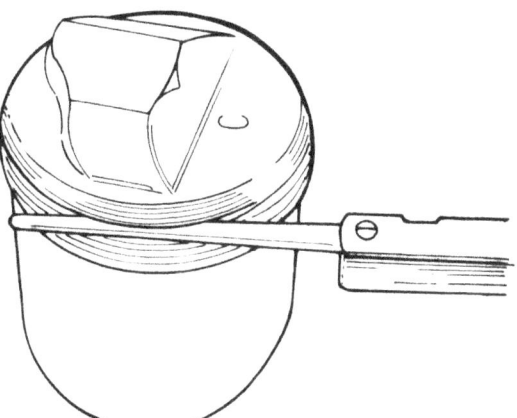

FIG 1 : 70   Checking piston ring side clearance

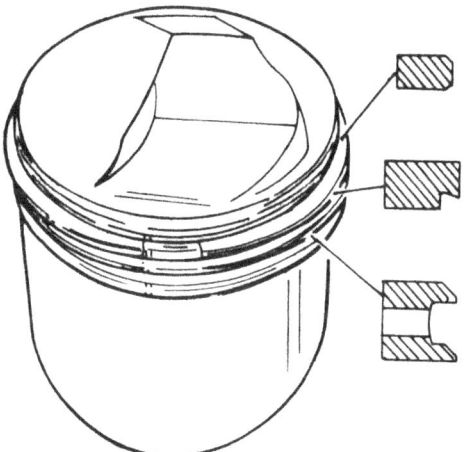

FIG 1 : 71   Piston ring installation

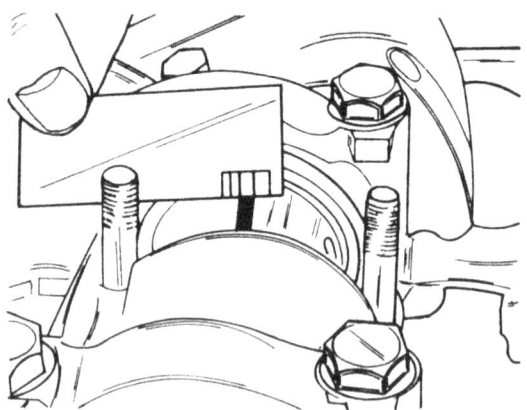

FIG 1:72 Checking bearing clearance

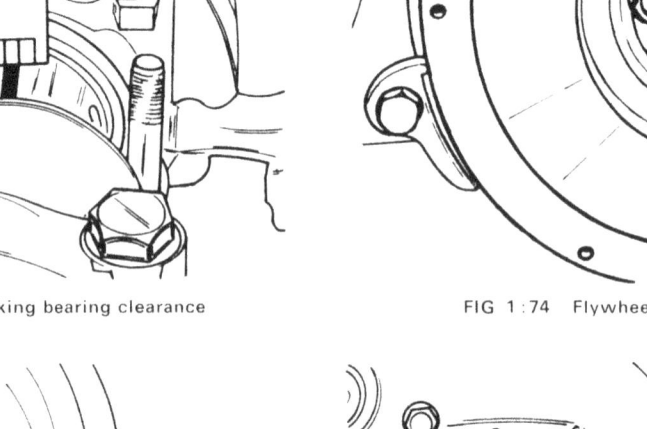

FIG 1:74 Flywheel installation

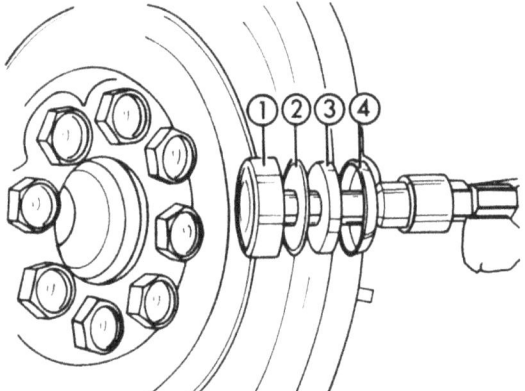

FIG 1:73 Pilot bearing removal

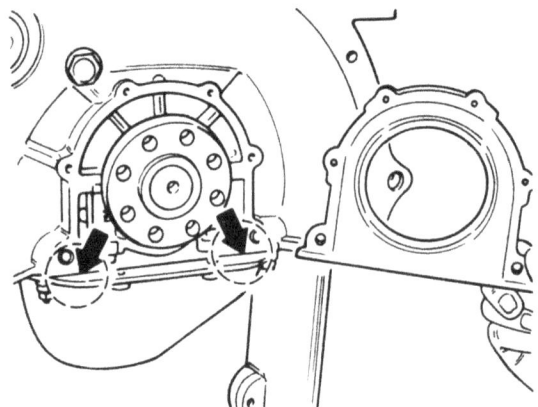

FIG 1:75 Crankcase rear cover installation

Note that each bearing must be measured separately and none of the remaining bearing caps must be fitted during the operation. The bearing surfaces must be clean and free from oil and the crankshaft must not be turned during the measuring procedure. The point at which the measurement is taken must be close to the respective dead centre position and no hammer blows must be applied to the bearing or cap.

Place a length of plastic filament identical to the width of the bearing on the crankshaft journal, then fit the main or big-end bearing cap with shell bearings and tighten to the specified torque. Remove the cap and measure the width of the flattened filament with the scale supplied to obtain the running clearance for that bearing. The clearance limits are given in **Technical Data**. If the bearing running clearance is too high, new bearing shells of the correct type must be fitted and the clearance rechecked. If undersize bearings are to be fitted to take up crankshaft wear, the crankshaft journals must be factory-reground, so the crankshaft should be taken to a BMW service station for attention. Early type crankshaft bearing shells were provided with an oil hole, later shells being provided with an oil pocket. When renewing shell bearings, always use the later type.

1:11 Flywheel and pilot bearing

Pilot bearing renewal:

Remove the clutch as described in **Chapter 5** or the automatic transmission as described in **Chapter 7**. Using a Kukko extractor or similar, remove the ball-bearing complete with cover plate, felt ring and cap as shown in **FIG 1:73**.

Install the bearing in the reverse order of removal, packing bearing 1 with good quality high melting point grease. Insert the cover plate 2 with embossed side outwards and soak felt ring 3 in hot tallow before installation. Tap bearing cap 4 into place until it seats firmly. On completion, refit the clutch as described in **Chapter 5** or the automatic transmission as described in **Chapter 7**.

Flywheel removal:

Remove the clutch as described in **Chapter 5** or the automatic transmission as described in **Chapter 7**. On models without flywheel locating sleeves, mark the installed position of the flywheel relative to the crankshaft as shown by the arrow in **FIG 1:74**. Use tool 7007 or other suitable means to lock the flywheel against rotation, then loosen the mounting bolts. Support the weight of the flywheel, then remove the bolts and detach the flywheel from the crankshaft, together with torque converter drive plate in the case of automatic transmission models. Note that the flywheel is mounted with special expansion bolts which must be used once only, so discard the bolts and obtain new ones to replace them.

If the flywheel ring gear is damaged, it can be renewed, but as it is shrunk onto the flywheel and the new gear must be accurately heated before installation, the work should be carried out by a service station.

Refit the flywheel, including drive plate for automatic transmission models, in the reverse order of removal, using new expansion bolts. Coat the bolt threads with Loctite LT red and install them finger tight, then tighten alternately and evenly to the specified torque.

1:12 Crankshaft oil seals

Front seal renewal:

Remove the crankshaft pulley and damper assembly as described in the instructions for lower timing case cover removal in **Section 1:6**. Lever out the seal, taking care not to damage the housing. Drive the new seal squarely into position, making sure that the lips run in front of or behind any scored areas on the damper hub.

Rear oil seal renewal:

Drain the engine oil. Remove the flywheel as described in **Section 1:11**. Refer to **Section 1:8** and loosen but do not remove the sump fixing bolts. Refer to **FIG 1:75**. Carefully lever the sump gasket away from the crankcase rear end cover, then remove the fixing bolts and detach the cover. Note that, if the sump gasket is damaged, the sump must be removed and the gasket renewed. Carefully drive the oil seal from the end cover and discard. Press the new oil seal into the end cover as shown in **FIG 1:76** until it seats firmly.

Install the rear cover and remaining components in the reverse order of removal, coating the junctions between end cover and sump with Atmosit or similar sealant at the points arrowed in **FIG 1:75**.

1:13 Crankshaft removal and refitting

Removal:

Remove the engine as described in **Section 1:2**, then remove the clutch assembly on manual transmission models as described in **Chapter 5**. Remove the cylinder head as described in **Section 1:3**, the timing chain as described in **Section 1:6**, the oil pump as described in **Section 1:9** and the crankshaft end cover as described in **Section 1:12**.

Invert the cylinder block and remove the big-end bearing caps as described in **Section 1:10**. Push the piston and connecting rod assemblies into the bores sufficiently to clear the crankshaft journals. Before removing the crankshaft, check crankshaft axial play which should be 0.085 to 0.174mm (0.0035 to 0.007in). If axial play is excessive, the crankshaft guide bearing should be renewed, referring to **Section 1:10** to select bearing shells with the correct running clearance.

Note that the crankshaft bearing caps are numbered 1 to 6 from front to rear of the engine for correct installation. Remove the bearing caps and lower bearing shells,

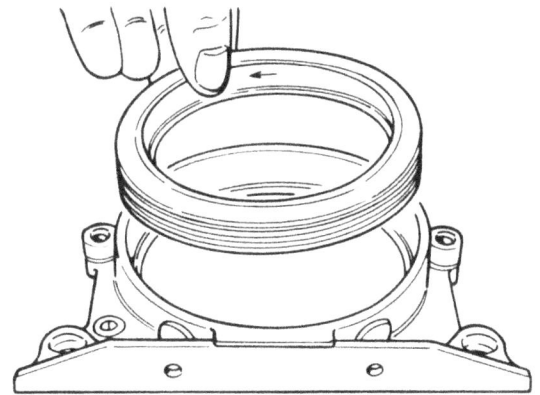

FIG 1:76   Rear oil seal installation

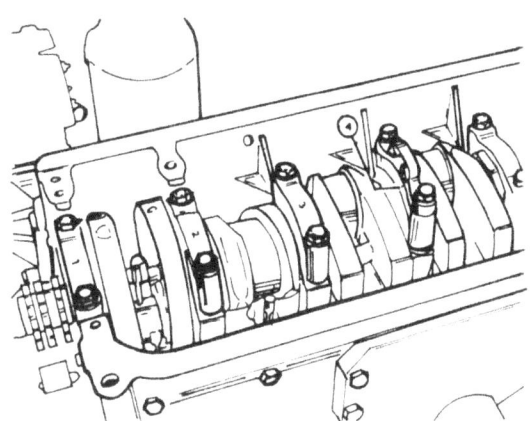

FIG 1:77   Crankshaft removal

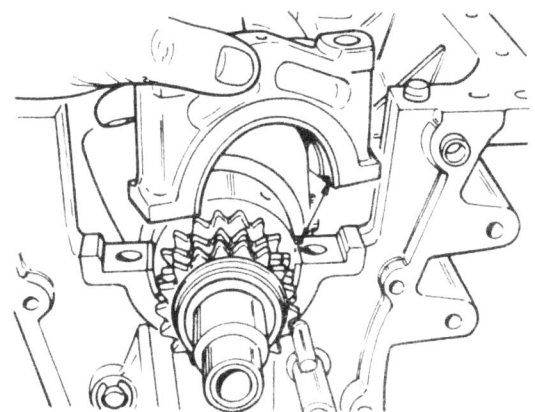

FIG 1:78   Main bearing cap installation

keeping the shells in the correct order for refitting in their original positions if they are not to be renewed. Lift the crankshaft from the crankcase and collect the upper bearings, keeping these in the correct order also (see **FIG 1 : 77**).

If there has been a crankshaft bearing failure, the journal must be checked for damage and for transfer of metal to its surface. The oilways in the crankshaft must be checked to ensure that there is no obstruction. Main bearing clearance can be checked by the use of Plastigage, in the manner described in **Section 1 : 10**. If there is any doubt about the condition of the crankshaft it should be taken to a specialist for more detailed checks.

Refitting :

Refit the crankshaft in the reverse order of removal, making sure that the bearing shells and main bearing caps are refitted in their original positions. Make sure that the grooves in the caps and crankcase are correctly aligned as shown in **FIG 1 : 78**. Lubricate the bearing shells with engine oil before installation.

1 : 14 Fault diagnosis

(a) Engine will not start

1 Defective coil
2 Faulty distributor capacitor
3 Dirty, pitted or incorrectly set contact points
4 Ignition wires loose or insulation faulty
5 Water on spark plug leads
6 Battery discharged, corrosion of terminals
7 Faulty or jammed starter
8 Sparking plug leads wrongly connected
9 Vapour lock in fuel pipes
10 Defective fuel pump
11 Overchoking or underchoking
12 Blocked fuel filter or carburetter jet
13 Leaking valves
14 Sticking valves
15 Valve timing incorrect
16 Ignition timing incorrect

(b) Engine stalls

1 Check 1, 2, 3, 4, 5, 10, 11, 12, 13 and 14 in (a)
2 Sparking plugs defective or gaps incorrect
3 Retarded ignition
4 Mixture too weak
5 Water in fuel system
6 Petrol tank vent blocked
7 Incorrect valve clearances

(c) Engine idles badly

1 Check 2 and 7 in (b)
2 Air leak at manifold joints
3 Carburetter adjustment wrong
4 Air leak in carburetter
5 Over-rich mixture
6 Worn piston rings
7 Worn valve stems or guides
8 Weak exhaust valve springs

(d) Engine misfires

1 Check 1, 2, 3, 4, 5, 8, 10, 12, 13, 14, 15 and 16 in (a)
2 Weak or broken valve springs

(e) Engine overheats (see **Chapter 4**)

(f) Compression low

1 Check 13 and 14 in (a) ; 6 and 7 in (c) ; and 2 in (d)
2 Worn piston ring grooves
3 Scored or worn cylinder bores

(g) Engine lacks power

1 Check 3, 10, 11, 12, 13, 14, 15 and 16 in (a) ; 2, 3, 4 and 7 in (b) ; 6 and 7 in (c) ; and 2 in (d). Also check (e) and (f)
2 Leaking joint washers or gaskets
3 Fouled sparking plugs
4 Automatic advance not working

(h) Burned valves or seats

1 Check 13 and 14 in (a) ; 7 in (b) ; and 2 in (d). Also check (e)
2 Excessive carbon round valve seats and head

(j) Sticking valves

1 Check 2 in (d)
2 Bent valve stem
3 Scored valve stem or guide
4 Incorrect valve clearances

(k) Excessive cylinder wear

1 Check 11 in (a)
2 Lack of oil
3 Dirty oil
4 Piston rings gummed up or broken
5 Badly fitting piston rings
6 Connecting rod bent

(l) Excessive oil consumption

1 Check 6 and 7 in (c) ; and check (k)
2 Ring gaps too wide
3 Oil return holes in piston choked with carbon
4 Scored cylinders
5 Oil level too high
6 External oil leaks

(m) Crankshaft and connecting rod bearing failure

1 Check 2 in (k)
2 Restricted oilways
3 Worn journals or crankpins
4 Loose bearing caps
5 Extremely low oil pressure
6 Bent connecting rod

(n) Internal water leakage (see **Chapter 4**)

(o) Poor water circulation (see **Chapter 4**)

(p) Corrosion (see **Chapter 4**)

(q) High fuel consumption (see **Chapter 2**)

(r) Engine vibration

1 Loose alternator or other belt driven component
2 Engine mountings loose or defective
3 Misfiring due to mixture, ignition or mechanical faults

CHAPTER 2

THE FUEL SYSTEM

2:1 Description

3.0 Si, Si A, CSi, CSiA and 3.0 CSL models with 3.15 litre engines are equipped with electronically controlled fuel injection systems, details of which are given in **Section 2:8**. That section also describes the maintenance and servicing procedures which can be carried out without the need for specialised testing equipment.

The remaining models covered by this manual are provided with twin downdraught carburetters fitted with automatic choke units. Fuel from the rear-mounted tank is supplied to the carburetters either by a mechanical (diaphragm) fuel pump mounted on the engine cylinder head and driven by a special eccentric on the lefthand side of the camshaft, or by an electrically operated pump mounted in the engine compartment. Twin renewable paper cartridge-type air filters are fitted in a pressed steel casing which is attached directly to the carburetters. On some models, the air cleaner intake pipe is provided with a main intake pipe and a secondary intake pipe which draws warm air from a point close to the exhaust manifold. A sensor linked to a flap valve operates to control air flow through either or both intakes to regulate the temperature of air supplied to the carburetters.

2:2 Routine maintenance

The air filter elements and fuel line filter cartridge (if fitted) should be renewed at the intervals recommended in the manufacturer's service schedule. The air filter elements should be inspected occasionally between servicing intervals and cleaned, if necessary, as described in **Section 2:3**. The filter gauze fitted to the fuel pump should be periodically cleaned and checked as described in **Section 2:4**

Fuel line filter renewal:

Slacken the hose clips and remove the mounting screw as shown by the arrows in **FIG 2:1**. Detach the hoses from the connectors then remove and discard the filter element. Fit the new element in the reverse order of removal, making sure that the direction of fuel flow is correct according to the markings on the ends of the filter casing.

2:3 Air cleaner

For access to the air filter elements, remove the top cover from the assembly by releasing the spring clips (see

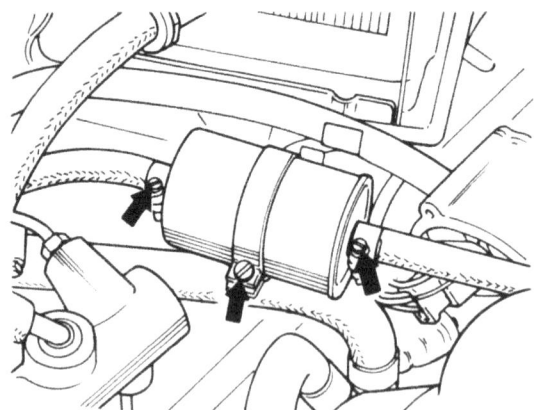

FIG 2:1   Fuel line filter installation

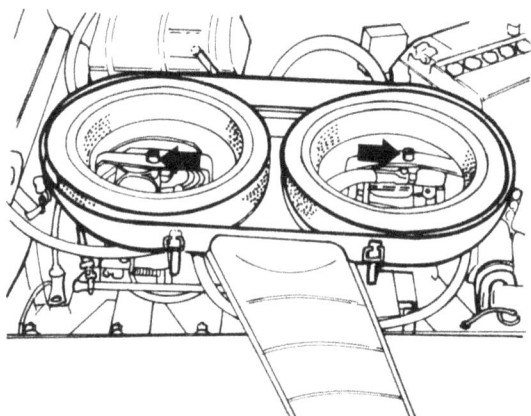

FIG 2:2   Air cleaner with top cover removed

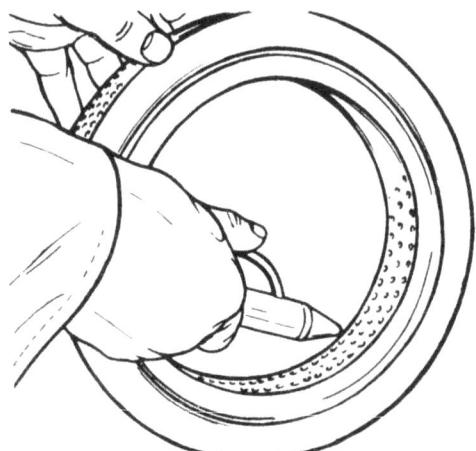

FIG 2:3   Cleaning air filter element

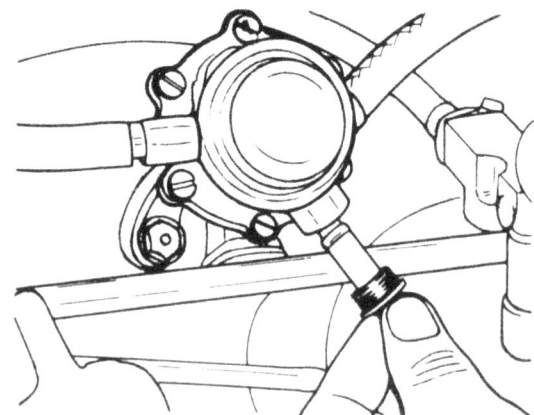

FIG 2:4   Filter removal, diaphragm pump

FIG 2:2). If the elements are to be renewed, remove and discard the old elements, wipe clean the inside of the housing and cover, then reassemble using new elements. To clean filter elements between renewal periods, hold the element flat and tap it gently against a solid surface to release loose dust, then blow air from the inside to outside using an air-line as shown in **FIG 2:3**. Air pressure should not be more than 5 atmospheres (71lb/sq in).

To remove the air cleaner assembly complete, remove the top cover then unscrew the two securing nuts arrowed in **FIG 2:2**. Lift the assembly from the carburetters and release the hoses from the fittings on the body. Refitting is a reversal of the removal procedure.

2:4 Fuel pump

Testing:

Before testing the pump, ensure that the fuel tank vent system is not blocked. A blockage is indicated if the removal of the fuel filler cap results in a sound of air being drawn into the tank. If so, the fuel tank vent system must be checked and cleaned.

If the vent system is clear and it is still suspected that fuel is not reaching the carburetters, disconnect the carburetter feed pipe and hold a suitable container under the end of the pipe. Turn the engine over a few times with the starter (mechanical pump), or switch on the ignition (electric pump), and watch for fuel squirting from the end of the pipe, which indicates that the pump is working. If so, check the float needles in the carburetters for possible sticking.

Reduced fuel flow can be caused by blocked fuel pipe or a clogged filter. If a clogged fuel line filter is suspected, remove the filter as described in **Section 2:2** and check that fuel can flow through it freely. Check the filter gauze at the fuel pump as described later in this section.

If an obstructed pipeline appears to be the cause of the trouble, it may be cleared with compressed air. Disconnect the pipeline at both ends. **Do not pass compressed air through the pump or the valves will be damaged.** Similarly, compressed air must not be passed through the fuel line filter, if fitted. If there is an obstruction between the pump and the tank, remove the tank filler cap before blowing the pipe through from the pump end.

If the pump delivers insufficient fuel, suspect an air leak between the pump and the tank, dirt under the pump valves or faulty valve seatings. If no fuel is delivered, suspect a sticking valve or a faulty pump diaphragm.

Test the action of the pump valves by blowing and sucking at the inlet and outlet points. Do this with the pump in situ, using a suitable piece of pipe connected to the pump inlet and outlet in turn. It should be possible to blow air in through the pump inlet but not to suck air out, and it should be possible to suck air out of the pump outlet but not to blow air in. If the valves do not work properly according to this test, or if the pump is defective in any other way, the unit must be overhauled or renewed as described later. Note that no servicing is possible in the case of electrically operated pumps.

Fuel pump filter:

If a diaphragm pump is fitted, remove the air cleaner assembly as described in **Section 2:3**. Unscrew and remove the cap and filter gauze as shown in **FIG 2:4**. If an electrically operated pump is fitted, disconnect the fuel inlet hose and remove the filter gauze as shown in **FIG 2:5**.

Carefully wash the filter gauze in clean petrol, using a small brush to remove stubborn deposits. If the filter is damaged or will not clean up properly it should be renewed.

Carefully install the filter in the reverse order of removal. If the air cleaner was removed, refit as described in **Section 2:3**.

Fuel pump removal:

Diaphragm pump:

Remove the air cleaner assembly as described in **Section 2:3**. Disconnect the fuel pipes from the pump, then plug or clamp the ends of the pipes to prevent fuel loss. Unscrew the two fixing nuts and remove the pump from the insulating flange. Check the condition of the pump pushrod and insulating flange, which are shown in **FIG 2:6**. If new components are required, note that pushrod length **A** and insulating flange thickness **B** for replacement parts must be the same as those of the originals.

Refit the pump in the reverse order of removal, using new gaskets at the insulating flange. Tighten the mounting nuts alternately and evenly to avoid distortion of the flange.

Electrically operated pump:

Disconnect the plug at the fuel pump as shown in **FIG 2:7** pulling on the plug body only, never directly on the cables. Disconnect the fuel inlet pipe and remove the filter gauze to prevent it from being damaged. Disconnect the fuel delivery hose from the expansion vessel attached to the pump, then plug or clamp the ends of the hoses to prevent fuel loss. Remove the fuel pump together with expansion vessel. Disconnect the expansion vessel from the pump as shown in **FIG 2:8**. Note that the fuel pump must be renewed complete if it is faulty, as no repairs are possible.

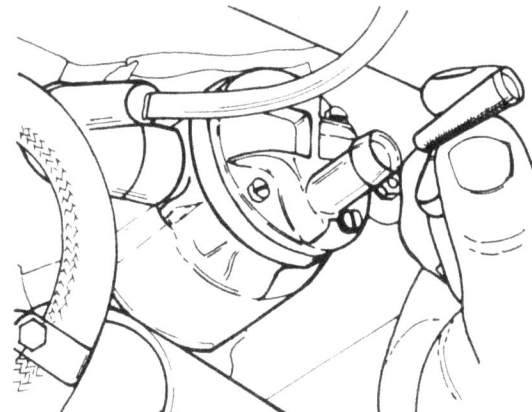

FIG 2:5   Filter removal, electrically operated pump

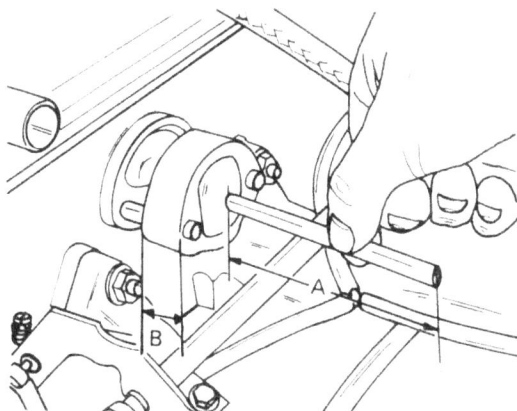

FIG 2:6   Diaphragm pump pushrod and insulating flange

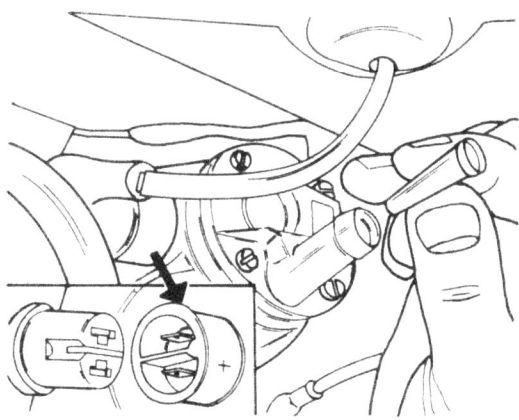

FIG 2:7   Electrically operated pump removal

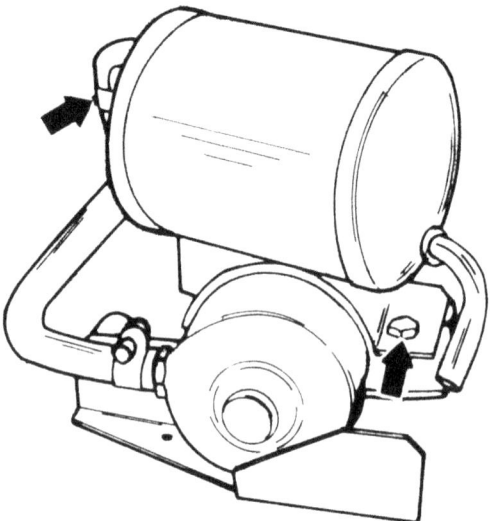

FIG 2:8   Removing expansion vessel

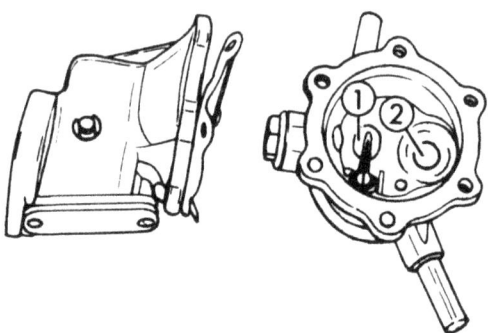

FIG 2:9   Inlet valve 1 and outlet valve 2

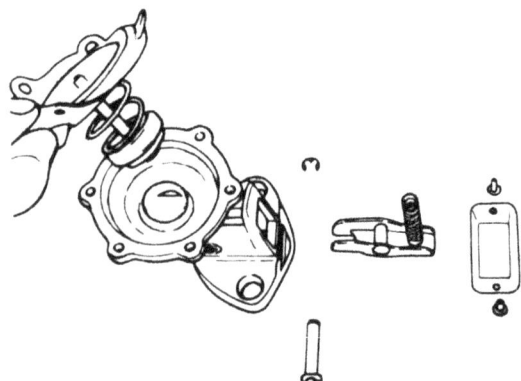

FIG 2:10   Pump lower components

Refit the pump in the reverse order of removal, making sure that the plug is correctly connected as shown in **FIG 2:7**. The projection in the socket must fit in the plug groove.

Diaphragm pump overhaul:

Remove the pump as described previously. Mark the pump upper and lower parts so that they can be reconnected in their original relative positions, then remove the screws and separate the two parts. Refer to **FIG 2:9**. Remove and check inlet valve 1 and make sure that its sealing surface is in good condition. Check outlet valve 2 for correct operation, by pushing gently against its spring and allowing it to return. Carefully wash the pump upper part in petrol to remove any dirt or sediment. Remove and clean the filter element as described previously.

Refer to **FIG 2:10** and dismantle the pump lower components. Remove the retaining washer, cup and spring from the diaphragm pushrod. The diaphragm should be discarded and a new one fitted whenever the pump is overhauled. Check all other components for wear or damage and renew as necessary. Clean the pump lower body with petrol to remove dirt and sediment.

Reassemble the pump in the reverse order of dismantling. Make sure that the rocker arm correctly engages the lower end of the diaphragm pushrod. When the two halves of the pump body are fitted together, the diaphragm should be properly positioned. This is best carried out by fitting the lower part of the pump to tool 5125. If this tool is not available operate the rocker arm by hand until the diaphragm is in the central (flat) position, then hold in this position while fitting the upper part of the pump and alternately and evenly tightening the retaining screws.

2:5 Carburetter tuning and adjustment

Note that tuning and adjustment procedures will only be effective if the sparking plugs, contact points and ignition system are in good order and the valve clearances correctly set. Accurate tachometer equipment will be needed to correctly set engine idle speed and suitable flow meter equipment will be necessary to ensure correct synchronising of the carburetters. If carburetters with mixture bypass system are fitted, suitable exhaust gas analysing equipment will be needed to check the CO (carbon monoxide) content of the exhaust gas to ensure that it is maintained at the specified level. If suitable equipment is not available, the work should be carried out at a fully equipped service station.

Slow-running adjustments:

Carburetters without mixture bypass system:

Make sure that the engine is at normal operating temperature. Switch off the engine, then remove the air cleaner assembly as described in **Section 2:3**. It may also be necessary to remove the air cleaner mounting studs from the carburetters, according to the type of flow meter equipment to be used. To obtain a basic setting, tighten the idle mixture screws indicated by the lower arrows in **FIG 2:11** until they gently contact their seats, then unscrew each by one and a half to two full turns.

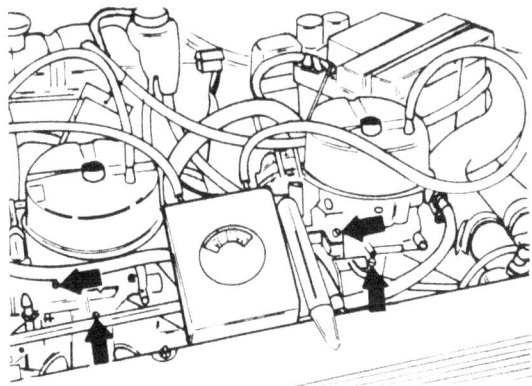

FIG 2:11 Typical installation of synchronising equipment. Carburetter adjustment screws are arrowed

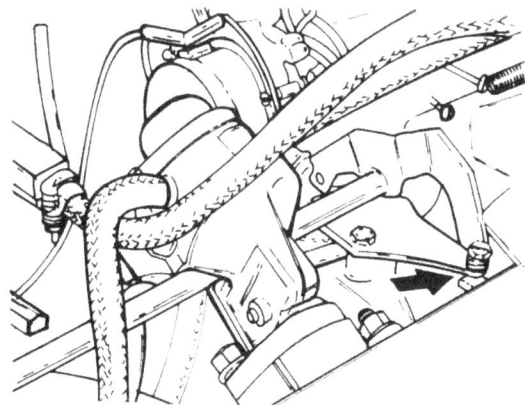

FIG 2:12 Rotary shaft adjustment screw

Make sure that the rotary shaft adjustment screw arrowed in **FIG 2:12** is well clear of its stop. Note that this screw is intended for use only when it is necessary to raise engine speed temporarily when checking such items as distributor vacuum advance and retard characteristics. The adjustment screw must never be used to modify engine idling speed for normal running conditions. Disconnect the linkage connector shown in **FIG 2:13**.

Connect the tachometer and flow meter equipment according to the manufacturer's instructions. Start the engine and allow it to idle. Adjust the screws indicated by the upper arrows in **FIG 2:11** equally to raise the idling speed to 900rev/min, then alternately as necessary to obtain the same flow meter reading at each carburetter. Now adjust the idle mixture screws indicated by the lower arrows to obtain the fastest possible idling speed, then readjust the idle speed screws to correct engine speed. Repeat these procedures as necessary until a smooth idle at the specified engine speed together with the same flow meter reading at each carburetter is obtained. Make adjustments a little at a time and always make final adjustments at the idle mixture screws.

When engine idle speed adjustments have been correctly carried out, adjust the length of the linkage connector at the knurled nut arrowed in **FIG 2:13** until the connector can be refitted to the linkage without moving the linkage and affecting idle speed. Make sure that clearance exists between the rotary shaft adjustment screw and the stop (see **FIG 2:12**). Switch off the engine, remove the flow meter equipment then refit the air cleaner assembly as described in **Section 2:3**. Idle speed will drop by approximately 100rev/min when the air cleaner is installed, so the engine should be restarted and the idle mixture screws readjusted by exactly equal amounts to increase idle speed to 900rev/min.

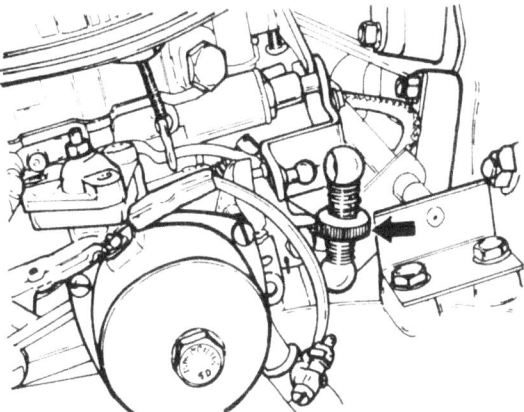

FIG 2:13 Carburetter linkage connector

Carburetters with mixture bypass system:

Make sure that the engine is at normal operating temperature, then switch off. Remove the air cleaner assembly as described in **Section 2:3**. Remove the screw plugs from the exhaust manifolds and insert test probes 7062 as shown in **FIG 2:14**. Connect the exhaust gas analysing equipment. Connect the tachometer and flow meter equipment according to the manufacturer's instructions.

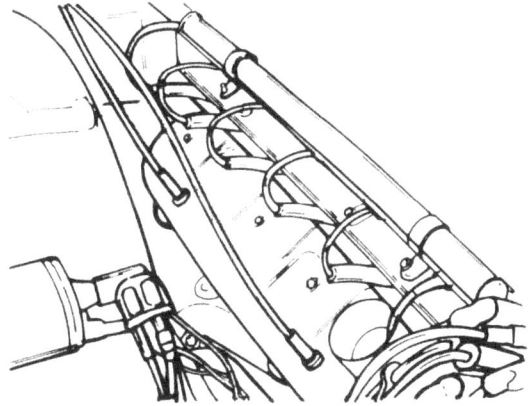

FIG 2:14 Installing test probes to exhaust manifold

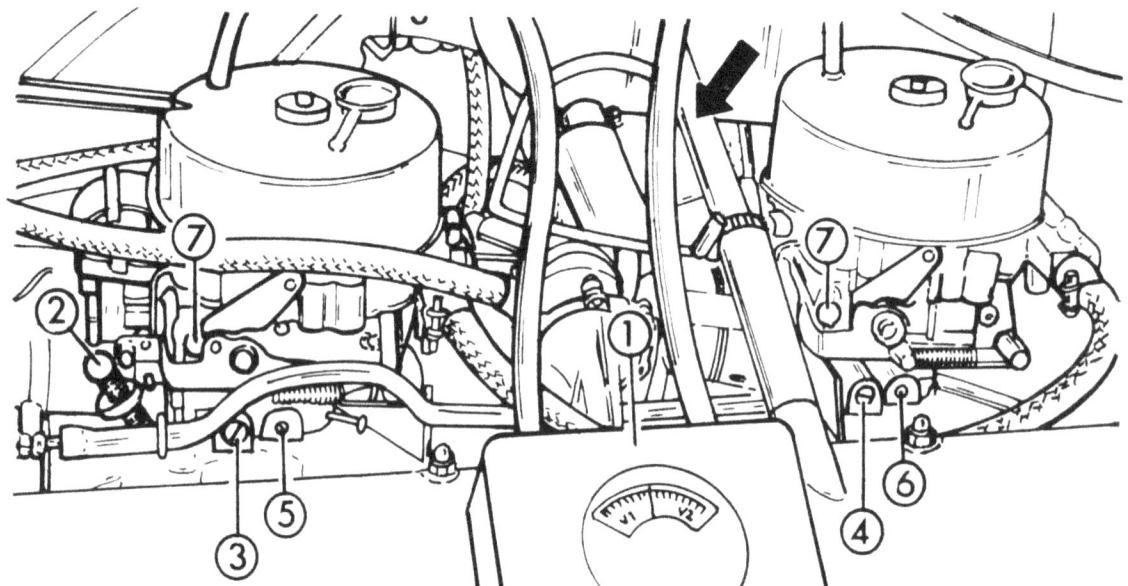

FIG 2:15 Adjusting carburetters having mixture bypass system. The tool used to compensate for the absence of the air cleaner is arrowed

Key to Fig 2:15   1 Synchroniser indicator   2 Connector   3, 4 Additional mixture regulating screws   5, 6 Idle mixture regulating screws   7 Stop screws

Refer to **FIG 2:15**. If tool 130000 is available, it can be installed as shown. This avoids the need for resetting idle speed after the air cleaner assembly has been refitted, but it is not essential. Detach connector 2 from the carburetter linkage.

Start the engine and adjust the two additional mixture regulating screws 3 and 4 until flow meter reading is the same at each carburetter and an idle speed of 900 to 1000rev/min is obtained. Now carry out further adjustments as necessary to the same screws until a CO reading of 2.0 ± 0.5 per cent is obtained, while maintaining equal flow meter readings at the carburetters. If these final adjustments cause the idle speed to alter, repeat the adjustment procedure. If repeated attempts to

obtain the correct settings are unsuccessful, check the stop screw adjustment as described later.

When slow-running adjustments are complete, adjust the length of linkage connector by means of knurled nut arrowed in **FIG 2:13** until it can be refitted without moving the linkage or changing the idle speed at all. Remove the flow meter equipment and install the air cleaner assembly as described in **Section 2:3**. When the air cleaner is fitted, idle speed will drop by approximately 100rev/min, so the additional mixture regulating screws 3 and 4 (see **FIG 2:15**) must be finally adjusted by exactly equal amounts until the specified engine idle speed is obtained, while maintaining the specified exhaust gas CO content.

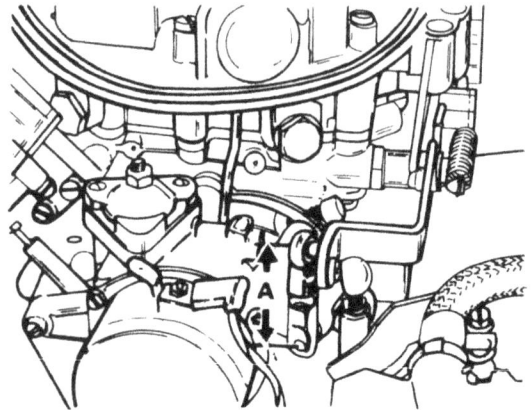

FIG 2:16   Pushrod length A must be 40mm (1.57in)

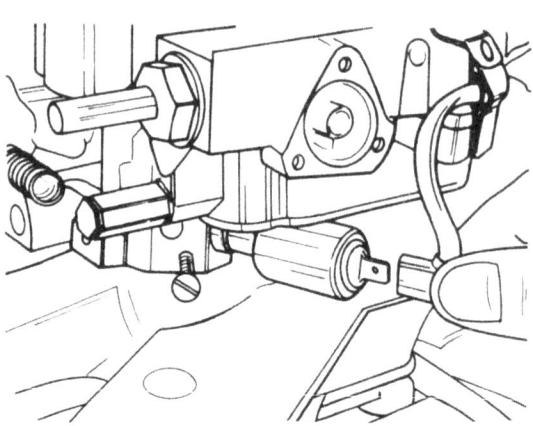

FIG 2:17   Disconnecting idle valve wiring

Stop screw adjustment:

The stop screws 7 on carburetters with mixture bypass system are correctly set by the manufacturers and their positions should not be modified except in exceptional circumstances, for instance if the specified idle speed and exhaust gas CO content cannot be obtained with the adjustment procedure described previously. If this is the case, detach connector 2 from the carburetter linkage and screw both additional mixture regulating screws 3 and 4 fully in. Remove the plastic caps and adjust stop screws 7 to obtain an engine idle speed of 700rev/min with the carburetters synchronised, at the same time adjusting the CO content to 3 per cent per carburetter by means of idle mixture regulating screws 5 and 6. This done, refit the plastic caps to screws 7 and reset idle speed to 900 to 1000rev/min and CO content to 2.0 ± 0.5 per cent using additional mixture regulating screws 3 and 4 and idle mixture regulating screws 5 and 6, making sure that the carburetters remain synchronised. If it is difficult to obtain the same flow meter reading for each carburetter, check the length of the pushrod shown in **FIG 2:16** and adjust if necessary so that dimension **A** is 40mm (1.57in).

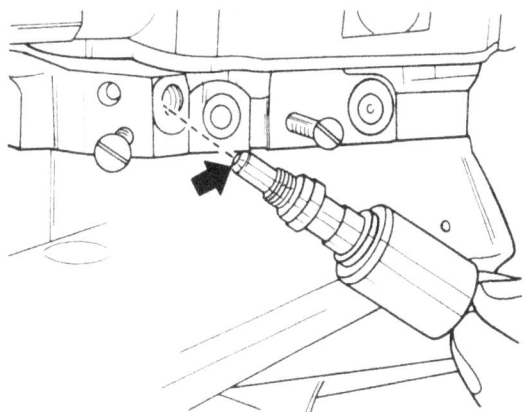

FIG 2:18   Idle valve taper sealing surface

Checking idle valves:

Electrically operated idle valves are fitted to the carburetters to prevent the engine from running on when it is hot and the ignition is switched off. A faulty valve will cause the engine to idle roughly and at a slower speed. If both valves are faulty the engine will cut when the throttle linkage is returned to the idle position.

To check valve operation, set the engine to run at idle speed and pull the connector from the idle valve on one of the carburetters as shown in **FIG 2:17**. When this is done, the engine should idle noticeably slower and less smoothly. When the cable is connected again, a slight clicking noise should be audible. Repeat the test at the second carburetter. If an idle valve does not operate correctly, it must be renewed. To do this, pull off the electrical connector and unscrew the valve from the carburetter. When installing a valve, make sure that the taper sealing surface arrowed in **FIG 2:18** is in perfect condition and thoroughly clean. Do not overtighten the valve, the correct torque figure being 0.25mkp (1.8lb ft).

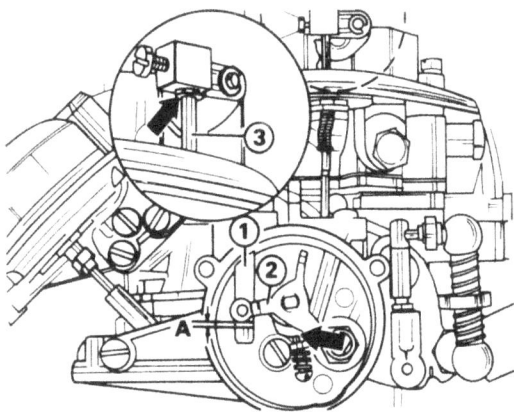

FIG 2:19   Choke adjustment, first stage

Choke flap adjustment:

Remove the air cleaner assembly as described in **Section 2:3**. Remove the three screws from the automatic choke flange and detach the choke cover leaving the water hoses connected. Do not loosen the choke housing central bolt. Hold the choke flap in the fully closed position by hand, then loosen the bolt for the pivot unit which is shown in the inset in **FIG 2:19**. With the adjustment screw aligned with the upper notch of the stepped disc as shown by the lower arrow, set the play between rod 1 and actuating disc lever 2 to 1.5mm (0.059in) as shown at **A**. With this position held, tighten the pivot unit bolt to lock against rod 3, then press the circlip on the rod firmly up against the pivot unit.

Refer to **FIG 2:20**. With the adjusting screw still against the upper notch on the stepped disc, press rod 1 upwards and actuating disc 2 as shown. Now use a drill or rod of the correct diameter to check the gap between

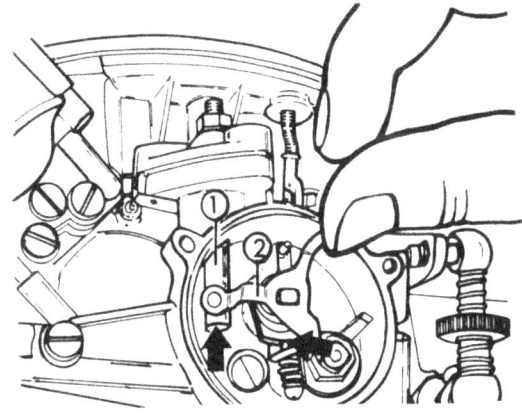

FIG 2:20   Choke adjustment, second stage

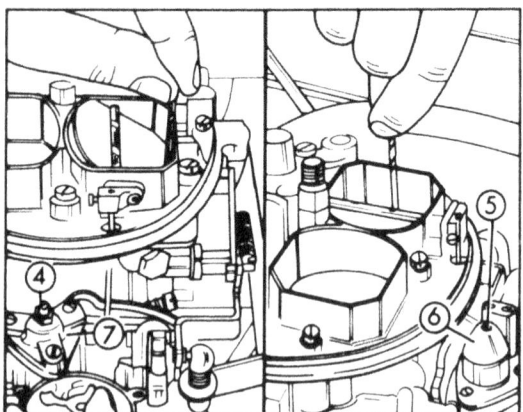

FIG 2:21   Choke adjustment, third stage

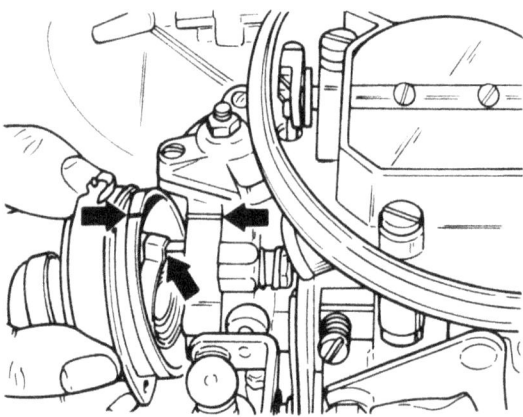

FIG 2:22   Installing choke cover

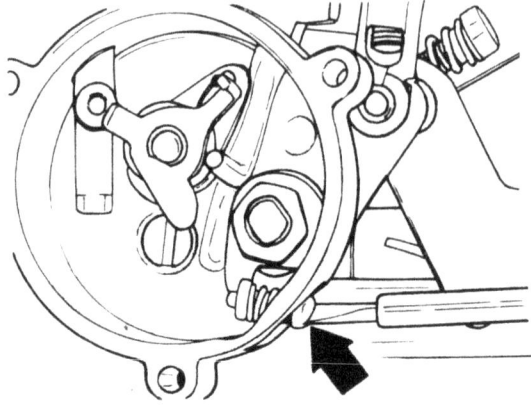

FIG 2:23   Fast-idle speed adjustment screw

choke flap and carburetter air intake as shown in FIG 2:21, referring to **Technical Data** to determine the correct measurement. To adjust the gap on earlier models, slacken the locknut and turn adjusting screw 4 as necessary. Tighten the locknut on completion. On later models, adjust by turning bolt 5 in cover 6. Lock the bolt after adjustment by applying a dab of paint or sealing compound. If the engine does not run smoothly when started from cold on models having the later type of choke mechanism 6, it is possible to convert to the earlier type with valve cover 7 as the necessary replacement parts can be obtained from a BMW agent.

When adjustments at both carburetters are complete, refit the choke cover, making sure that the peg on the mechanism engages the spring correctly and that the notch on the cover aligns with the projection on the housing as shown in FIG 2:22. Install the air cleaner assembly as described in **Section 2:3**.

Fast-idle speed adjustment:

The fast-idle linkage serves to increase engine idle speed when the automatic choke is operating. This prevents the engine from cutting out after starting from cold. Linkage adjustments must only be carried out when the engine is at normal operating temperature and after the slow-running adjustments have been correctly carried out as described previously. The air cleaner assembly must be removed as described in **Section 2:3**. On models fitted with distributors having vacuum advance and retard, the vacuum retard hose must be pulled from the fitting at the distributor (see **Chapter 3**).

Run the engine until it is at normal operating temperature, then switch off. Remove the cover from the choke unit as described previously. Detach the connector from the carburetter linkage as shown in FIG 2:13. Lift the throttle linkage for the rear carburetter by approximately $\frac{1}{8}$in, then close the choke flap by hand until there is a gap of 2.4mm (0.094in) between the edge of the flap and the air intake. Measure the gap in the manner shown in FIG 2:21, using a drill or rod of the correct diameter. This procedure will set the fast-idle adjustment screw on the second step of the cam in the choke unit. Release the choke flap.

Without touching the throttle linkage, start the engine. The fast-idle speed should be 1400rev/min. If above or below this figure, switch off the engine to make adjustments, which are carried out as shown in FIG 2:23. Push the carburetter linkage to the full throttle position to bring the screw to the adjustment position shown. Turn the screw anticlockwise to reduce fast-idle speed, clockwise to increase. One turn of the screw corresponds to approximately 300rev/min. After each adjustment, reset the linkage as described previously and check fast-idle speed. When the speed is correct, switch off the engine and raise the throttle linkage at the rear carburetter approximately $\frac{1}{8}$in then release, so that the fast-idle linkage disengages. Repeat the entire operation at the front carburetter.

On completion, attach the connector to the carburetter linkage and set both carburetters to the fast-idle position as described previously. Start the engine without touching the accelerator linkage and check that fast-idle speed is 1800 to 2000rev/min. Refit the choke covers and air cleaner assembly as described previously.

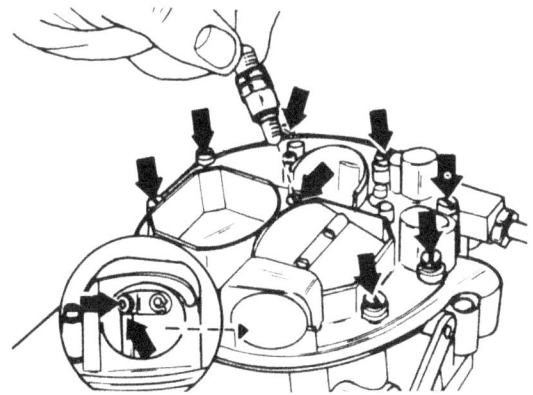

FIG 2:24 Carburetter top cover attachment screws and choke linkage connection

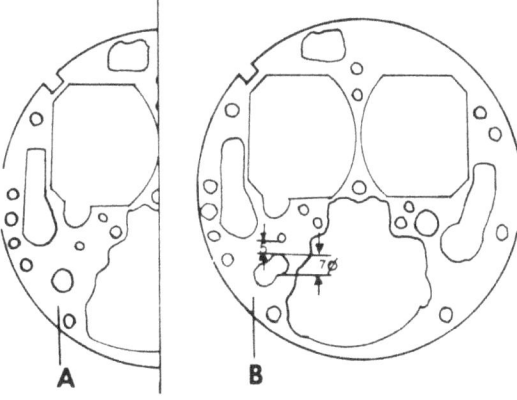

FIG 2:26 Alternative carburetter cover gaskets A and B

2:6 Carburetter servicing

It is not necessary to remove the carburetters to carry out this work. If poor engine performance is traced to carburetter operational faults which cannot be cured by the servicing procedures described in this section and the tuning and adjustment procedures described in **Section 2:5**, the car should be taken to a BMW service station for more detailed checks to be carried out.

Remove the air cleaner assembly as described in **Section 2:3**, then disconnect the fuel pipe from the carburetter. Refer to **FIG 2:24**. Unscrew the air cleaner mounting stud and fixing screws for the top cover. Press the circlip shown by the lower arrow in the inset hard against the joint, then slacken the bolt on the joint to release the rod. The top cover can then be detached When the cover is installed, the choke flap should be held in the fully closed position then the joint pushed on to the rod until it contacts the circlip before tightening the bolt. This ensures that the choke linkage is reconnected in the original position.

Note that the carburetter may be fitted with either of the types of float chamber vent shown in **FIG 2:25**, the appropriate gaskets being shown in **FIG 2:26**. Cover type **A** may be fitted with gasket **A** or **B**, but cover type **B** must be fitted with gasket **B** or a gasket **A** suitably modified as shown in the illustration, the dimensions being in millimetres.

Refer to **FIG 2:27** and remove the idling jet, then remove the two securing screws arrowed and detach the carburetter body. Refer to **FIG 2:28** and remove main jet 1 pump suction valve 2, pump pressure valve 3 and

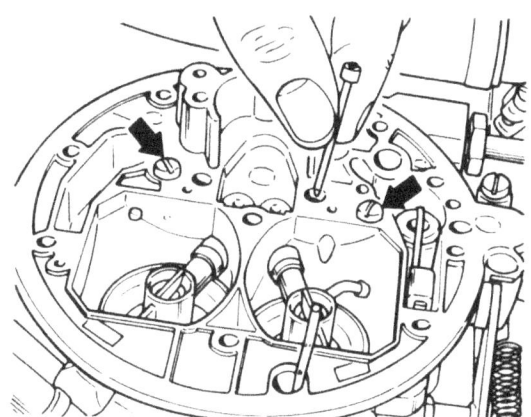

FIG 2:27 Idle jet and body securing screws

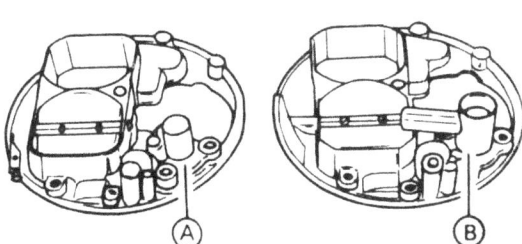

FIG 2:25 Alternative carburetter vents A and B

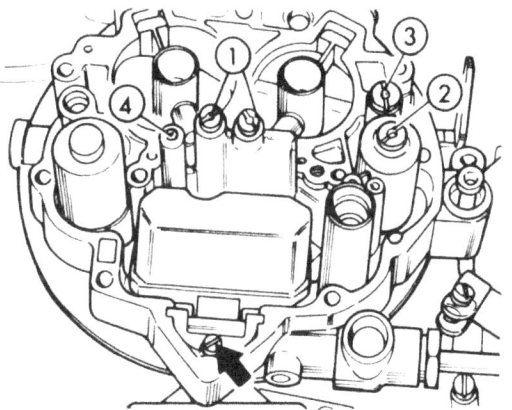

FIG 2:28 Removing float, jets and valves

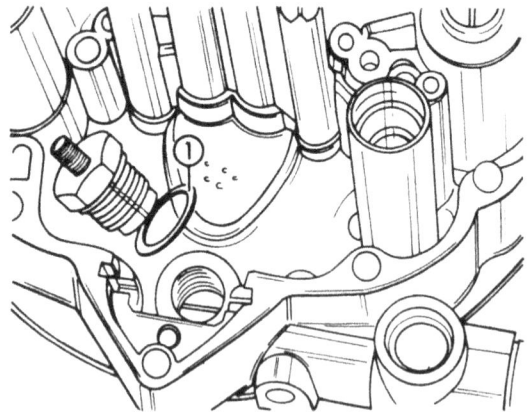

FIG 2:29   Needle valve assembly

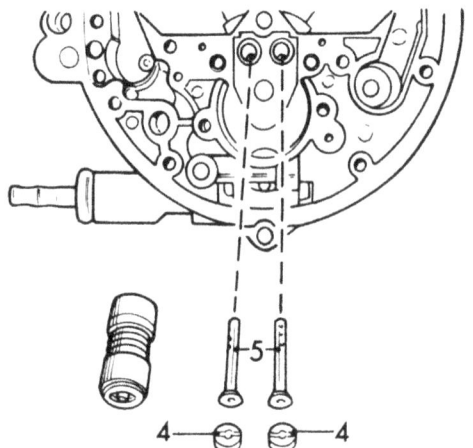

FIG 2:30   Removing air corrector jets. mixture tubes and pump plunger

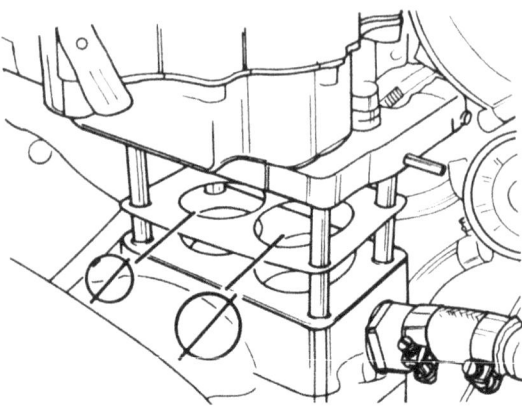

FIG 2:31   Carburetter flange gasket

intermediate jet 4, taking care to keep these parts in the correct order for installing in their original positions. Remove the fixing screw arrowed and detach the float. Unscrew and remove the needle valve assembly, collecting sealing washer 1 (see **FIG 2:29**). A sealing washer of the correct thickness must always be fitted to the needle valve assembly as this ensures correct float level. Refer to **FIG 2:30** and remove air corrector jets 4, mixture tubes 5 and pump plunger. Take care not to mix the tubes and jets as they are differently calibrated for primary and secondary bores.

Clean all dismantled parts in petrol or an approved carburetter cleaner, then examine them for wear or damage. Renew any faulty parts. Clean jets, mixture tubes, valves and passages thoroughly using compressed air, clean petrol and a small stiff brush. **Do not use cloth for cleaning purposes as small fibres may remain after cleaning and clog the jets or passages. Never use a wire probe as this will damage or enlarge the jets or passages.**

Make sure that all sediment is cleared from the float chamber and inspect the float for damage or leakage, either of which will dictate renewal of the float. Float leakage can usually be detected by shaking the float and listening for the sound of fuel splash inside. Another method is to immerse the float in warm water and look for a stream of air bubbles which will indicate a hole in the unit.

The needle valve assembly should be cleaned thoroughly and inspected for wear or damage. Check that the valve operates correctly by blowing through from the feed end. The air flow should be cut off completely when the needle is held in to the body by gentle finger pressure. Renew the assembly if there is any doubt about its condition.

When servicing is complete, reassemble the carburetter in the reverse order of dismantling, then carry out the tuning and adjustment procedures described in **Section 2:5**.

2:7 Removing and refitting carburetters

Remove the air cleaner assembly as described in **Section 2:3**, then disconnect the fuel and vacuum hoses, and the electrical connector if fitted, from the carburetter. Note the connections of the vacuum hoses on the carburetter fittings, so that they can be reconnected correctly when the carburetter is refitted. Disconnect the linkage connector as shown in **FIG 2:13**.

If the carburetter is being removed to renew flange gaskets or for access to other components, there is no need to disconnect the water hoses to the automatic choke unit. Instead, detach the choke cover with hoses attached as described in **Section 2:5**. Remove the fixing nuts and detach the carburetter and flange gasket as shown in **FIG 2:31**. If the insulating flange is to be renewed, disconnect the pushrod shown in **FIG 2:16** and disconnect the joint from the rod shown in the inset of **FIG 2:19**. Remove the throttle valve housing from the main carburetter body, then detach the insulating flange. Refit the carburetter in the reverse order of removal, noting the following points:

Always renew all gaskets. When installing the flange gasket, the graphite-coated side must face towards the inlet manifold (see **FIG 2:31**). Earlier type gaskets had holes of different sizes, which must be correctly located with the smaller hole towards the cylinder head as shown in the illustration. Later type gaskets have holes of equal size and an interrupted centre web, which enables them to be fitted either way round, and they may be used to replace the earlier type. On completion, adjust the automatic choke and carry out the slow-running adjustments described in **Section 2:5**.

If the carburetter is to be detached complete, drain the cooling system as described in **Chapter 4** and disconnect the two water hoses from the automatic choke unit. Detach fuel return hose, if fitted. Remove the complete carburetter assembly from the inlet manifold, collecting the flange gasket. When refitting, make sure that the flange gasket is correctly installed carrying out tuning and adjustment as described in **Section 2:5**.

2:8 Fuel injection system

Fuel from the rear-mounted tank is supplied to the injector pump for the system by means of an electric fuel pump. The injector pump is responsible for the delivery of a timed and metered quantity of fuel to each of the six cylinders in the engine in the correct firing order. There are a number of control devices to ensure the correct timing and metering of this fuel injection charge, according to the ambient and engine temperature and the engine operating conditions at any moment. Apart from the items covered in this section, no attempts should be made to dismantle or adjust any part of the system. All such work should be carried out only by a BMW service station having the necessary special equipment and trained personnel.

Air cleaner:

The air filter element should be renewed at the intervals recommended in the manufacturer's service schedule. Between these periods, the filter element should occasionally be examined, and cleaned if necessary. To remove the element, release the spring clips and detach the air cleaner cover. Lift out the element. If renewal is necessary, discard the old element, wipe the inside of the air cleaner body and cover to remove dirt and grease, then reassemble using a new element. Note that the side of the element marked 'TOP' must be uppermost.

If the element is to be cleaned and refitted, blow out dirt using an air-line with pressure not more than 5 atmospheres (71lb/sq in). Apply the air jet from the bottom of the filter element only. Install the element as described previously.

To remove the air cleaner assembly complete, refer to **FIG 2:32**. Loosen the clamp on the throttle butterfly manifold and lift the air cleaner assembly from the guide rails. Detach the assembly by pulling the hose from the front panel. Refit in the reverse order of removal, releasing the catches securing the top cover before doing so. Relocate the catches on completion.

Slow-running adjustment:

Note that slow-running adjustments will only be effective if the sparking plugs, contact points and ignition system are in good order and the valve clearances correctly set. The injection system must also be operating correctly. Note that an accurate tachometer will be

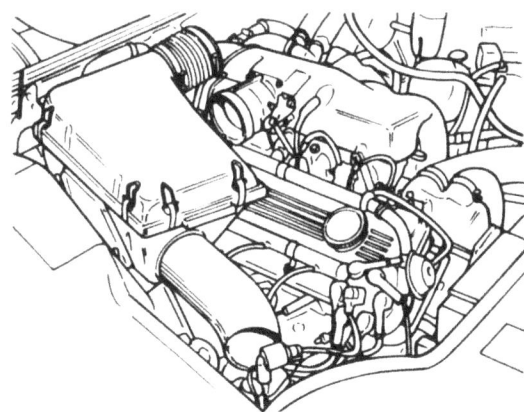

FIG 2:32   Air cleaner used with fuel injection system

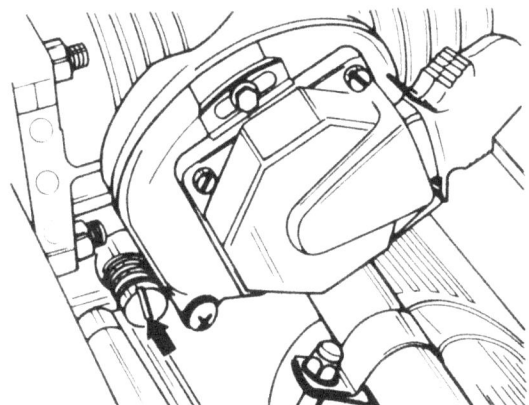

FIG 2:33   Idle air adjustment screw

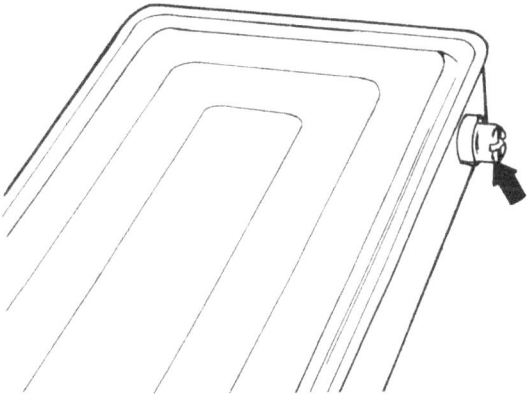

FIG 2:34   Fuel flow potentiometer

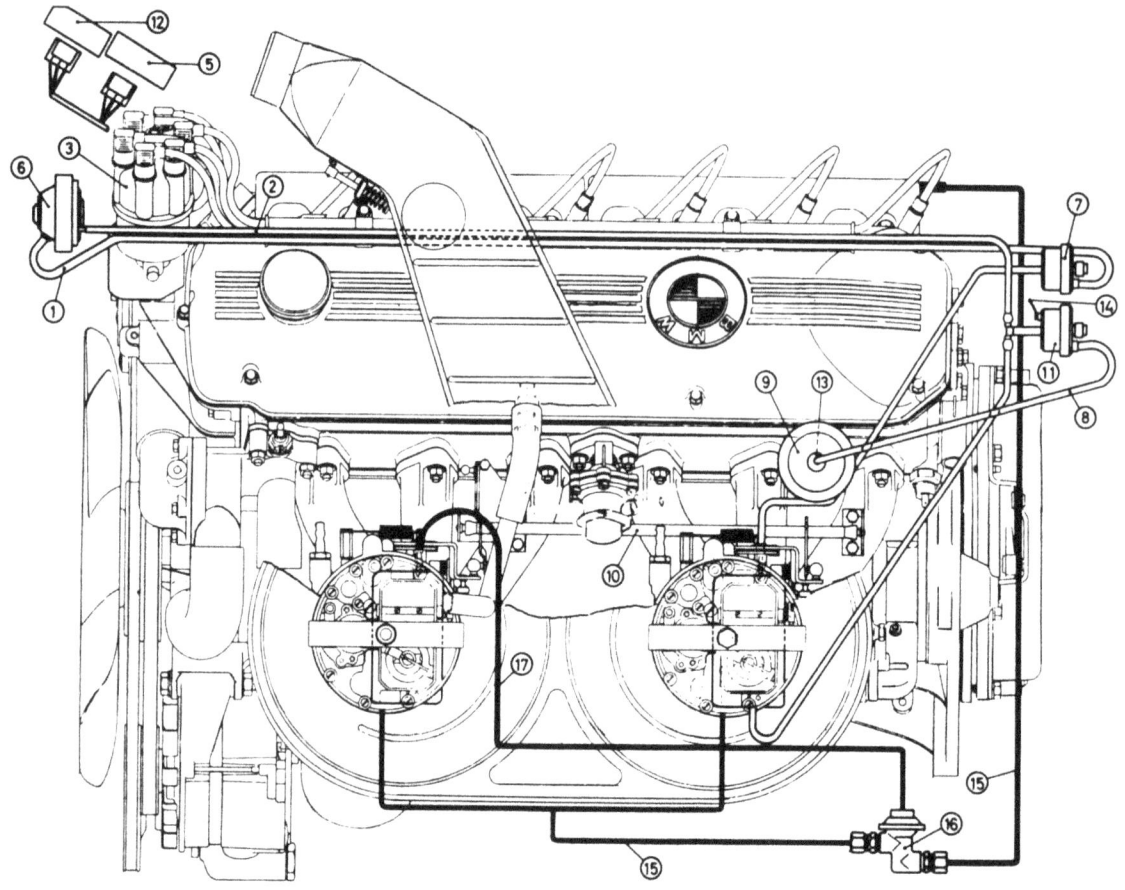

FIG 2:35 Layout of emission control system for 3.0 S-US and 3.0 CS-US models

Key to Fig 2:35 1 Vacuum hose, advance side   2 Vacuum hose, retard side   3 Ignition distributor   4 Stop screw (not shown)
5 Speed relay for solenoid valve 7   6 Double-acting vacuum unit   7 Two-way solenoid valve (advance side)   8 Vacuum hose
from closure damper to two-way solenoid valve   9 Closure damper   10 Throttle control linkage   11 Two-way solenoid valve
(retard side)   12 Speed relay for solenoid valve 11   13 Adjustment pad of closure damper   14 Cable connection   15 Exhaust
recirculation line   16 Control valve   17 Control pressure line

needed to check engine idle speed and suitable analytical
equipment will be necessary to measure CO (carbon
monoxide) content of the exhaust gas. If suitable
equipment is not available for this purpose, the work
should be carried out by a fully equipped service station.

It is most important that the engine is at normal
operating temperature, with a coolant temperature of
approximately 80°C (176°F) and an oil temperature of
approximately 60°C (140°F). Make sure that the air
cleaner element is in good condition as described
previously.

Start the engine and adjust to an idle speed of 850 to
1000rev/min for European models, 900 to 950rev/min
for USA models, using the idle air screw arrowed in
FIG 2:33. Now adjust the fuel flow potentiometer
arrowed in **FIG 2:34** to adjust the CO content of the
exhaust gas. Turning anticlockwise will reduce emissions.
CO content must be 1 to 2 per cent by volume for Europe,

1.5 to 2.0 per cent by volume for USA. Repeat the entire
adjustment procedure if adjustment at the potentiometer
alters engine idle speed beyond the stated limits. If the
correct CO content cannot be obtained at the specified
idle speed, the car should be taken to a service station for
detailed checks to be made on the fuel injection system.

2:9 Emission control systems

The layout of the emission control system on USA
export models is shown in **FIG 2:35**, a slightly simpler
system using fewer components being fitted to later
European models. The system functions to finely control
fuel/air mixture at the carburetters and ignition timing
advance and retard at the distributor. This ensures
optimum engine operating conditions throughout the
speed range to maintain toxic emissions from the engine
and fuel system at the low level required by legislation.

The hoses and pipes in the system should periodically be checked for leaks or other damage and for tightness at the connections. If faulty operation of any of the components in the system is suspected, the car should be taken to a fully equipped service station so that the system can be thoroughly checked using special equipment.

2:10 Fault diagnosis

(a) Leakage or insufficient fuel delivered

1 Tank vent system blocked
2 Fuel pipes blocked
3 Air leaks at pipe connections
4 Fuel filter blocked
5 Pump diaphragm defective
6 Pump valves sticking or seating badly
7 Electric pump wiring or connections defective

(b) Excessive fuel consumption

1 Carburetter(s) incorrectly adjusted
2 Fuel leakage
3 Sticking or incorrectly adjusted choke unit
4 Dirty air cleaner
5 Worn carburetter jet(s)
6 Excessive engine temperature

(c) Idling speed too high

1 Rich fuel mixture
2 Throttle control sticking
3 Mixture control or choke sticking
4 Worn throttle valves

(d) Poor idling

1 Carburetter(s) incorrectly adjusted
2 Faults in ignition system
3 Engine valve clearances incorrect
4 Faulty or maladjusted choke unit
5 Faulty idle valve(s)

(e) Noisy fuel pump

1 Loose pump mountings
2 Air leaks on suction side of pump
3 Obstruction in fuel pipeline
4 Clogged fuel filter

(f) No fuel delivery

1 Float needle valve stuck
2 Tank vent system blocked
3 Defective fuel pump
4 Pipeline obstructed
5 Bad air leak on suction side of pump

NOTES

CHAPTER 3

THE IGNITION SYSTEM

3:1 Description

The ignition system is conventional, comprising an ignition coil, distributor and contact breaker system. The distributor incorporates automatic timing control by means of centrifugal mechanism and a vacuum operated unit. As engine speed increases, the centrifugal action of rotating weights pivoting against the tension of small springs moves the contact breaker cam relative to the distributor drive shaft and progressively advances the ignition. Small bore pipe(s) connect between fittings on the vacuum unit and the carburetter. At high degrees of vacuum the unit advances the ignition, but under load, at reduced vacuum, the unit progressively retards the ignition

Some later models are fitted with a rotor arm which incorporates an engine speed governor. This consists of a sliding weight which is thrown outwards by centrifugal force to contact a metal blade on the outer part of the rotor at a predetermined engine speed. This shortcircuits the ignition current to earth to prevent any further increase in engine speed. On engines equipped with fuel injection systems instead of carburetters, the distributor is additionally fitted with a set of trigger contacts which transmit timed current pulses to the fuel injection system control unit.

The ignition coil is wound as an auto-transformer with the primary and secondary windings connected in series, the common junction being connected to the contact breaker with the positive feed from the battery going to the opposite terminal of the LT windings via the ignition switch. On later models, LT current supply to the coil is via a resistor which reduces nominal battery voltage considerably. This resistance is bypassed when the starter is in operation, so that full battery voltage is supplied to the coil. The coil then provides increased voltage to the HT system for maximum sparking plug efficiency when the engine is being started. If a resistor is not incorporated, full battery voltage is supplied to the coil at all times.

When the contact breaker points are closed, current flows in the coil primary winding, magnetising the core and setting up a fairly strong magnetic field. Each time the contacts open, the battery current is cut off and the magnetic field collapses, inducing a high current in the primary winding and a high voltage in the secondary. The primary current is used to charge the capacitor connected across the contacts and the flow is high and virtually instantaneous. It is this high current peak which induces the surge in the secondary winding to produce the sparking plug voltage across the plug points. Without the

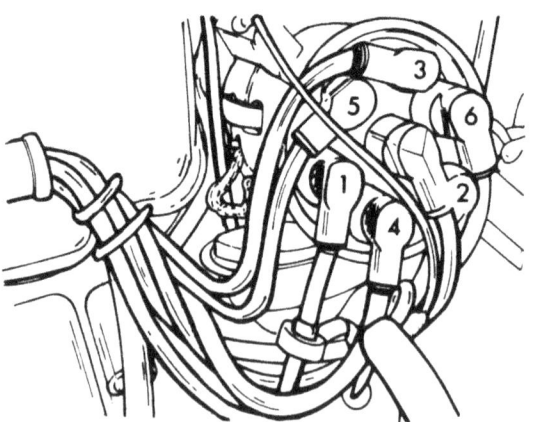

FIG 3:1   HT lead connections at distributor cap

capacitor the current peak would be much smaller and the sparking voltage considerably reduced, in fact to a point where it would be insufficient to fire the mixture in the engine cylinders. The capacitor, therefore, serves the dual purpose of minimising contact breaker wear and providing the necessary high charging surge to ensure a powerful spark.

3:2 Routine maintenance

Pull off the two spring clips to release the cap from the distributor body. On models provided with stereo suppression, detach the two thin wires from their connections on the distributor body. Remove the distributor cap leaving the HT leads attached, if the cap is to be removed complete, detach the HT leads by pulling off the plug-in connectors. Each lead is marked with the appropriate cylinder number and leads must be connected to the distributor cap in the correct firing order, as shown in **FIG 3:1**. For access to the contact breaker points, pull the rotor from the top of the distributor shaft and remove the dust cover if fitted.

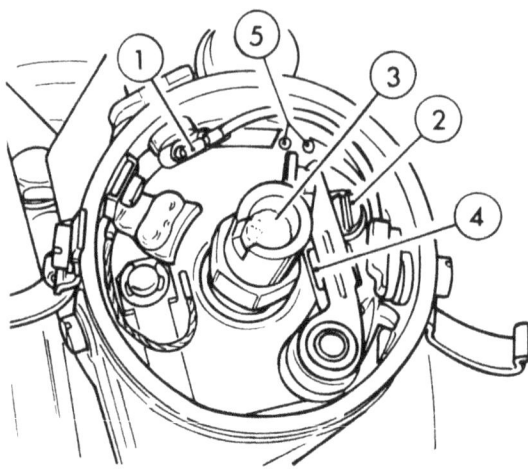

FIG 3:2   Upper distributor components

Lubrication:

This should be carried out at the intervals recommended in the manufacturer's service schedule. Remove the distributor cap as described previously. **FIG 3:2** shows the upper distributor components. Apply just enough engine oil to the felt pad 3 to soak it. Apply a thin smear of an approved grade of grease to cam follower 4 and the six-sided cam against which it operates. When lubricating the internal parts of the distributor, take great care to avoid oil or grease contaminating the contact breaker points, lubricating sparingly for this reason.

Adjusting the contact breaker points:

Turn the engine until one of the cams has opened the contact breaker points to their fullest extent, then check the gap between the points with clean feeler gauges. The correct gap is 0.35 to 0.40mm (0.014 to 0.016in). To adjust the gap, slacken the screw shown at 2 in **FIG 3:2** and insert the point of a screwdriver between the pips and cut-out provided (5). Turn the screwdriver to open or close the points gap as necessary, then tighten the retaining screw and recheck the gap. If dwell meter equipment is available, adjusting the points to give the correct dwell angle (see **Technical Data**) will provide the most accurate setting.

Cleaning the contact breaker points:

Use a fine carborundum stone or special contact point file to polish the points if they are dirty or pitted, taking care to keep the faces flat and square. If the points are too worn to clean up in this manner, they should be renewed. On completion, wipe away all dust with a cloth moistened in petrol then set the points gap as described previously.

Renewing the contact breaker points:

Refer to **FIG 3:2**. Pull off the connector 1, then remove screw 2 and lift out the contact breaker points. Wash the mating faces of the new contact points with methylated spirits to remove the protective coating. Fit the contact points set to the base plate and secure with the single screw. Push the connector on to the terminal. Set the contact points to the correct gap as described previously.

Checking rotor arm:

To test rotor insulation, connect an ohmmeter between the rotor centre and outer contacts. Resistance should be approximately 5000 ohms.

Alternatively, check by fitting the rotor in position and removing the central HT lead from the distributor cap. Hold the end of the lead approximately 12mm (0.5in) from the rotor centre contact. To avoid shocks, hold the lead with insulated pliers or a thick glove. With the ignition switched on, flick open the contact points. If a spark jumps the gap the rotor is faulty and must be renewed. Always fit a new rotor if the original is cracked or the brass parts are badly eroded.

On models having a rotor equipped with an engine speed governor, check that the centrifugal weight 1 (see **FIG 3:3**) and contact blade 2 are in good condition. Check that the weight moves out towards the contact freely and returns unaided when released. If any faults are found, renew the rotor.

3:3 Ignition faults

If the engine runs unevenly, set it to idle at about 1000rev/min and, taking care not to touch any conducting parts of the sparking plug leads, remove and replace each lead from its plug in turn. To avoid shocks during this operation it is best to wear a pair of thick gloves or to use insulated pliers. Doing this to a plug which is firing correctly will accentuate the uneven running but will make no difference if the plug is not firing.

Having by this means located the faulty cylinder, stop the engine and remove the plug lead. Pull back the insulation or remove the connector so that the end of the lead is exposed. Alternatively, use an extension piece, such as a small bar or drill, pushed into the plug connector. Hold the lead carefully to avoid shocks, so that the end is about 3mm ($\frac{1}{8}$in) away from the cylinder head. Crank the engine with the starter or flick open the contact points with the ignition switched on. A strong, regular spark confirms that the fault lies with the sparking plug which should be removed and cleaned as described in **Section 3:7**, or renewed if defective.

If the spark is weak and irregular, check the condition of the lead and, if it is perished or cracked, renew it and repeat the test. If no improvement results, check that the inside of the distributor cap is clean and dry and that there is no sign of tracking, which can be seen as a thin black line between the electrodes or to some metal part in contact with the cap. Tracking can only be cured by fitting a new cap. Check the carbon brush inside the cap for wear or damage, and check that it moves in and out freely against the pressure of its internal spring. Check the brass segments in the cap for wear or burning. Renew the cap if any fault is found. Wipe the cap clean both inside and outside before refitting.

If these checks do not cure a weak HT spark, or if no spark can be obtained at the plug or lead, check the LT circuit as described next.

Testing the LT circuit:

The LT circuit connects the battery, ignition switch, coil primary winding and the contact breaker assembly and provides timed pulses of current to the coil primary windings as the contacts open and close. These pulses control the secondary coil winding which provides current at high voltage to the distributor, where the distributor rotor directs it through the HT leads to the sparking plugs.

Remove the distributor cap and check that the contact breaker points are clean and correctly set, as described in **Section 3:2**. Disconnect the thin wire from the coil that connects to the distributor. Connect a 12-volt test lamp between the terminals to complete the circuit, switch on the ignition and turn the engine slowly. If the lamp lights and goes out as the points close and open, the circuit is in order. If the lamp fails to light, there is a fault in the LT circuit. Note that a 12-volt bulb will not glow with full brightness on models which have a resistor in circuit with the coil. This resistor is cut out of the circuit when the starter motor is operating, so that extra current is supplied to the coil to ensure a quick start. Full brightness of the lamp should be achieved when the switch is turned to crank the engine with the starter motor.

Remove the lamp and reconnect the wire to the coil and distributor. If the fault lies in the LT circuit, use the lamp

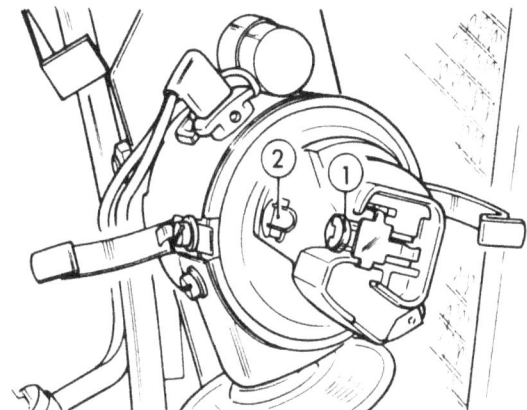

FIG 3:3   Rotor arm centrifugal weight 1 and contact 2. Later type shown

to carry out the following tests with the ignition switched on. Remove the wire from the ignition switch side of the coil and connect the lamp between the end of this wire and earth. If the lamp fails to light, it indicates a fault in the wiring between the battery and the coil or in the ignition switch. Reconnect the wire if the lamp lights.

Disconnect the wire from the coil that connects to the distributor. Connect the lamp between the coil terminal and earth. If the lamp fails to light it indicates a fault in the coil primary winding and a new coil must be fitted. Reconnect the wire if the lamp lights and disconnect its other end from the distributor. If the lamp does not light when connected between the end of this wire and earth it indicates a fault in the section of wire.

Capacitor:

The best method of testing a capacitor (condenser) is by substitution. Disconnect the original capacitor and connect a new one between the LT terminal on the distributor and earth for test purposes. If a new capacitor is proved to be required, it can then be properly fitted. The capacitor is recognised as a small cylinder attached to the outside of the distributor body.

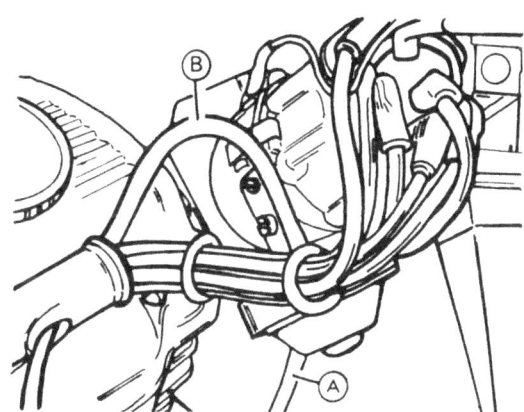

FIG 3:4   Double acting vacuum unit hose connections

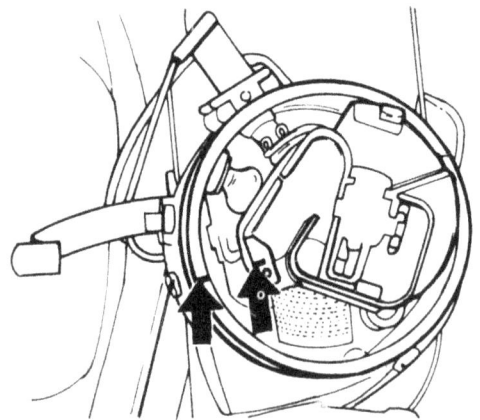

FIG 3:5 Aligning rotor and housing timing marks, later type shown

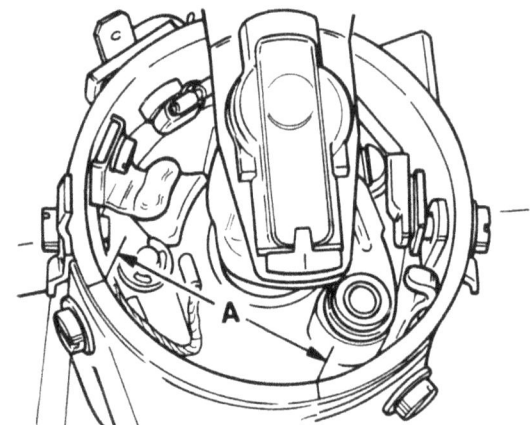

FIG 3:6 Aligning rotor for distributor refitting, early type shown

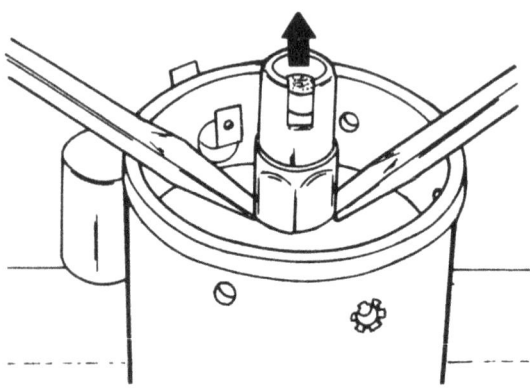

FIG 3:7 Removing cam assembly on later models

An alternative check for the capacitor is to charge it from a DC source, such as the car battery, then leave it for about 5min. The terminal and case of the capacitor should then be shorted with a piece of wire and, if the capacitor is in good condition, a noticeable spark should result.

3:4 Removing and refitting distributor

Removing:

Remove the distributor cap as described in **Section 3:2**. On models fitted with a double-acting vacuum unit, refer to **FIG 3:4** and remove pipes **A** and **B** from the unit, taking care not to mix the hoses so that they can be refitted correctly. On standard models fitted with this type of unit, hose **A** connects to a fitting on the front carburetter at lefthand side of idle shut off valve, hose **B** to the same carburetter at righthand side of valve. On models with this type of vacuum unit which are also equipped with exhaust emission control systems, hose **A** leads to the vacuum connection on the carburetter and hose **B** to the electromagnetic change-over valve. Disconnect the distributor LT wiring. On fuel-injection models, pull off the trigger contact plug at the distributor.

Turn the engine until the mark on the rotor aligns with the mark on the distributor body as shown in **FIG 3:5**. This is the TDC point on the firing stroke for No 1 (front) cylinder. Remove the bolt securing the clamp at the base of the distributor, then lift the distributor assembly from the engine. To avoid altering the timing settings, do not turn the engine while the distributor is removed.

Refitting:

If the engine has not been turned while the distributor was removed, align the rotor and shaft assembly as shown in **FIG 3:6** so that distance **A** between marks on rotor and body is approximately 35mm (1.4in). Offer the distributor into position and turn the rotor as little as necessary until the gear on the shaft aligns with the drive gear. Push the distributor body fully home, when the rotor should turn to the position shown in **FIG 3:5**. Turn the distributor body as little as necessary to exactly align the marks, then refit the clamp and tighten the bolt just sufficiently to secure the body. Reconnect the LT wiring. Carry out the ignition timing procedure described in **Section 3:6**.

If the engine has been turned and the timing setting lost, the engine must be reset to the firing point for No 1 cylinder. To do this, either remove the rocker cover and turn the engine until both valves for No 1 (front) cylinder are closed (see **Chapter 1**), or remove the sparking plug from No 1 cylinder and turn the engine until compression can be felt by a thumb placed over the plug hole. Now turn the engine as little more as necessary to align the central mark on the crankshaft vibration damper pulley in line with the pointer on the timing cover as described in **Section 3:6**. Install the distributor as described previously then check the ignition timing as described in **Section 3:6**.

3:5 Distributor overhaul

Remove the distributor as described in **Section 3:4**, then pull off the rotor arm and remove the dust cap if fitted. Remove the contact points set as described in **Section 3:2**.

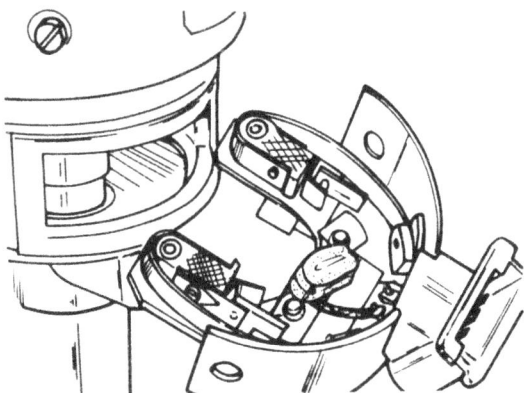

FIG 3:8 Removing trigger contacts on fuel injection models

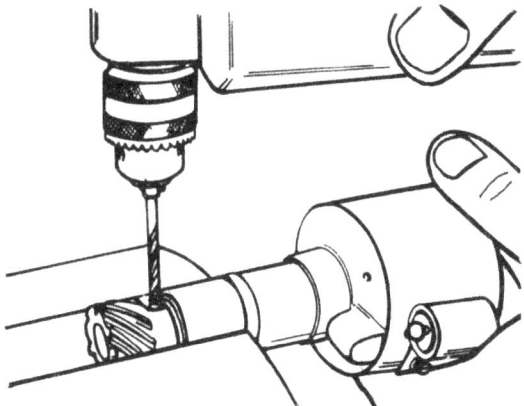

FIG 3:9 Drilling out grooved dowel pin

Remove the small circlip to detach vacuum unit operating arm from contact breaker base plate, then remove the screws and detach the vacuum unit from distributor body. Remove the contact breaker plate. On later models, the cam assembly is separate from the distributor shaft and can be removed by levering upwards with two screwdrivers as shown in **FIG 3:7**. When this is done, do not remove the lubricating felt pad from the centre of the cam assembly or the circlip beneath it will escape. On later models the cam is an integral part and must be removed complete with the distributor shaft.

On distributors used with fuel injection engines, the trigger contacts can be removed as shown in **FIG 3:8**.

To remove the shaft from the distributor body, the grooved dowel pin must first be drilled out as shown in **FIG 3:9**, taking care not to damage the gear or shaft. Remove the gear and extract the shaft and centrifugal mechanism through the top of the distributor body. When doing so, refer to **FIG 3:10** and collect thrust washers 1 and insulating washers 2, noting their positions for correct reassembly.

Examine all components for wear or damage. Note that, on units fitted with trigger contacts as shown in **FIG 3:8**, if the contacts are badly oiled, the distributor shaft sealing ring must have failed, this dictating renewal of the complete distributor assembly. Note that the trigger contact assembly must not be lubricated at all, and that the assembly should be renewed complete at intervals of approximately 60,000km (40,000 miles).

Check the fit of the distributor shaft in the bearing bushes and renew bushes if excessive play exists or if they are worn or damaged. If faults are found in the centrifugal advance mechanism on early models, the complete distributor shaft assembly must be renewed. On later models the centrifugal mechanism can be dismantled as follows, referring to **FIG 3:11**. Disconnect springs 2 and pull off lubricating felt 3, circlip 4, washer 5 and the cam assembly. Remove clips 6 and detach the centrifugal weights 7. Note that, if the holders or springs are renewed, the centrifugal advance curve should be checked on special equipment at a service station after the distributor is reassembled.

When servicing is complete, reassemble the distributor in the reverse order of dismantling, using a new grooved

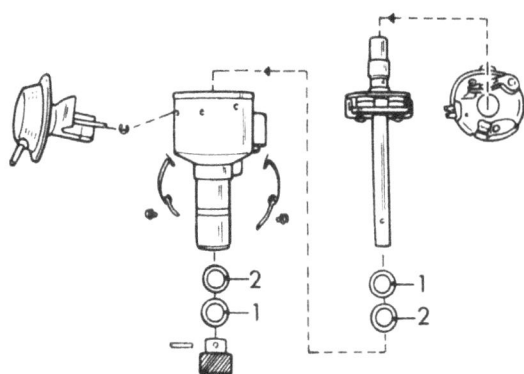

FIG 3:10 Distributor components

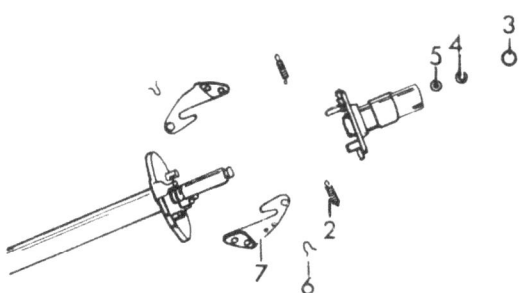

FIG 3:11 Centrifugal advance mechanism components, later models

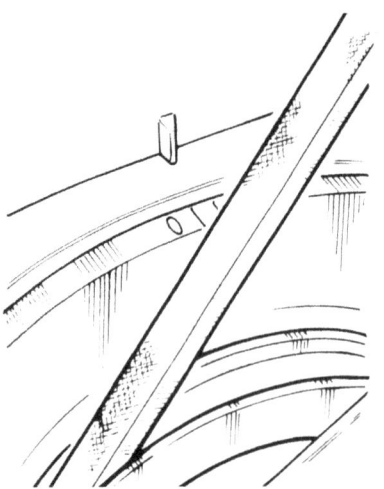

FIG 3:12   Aligning timing marks on vibration damper pulley

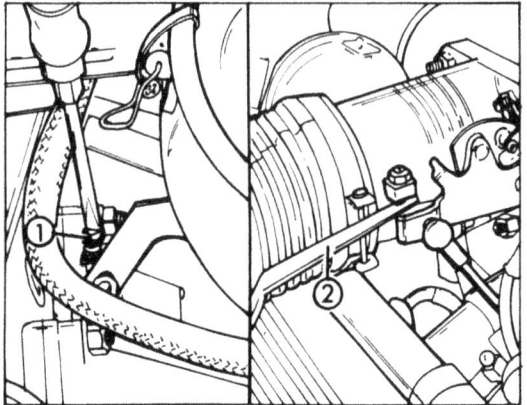

FIG 3:13   Raising idle speed with screw 1 (carburetters) or feeler 2 (fuel injection)

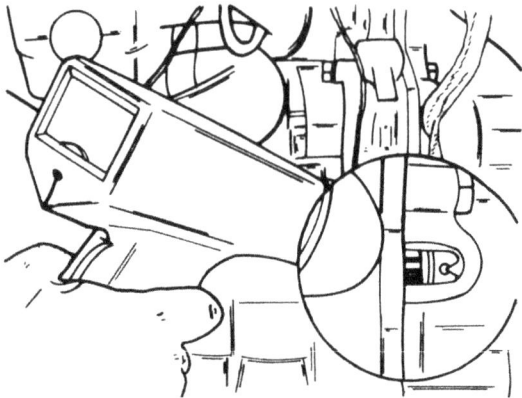

FIG 3:14   Checking timing with stroboscopic light

dowel pin to secure the gear to the shaft. Lightly lubricate the shaft with engine oil and the centrifugal weights with approved grease. On completion, adjust the contact points and lubricate the upper distributor components as described in **Section 3:2**, then refit the distributor as described in **Section 3:4**.

3:6 Timing the ignition

Static timing:

This method should be used to obtain a basic setting to allow the engine to be started and run up to normal operating temperature after servicing operations have been carried out. If the engine can be started and run, check the timing using the stroboscopic method described later.

Remove the distributor cap as described in **Section 3:2**. Make sure that the LT lead from the coil is properly connected at the distributor. Turn the engine until the centre timing mark on the crankshaft vibration damper pulley aligns with the pointer on the timing cover as shown in **FIG 3:12** and the mark on the rotor is aligned with the mark on the distributor body as shown in **FIG 3:5**. The pulley and rotor marks will align correctly once in every two engine revolutions. Slacken the distributor clamp bolt so that the distributor body can just be turned by hand.

Connect a 12-volt test lamp in parallel with the contact breaker points. One lead will connect to the terminal on the side of the distributor and one to earth. Turn the distributor body clockwise as far as possible to ensure that the contact points are fully closed. Now switch on the ignition and turn the distributor body very slowly in an anticlockwise direction until the lamp just lights. Without moving the distributor from this position, tighten the clamp bolt.

Disconnect the timing lamp and refit the parts removed, then start the engine and allow it to run until it reaches normal operating temperature. Check the timing by means of the stroboscopic method described next.

Stroboscopic timing:

This work requires the use of special stroboscopic light equipment which is wired into the ignition circuit for No 1 cylinder. If such equipment is not available, the work should be carried out by a service station. Run the engine until it reaches normal operating temperature. Refer to **FIG 3:4** and pull off vacuum hose **A** and, if fitted, vacuum hose **B**. Make sure that the contact points are clean and correctly set as described in **Section 3:2**. Connect up the stroboscopic timing lamp according to the instructions supplied with it.

Start the engine and allow it to idle. Refer to **FIG 3:13** and raise engine idle speed to 1700rev/min on carburetter engine by turning screw 1, or increase engine speed to 2500rev/min on fuel injection engine by using a feeler gauge 2 of suitable thickness between screw and stop.

Direct the timing light through the aperture provided in the flywheel or automatic transmission drive plate cover as shown in **FIG 3:14**. Turn the distributor body by hand until, for manual transmission models, the ball appears in exact alignment with the pointer as shown in the inset. On automatic transmission models, note that the long pin indicates ignition firing point, the short pin indicates TDC.

When the timing is correct, tighten the clamp bolt to secure the distributor body and make sure that the setting has not altered. On models with double acting vacuum unit, which can be recognised by provision of hose **B** shown in **FIG 3:4**, reduce the idle speed appropriately and check that at 1000rev/min the TDC mark is visible through the timing aperture.

On completion, switch off the engine and restore the ignition circuit to normal. Refer to **FIG 3:13** and slacken screw 1 on carburetter engines until there is a small amount of play between the shaft and the stop, or remove the feeler gauge 2 on fuel injection engine. Reconnect the hose or hoses removed from the distributor vacuum unit.

3:7 Sparking plugs

Sparking plugs should be of the recommended type, details of which are given in **Technical Data**. Inspect and clean the plugs regularly. When removing them, ensure that their recesses are clean and dry so that nothing can fall into the cylinders. Have the plugs cleaned on an abrasive blasting machine and tested under pressure with the electrode gaps correctly set at 0.6 to 0.7mm (0.024 to 0.028in). The electrodes should be filed until they are bright and parallel. The gaps must always be set by bending the outer electrode only. As a general rule, plugs should be cleaned and tested at about 6000 mile intervals and renewed at about 12,000 mile intervals, or before if badly worn.

The HT leads from the distributor to sparking plugs and coil should be examined for cracks and defective insulation. Renew any lead found to be defective in any way. Lead connectors are of the plug-in type.

3:8 Fault diagnosis

(a) Engine will not fire

1 Battery discharged
2 Contact breaker points dirty, pitted or maladjusted
3 Distributor cap dirty, cracked or tracking
4 Carbon brush in cap worn or stuck in mounting
5 Faulty cable or loose connection in LT circuit
6 Distributor rotor arm cracked
7 Faulty coil
8 Broken contact breaker spring
9 Contact points stuck open

(b) Engine misfires

1 Check 2, 3, 5 and 7 in (a)
2 Weak contact breaker spring
3 HT plug or coil lead cracked or perished
4 Loose sparking plug
5 Sparking plug insulation cracked
6 Sparking plug gap incorrect
7 Ignition timing too far advanced

(c) Poor acceleration

1 Ignition retarded
2 Centrifugal advance weights seized
3 Centrifugal advance springs weak, broken or disconnected
4 Distributor clamp bolt loose
5 Excessive contact points gap
6 Worn sparking plugs
7 Faulty vacuum unit or leaking hose

NOTES

CHAPTER 4
THE COOLING SYSTEM

4:1 Description

The cooling system is of the pressurised sealed type. Coolant circulation is assisted by a water pump driven by a belt, a thermostat preventing full circulation until normal engine operating temperature is reached, thus ensuring a rapid warm-up and good heater operation.

Air flow through the radiator is assisted by a cooling fan, which is driven through a coupling provided with a clutch unit operated by an integral thermal sensor. When the engine is cool, the coupling clutch is disconnected so that the fan is inoperative, ensuring that the engine reaches normal operating temperature as quickly as possible. When engine coolant reaches a temperature of approximately 55°C (131°F), the clutch is automatically engaged and the fan is driven to provide additional cooling.

An expansion tank containing a quantity of coolant is connected to the radiator by means of a hose. At high operating temperatures, when the coolant in the sealed system expands, excess coolant passes through the hose into the expansion tank. When the system cools, coolant from the expansion tank flows back into the radiator. With this system, no coolant loss should occur during normal operation.

4:2 Routine maintenance

Apart from an occasional check on the condition of the hoses and hose clips and a visual check on coolant level in the expansion tank, very little maintenance should be necessary. There should also be no need for regular topping up of the coolant. If regular topping up is required, the system should be examined for leaks before adding coolant.

Check the level of coolant in the expansion tank when the system is cold and top up as necessary. Note that the coolant level will rise when the engine is hot. If for any reason it is necessary to remove the expansion tank pressure cap when the engine is hot, hold the cap with a large piece of rag. Turn the cap anticlockwise and wait a few moments for the pressure to release before lifting off the cap.

It is recommended that an antifreeze solution is maintained in the system all year round. Topping up should therefore be carried out with the correct mixture of antifreeze and water to avoid weakening the solution in use.

Every two years the cooling system should be drained, flushed to remove sediment then refilled with fresh anti-freeze mixture. Check that the clips are tight on all hoses

FIG 4:1 Bottom hose clip (above) and radiator drain plug (below)

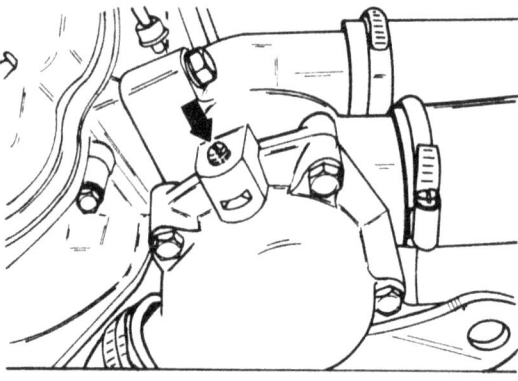

FIG 4:2 Cooling system bleed screw

FIG 4:3 Upper hose connections

and that the expansion tank pressure cap is in good condition and sealing effectively. Loss of system pressure due to a leaking filler cap can be a cause of overheating.

Regular checks on drive belt condition and tension should be made as described in **Section 4:4**.

Draining the system:

Set the heater controls to the maximum heat position and remove the cap from the expansion tank. Remove the radiator drain plug shown by the lower arrow in **FIG 4:1** and allow the coolant to drain fully, collecting it in a clean container if it is to be re-used. Remove the expansion tank and rinse out with clean water.

Flushing:

When old coolant has drained, refit and tighten the radiator drain plug and refit the expansion tank. Fill the system with clean water through the expansion tank filler until the level in the tank is correct. Run the engine until the top radiator hose feels warm, which indicates that the thermostat has opened for complete circulation. Now completely drain the system again before the sediment has time to settle.

Filling and bleeding:

Check that the drain plug is properly fitted and that all hose clips are tight. Leave the heater control in the maximum heat position. Prepare the new antifreeze mixture according to the manufacturer's instructions. If the system is still warm, allow it to cool down as adding the cold liquid when the system is warm may crack the engine cylinder block. Fill until the level is correct in the expansion tank, then start the engine and allow it to run at a fast-idle speed. Slacken the bleed screw arrowed in **FIG 4:2** and wait until the coolant leaking past the screw is completely free of air bubbles before retightening. During the operation, add coolant as necessary to maintain the correct level in the expansion tank. On completion, switch off the engine and refit the expansion tank cap. Check the coolant level after running the engine for some time and top up if necessary.

4:3 The radiator

Removal:

Drain the cooling system as described in **Section 4:2**. Slacken the hose clip shown by the upper arrow in **FIG 4:1**, then remove the lower hose from the radiator. Refer to **FIG 4:3** and remove the upper hose and expansion tank hose from the radiator.

If a transmission oil cooler is incorporated in the radiator, detach the supply and return lines at the connections arrowed in **FIG 4:4**, plugging the lines to prevent leakage or the entry of dirt.

Detach the radiator supports on each side then carefully lift out the radiator. Note that when refitting the retainer stays must press on the radiator mounting.

Refitting:

Refitting is a reversal of the removal procedure, after which the system should be refilled with coolant and bled as described in **Section 4:2**. On models fitted with transmission cooler, check and if necessary, top up transmission fluid level as described in **Chapter 7**.

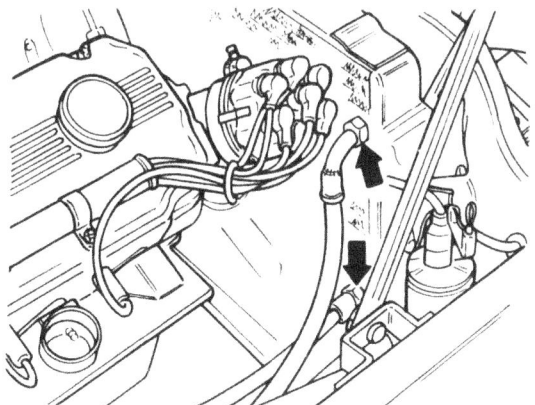

FIG 4:4 Transmission cooler line connections

FIG 4:5 Alternator drive belt tensioning

4:4 Drive belt tensioning

The instructions in this section concern the drive belt for the alternator and water pump and fan. Drive belts for power steering pump and air conditioning system compressor, if fitted, should be checked and adjusted as described in **Chapters 10** and **13**. Correct drive belt tension is important, as a tight drive belt will cause undue wear on pulleys and component bearings, a slack belt will cause slip and, possibly, lower output from the driven components.

Alternator drive belt tension is correct when the belt can be deflected a distance of 5 to 10mm (0.2 to 0.4in) under firm hand pressure at the centre of the upper run, as shown in **FIG 4:5**. To adjust the belt tension, slacken the two alternator mounting bolts arrowed in **FIG 4:5** and swing the alternator away from the engine as required, then tighten the mounting bolts and recheck the tension. If a lever is used to move the alternator, it is important that it be used between the engine and alternator bracket only, never against the alternator body.

The belt can be removed by slackening the mountings, moving the alternator as far as possible towards the engine then releasing the belt from the pulleys. Note, however, that drive belts for air conditioning compressor and power steering pump, if fitted, must be removed first as described in **Chapters 10** and **13**.

Pulley modifications:

To improve engine cooling, later models are fitted with pulleys which differ in size from the original items to provide a higher cooling fan speed. It is recommended that earlier models be fitted with these later type pulleys to improve efficiency of the cooling system.

Pulleys can be checked by measuring their diameters as shown in **FIG 4:6**. Later pulley sizes are 162mm (6.378in) for vibration damper pulley **A** and 102mm (4.016in) for water pump and cooling fan pulley **B**. These replace pulley sizes 138mm (5.433in) and 134mm (5.276in) respectively. The correct lengths for drive belts to be used with the new pulleys are 12.5 × 1050 (**A**) and 9.5 × 1075 (**B**). Lengths for belts used with earlier pulleys are 12.5 × 1025 (**A**) and 9.5 × 1125 (**B**).

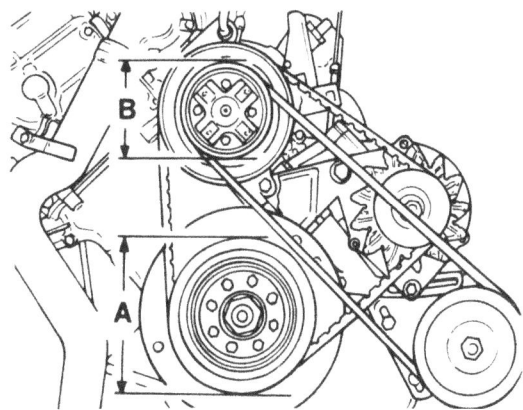

FIG 4:6 Checking pulley diameters

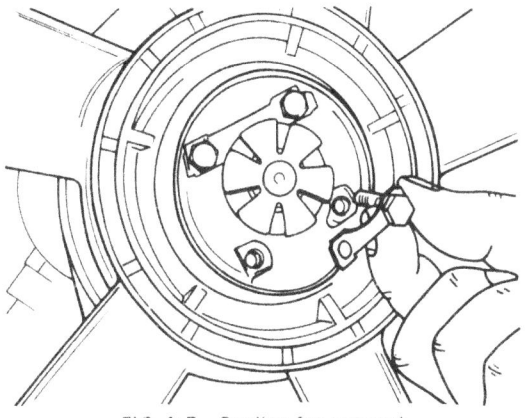

FIG 4:7 Cooling fan removal

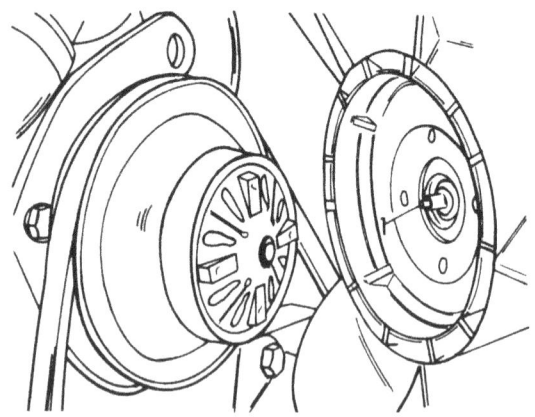

FIG 4:8 Cooling fan installation

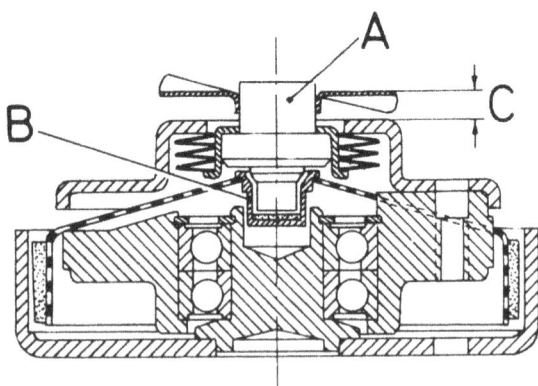

FIG 4:10 Section through fan coupling

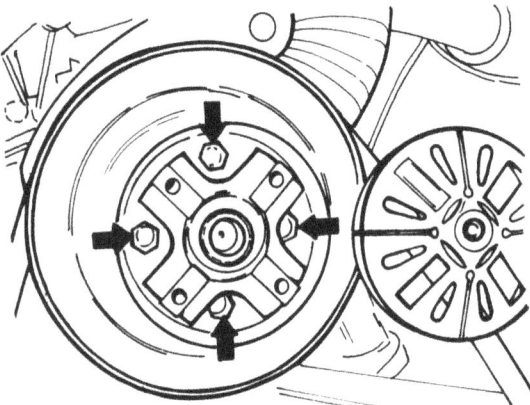

FIG 4:9 Fan coupling removal

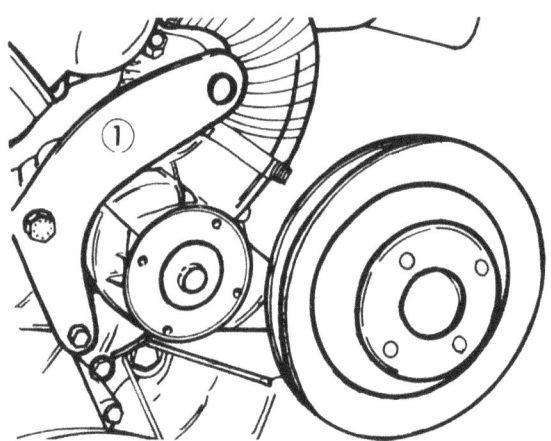

FIG 4:11 Water pump pulley and bracket

Always make sure that the correct drive belt is fitted when replacement is necessary, preferably by comparing with the original belt.

4:5 Cooling fan and coupling

Cooling fan:

To remove the fan, straighten the lockplates and remove the four fixing bolts, then detach the lockplates and pull the fan from the coupling (see **FIG 4:7**).

Refitting is a reversal of the removal procedure, making sure that piston 1 is in the correct position in the heat-sensing element (see **FIG 4:8**). Use new lockplates if the originals are not in good condition. Always use fixing bolts of the correct type, which is M6 × 25mm, otherwise it is possible for the fan to be permanently locked to the coupling. Tighten the bolts alternately and evenly then lock by bending up the lockplates.

Fan coupling:

To remove the coupling, first remove the cooling fan as described previously. Take off the drive plate then remove the clutch drum (see **FIG 4:9**).

If a coupling is faulty in any way it must be renewed complete, as slave element **A** is adjusted exactly to fit

drive plate **B** (see **FIG 4:10**). Note that gap **C** must be 5mm (0.197in). A faulty or inoperative coupling can be responsible for engine overheating, by failing to engage the cooling fan at the specified coolant temperature. If, for any reason, a replacement coupling assembly is not available, the fan should be temporarily locked to the coupling to prevent engine overheating. To do this, remove two of the fan securing bolts (see **FIG 4:7**) and replace them with two M6 × 30mm bolts. These bolts should be positioned opposite each other to maintain cooling fan balance. The fan will then be locked to the coupling and will operate at all times. This will prevent engine overheating, but may not allow the engine to reach normal operating temperature, especially during short journeys. This can be a cause of increased engine wear and high fuel consumption, so a new coupling should be installed with four bolts of the correct length as soon as possible.

4:6 The water pump

Removal:

Drain the cooling system as described in **Section 4:2**, then remove cooling fan coupling as described in **Section 4:5**. Remove the alternator drive belt as described in **Section 4:4**. Remove the pulley from the water pump, then detach bracket 1 (see **FIG 4:11**). Disconnect the water hose from the pump, then remove the five fixing bolts and detach the pump and gasket (see **FIG 4:12**). As special press tool equipment is needed to dismantle and reassemble the water pump, the work should be carried out by a service station.

Refitting:

Clean the contact faces of the water pump and cylinder block to remove all traces of old gasket, taking care not to damage the surfaces. Refit the water pump, using a new gasket, then tighten the fixing bolts alternately and evenly. Refit the remaining components in the reverse order of removal and refill and bleed the cooling system as described in **Section 4:2**.

4:7 The thermostat

Removal:

Drain the cooling system as described in **Section 4:2**. Remove the four fixing bolts and detach the thermostat cover, there being no need to detach the hose (see **FIG 4:13**). Remove the thermostat from the housing.

Testing:

Clean the thermostat and immerse it in a container of cold water together with a 0-100°C thermometer. Heat the water and check thermostat operation. The thermostat should begin to open at 84°C (183°F) for manual transmission models, 80°C (176°F) for automatic transmission models. If the thermostat is removed from the hot water and placed into cold water it should quickly return to the closed position. If the thermostat operates satisfactorily it may be refitted, if not it must be renewed.

Refitting:

Install the thermostat in the housing, making sure that the clamp and the arrow are facing in the direction of travel (see **FIG 4:13**). Clean the housing and cover mating faces, then refit the cover using a new gasket, if fitted. Tighten the fixing bolts alternately and evenly. Fill and bleed the system as described in **Section 4:2**.

4:8 Frost precautions

With the correct coolant solution in use as described in **Section 4:2**, no additional frost precautions should be necessary. However, it is advisable to have the solution tested at intervals during the winter to make certain that it has not weakened. A hydrometer calibrated to read both specific gravity and temperature for the type of coolant in the system must be used, most garages having such equipment. Always ensure that the anti-freeze mixture used for filling the system is of sufficient strength to provide protection against freezing, according to the manufacturer's instructions.

4:9 Fault diagnosis

(a) Internal water leakage

1 Cracked cylinder wall
2 Loose cylinder head bolts
3 Cracked cylinder head
4 Faulty head gasket

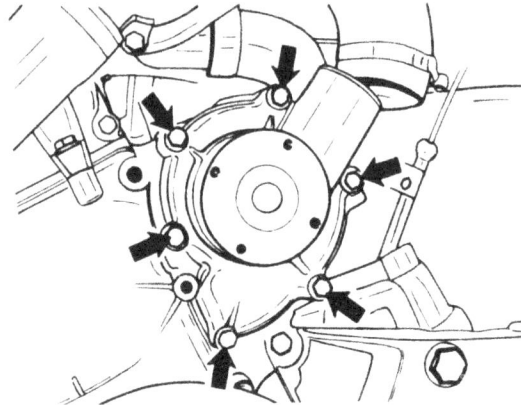

FIG 4:12   Water pump removal

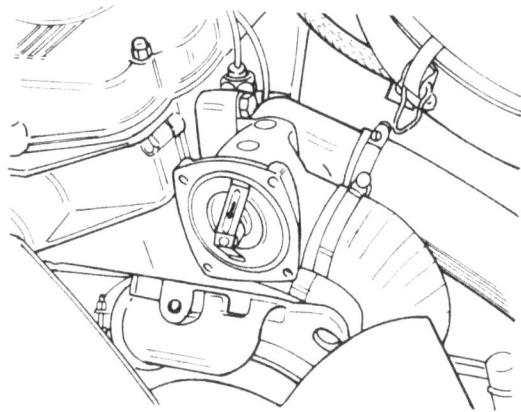

FIG 4:13   Thermostat removal

(b) Poor circulation

1 Radiator core blocked
2 Engine water passages restricted
3 Low water level
4 Loose drive belt
5 Defective thermostat
6 Perished or collapsed radiator hoses

(c) Corrosion

1 Impurities in the coolant
2 Infrequent draining and flushing

(d) Overheating

1 Check (b)
2 Faulty fan coupling
3 Sludge in crankcase
4 Faulty ignition timing
5 Low oil level in sump
6 Tight engine
7 Choked exhaust system
8 Binding brakes
9 Slipping clutch
10 Incorrect valve timing
11 Weak fuel mixture

NOTES

CHAPTER 5

THE CLUTCH

5 : 1 Description

A single dry plate clutch of diaphragm spring type is fitted, the main components being the driven plate, pressure plate assembly and release bearing.

The driven plate consists of a resilient steel disc attached to a hub which slides on the splined gearbox input shaft. The friction linings are riveted to both sides of the disc. The pressure plate assembly consists of the pressure plate, diaphragm spring and housing, this housing being attached to the rear face of the engine flywheel. The release bearing is a ballbearing of special construction with an elongated outer ring that presses directly against the diaphragm spring when the clutch pedal is operated.

The clutch operating mechanism is hydraulic, the clutch pedal actuating a master cylinder where pressure on the fluid is generated, this pressure being transmitted through a hose to the clutch slave cylinder mounted on the clutch housing. Slave cylinder action is transmitted to the release bearing by a release lever. On some models the release lever is fully enclosed inside the clutch housing, on others it operates through a hole in the side of the housing.

When the clutch is fully engaged, the driven plate is nipped between the pressure plate and the flywheel and transmits torque to the gearbox by turning the splined input shaft. When the clutch pedal is depressed the pressure plate is withdrawn from the driven plate by hydraulic pressure, the driven plate then ceasing to transmit torque.

5 : 2 Routine maintenance

As the clutch operating mechanism is self-adjusting, no routine maintenance is required apart from a regular check on the level of hydraulic fluid in the system. The clutch and brake hydraulic systems share a common fluid reservoir, topping up being carried out as described in **Chapter 11**.

Checking clutch plate wear:

It is possible to make a simple check on clutch driven plate friction lining wear, without the need for component dismantling.

Models with external release lever:

Working from beneath the car, press the release lever in a forward direction until it touches the stop (see **FIG 5 : 1**). With a new clutch driven plate, dimension **A**

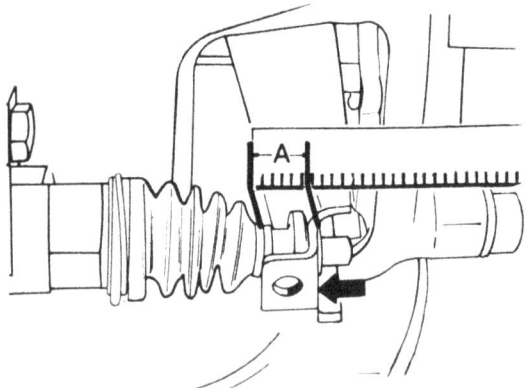

FIG 5:1 Checking friction lining wear, models with external release lever

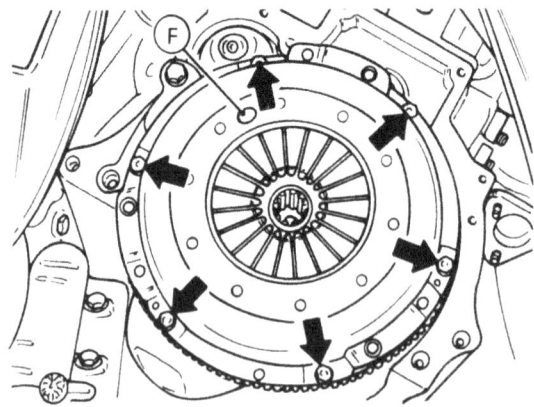

FIG 5:4 Removing clutch assembly from flywheel

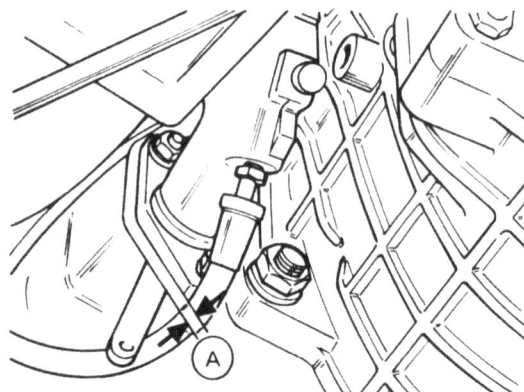

FIG 5:2 Checking friction lining wear, models with internal release lever

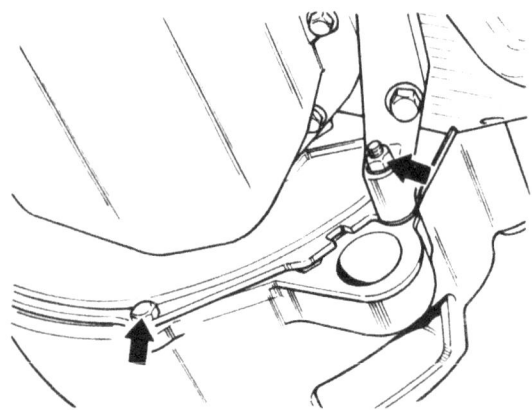

FIG 5:3 Coverplate attachments

should be 17 to 19mm (0.67 to 0.75in), measured at the slave cylinder pushrod. If the dimension is less than 5mm (0.2in), the driven plate should be renewed.

Models with internal release lever:

Checking on these models must be carried out using special tool BMW 7061 (see **FIG 5:2**). If the tool can be inserted into the opening on the slave cylinder as far as its handle, as shown in the illustration, sufficient driven plate lining thickness exists for further service. If a gap of approximately 5mm (0.2in) remains between the gauge handle and slave cylinder as shown at **A**, the friction linings are worn to the limit and a new driven plate must be fitted.

5:3 Removing and dismantling clutch

Refer to **Section 5:5** and remove the slave cylinder, but do not disconnect the fluid hose. Wire the slave cylinder to the underbody to prevent strain on the hose. Remove the gearbox as described in **Chapter 6**.

On models fitted with an external clutch release lever, loosen the clutch housing mounting bolts, then refer to **FIG 5:3** and remove the coverplate. Remove the clutch housing. On models fitted with an internal clutch release lever, remove the fixing bolts and detach the clutch housing.

Refer to **FIG 5:4**. Lock the flywheel against rotation using tool BMW 7007 or other suitable means, then mark the relationship of the clutch cover to engine flywheel so that it can be easily realigned to retain the original balance when refitted. Slacken the clutch cover retaining bolts (arrowed) alternately and evenly until spring pressure is released. Remove the bolts and lift off the clutch pressure plate assembly and driven plate, taking care not to get grease or oil on to the friction linings.

To remove the release bearing on models fitted with external release lever, refer to **FIG 5:5** and lift the spring ends over spherical pin collar. Take care not to damage angular seal 1. Remove the arm and bearing assembly by pulling to the side as shown in **FIG 5:6**. Disconnect the bearing from the retaining springs as shown in **FIG 5:7**.

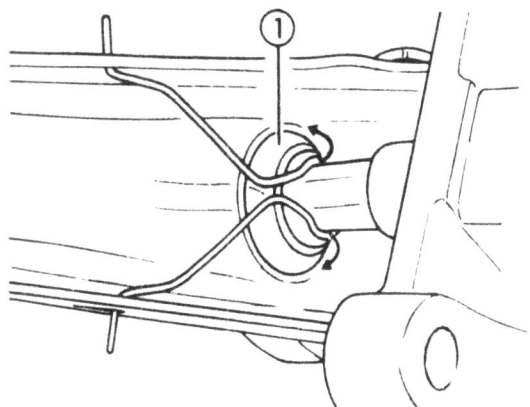

FIG 5:5   Disconnecting retaining spring

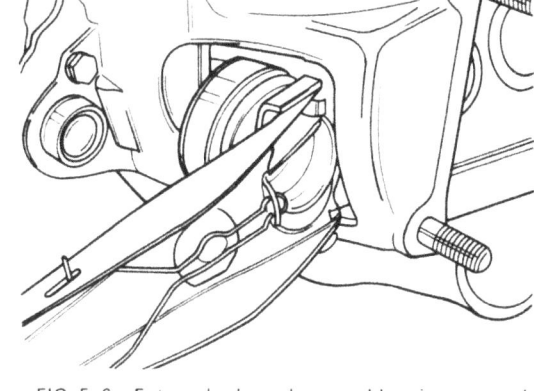

FIG 5:6   External release lever and bearing removal

To remove the release bearing on models fitted with internal release lever, refer to **FIG 5:8** and detach the spring retainer. Detach the release lever, then remove the release bearing (see **FIG 5:9**).

Servicing:

Inspect the clutch cover for loose rivets and for damage or distortion of the diaphragm spring. Inspect the spring link between pressure plate and cover for distortion or loose rivets (see **FIG 5:10**). Check the pressure plate for scoring or damage and check that the working surface is flat and true. using a metal straightedge. Make the check at several points. Note that the clutch cover, pressure plate and diaphragm spring assembly must not be dismantled. If any part is faulty the assembly must be renewed complete. Note that the assembly is colour coded with a paint mark for correct renewal, as shown at F in **FIG 5:4**.

Inspect the surfaces of the flywheel where the driven plate makes contact. Small scratches on the surface are unimportant, but if there are deep scratches the flywheel must be machined smooth or renewed.

Check the release bearing for roughness when it is pressed and turned by hand. Clean the release bearing by wiping with a cloth only. Do not use solvents for this purpose as they would wash the internal lubricant from the bearing. If a new bearing is to be installed, note that height H (see **FIG 5:11**) of installed bearing must be 38 + 0.050 - 0.075mm (1.496 + 0.002 - 0.003in).

Check the driven plate for loose rivets and broken or very loose torsional springs. Check the plate for distortion, preferably by mounting the plate between centres and using a dial gauge. Alternatively, hold the plate in position against the pressure plate surface and use feeler gauges at several points around the circumference. Distortion should not exceed 0.6mm (0.024in) at the periphery. The friction linings should be well proud of the rivets and have a polished glaze through which the grain of the material is clearly visible. A dark, glazed deposit indicates oil on the linings and, as this condition cannot be rectified, a new or relined plate will be required. Any sign of oil in the clutch indicates leakage from the engine or gearbox which must be traced and rectified. Check the

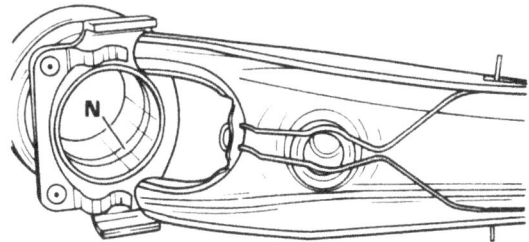

FIG 5:7   Detaching bearing from lever

FIG 5:8   Detaching spring retainer, internal release lever

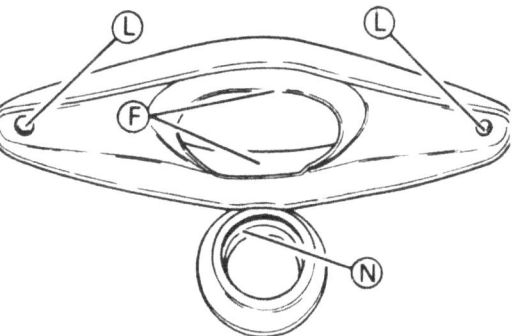

FIG 5:9   Internal release lever and bearing

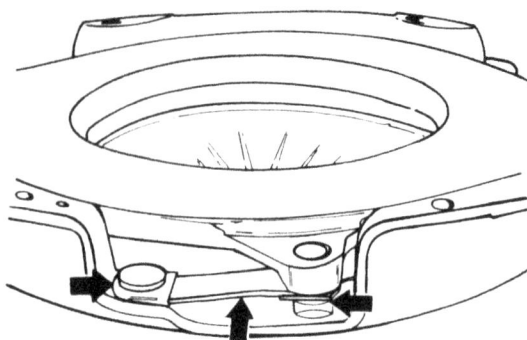

FIG 5:10   Inspecting spring link and rivets

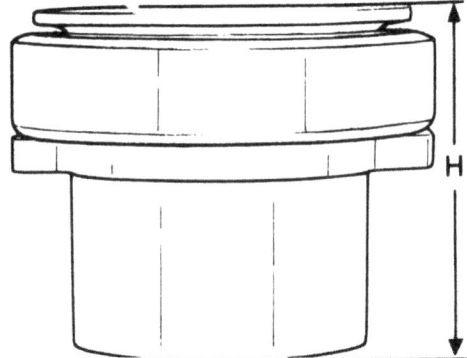

FIG 5:11   Release bearing installed height

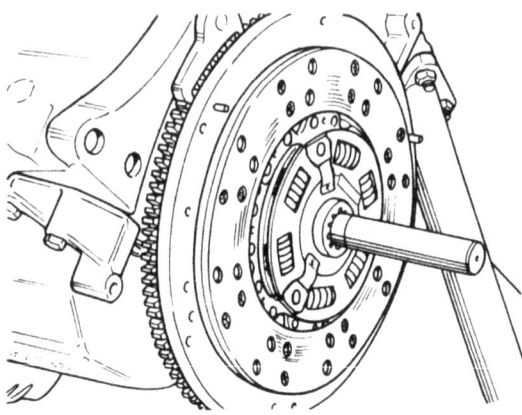

FIG 5:12   Driven plate installation

splines in the driven plate hub and on the gearbox input shaft, removing any burrs or, if there are signs of heavy wear, renewing parts as necessary.

It is not recommended that owners attempt to reline the clutch driven plate themselves, as the linings must be riveted and trued on the disc and the whole checked under a press. For this reason the driven plate should be relined at a service station or an exchange unit obtained and fitted.

5:4 Assembling and refitting clutch

When the clutch is refitted to the engine flywheel, the driven plate must be centralised before the cover is tightened down, using the special tool BMW 603 or a spare gearbox input shaft, as shown in FIG 5:12.

Place the driven plate in position on the flywheel and centralise by passing the special tool through the hub and into the pilot bearing in the crankshaft. Fit the clutch cover and pressure plate assembly, aligning the reference marks made during dismantling. Engage the locating pegs on the cover into the holes in the flywheel, then fit the retaining bolts finger tight (see FIG 5:4). Tighten the bolts alternately, one turn at a time, to the specified final torque.

On models with an external clutch release lever, install the release bearing in the reverse order of removal, filling the lubricating groove shown at N in FIG 5:7 with Molykote Longterm 2. It is essential to lubricate correctly, otherwise the release bearing may seize in service. When installing the release lever, make sure that the angular seal 1 is between the spherical pin and release lever (see FIG 5:5).

On models with an internal clutch release lever, fit the release bearing to the lever in the reverse order of removal. Refer to FIG 5:9 and pack lubricating groove N with Molykote Longterm 2 and coat guides F in release lever and bearing points L with similar lubricant. It is essential that lubrication is carried out as specified otherwise the release bearing may seize in service.

On models with external clutch release lever, install the clutch housing then refit the gearbox as described in Chapter 6. Refit the slave cylinder as described in Section 5:5.

On models with an internal clutch release lever, move the release lever to its correct installed position with the aid of the clutch slave cylinder. When slave cylinder pushrod and release lever are correctly positioned, align the thrust bearing to accept the gearbox input shaft. Make sure that sufficient lubricant is applied to the thrust bearing groove, as described previously. Operate the linkage to engage a gear. Supporting the weight of the gearbox, insert the input shaft and guide sleeve carefully into the thrust bearing. Turn the gearbox output flange until the input shaft slides through the driven plate hub and into the pilot bearing at the rear of the engine crankshaft. Remove the clutch slave cylinder again, attach the gearbox firmly to the clutch housing, then finally refit the slave cylinder as described in Section 5:5.

5:5 Servicing hydraulic system
Master cylinder:
Removal:

Siphon sufficient fluid from the reservoir to bring the level just below the pipe connection on the reservoir

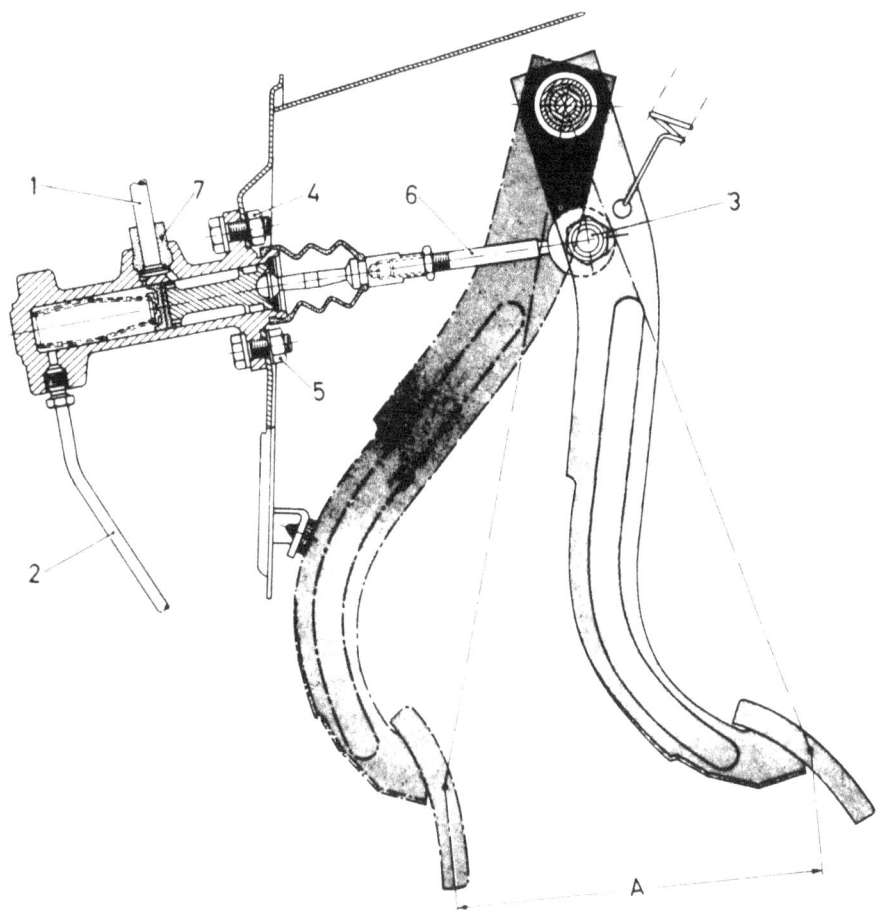

FIG 5:13 Section through master cylinder and pedal assembly

which supplies the clutch master cylinder. Note that brake fluid is poisonous and that it can damage paintwork. Keep fluid perfectly clean if it is to be re-used. Detach the lower dashboard panelling on the driver's side for access to the master cylinder attachment points.

Refer to **FIG 5:13**. Pull out pipe 1 with sealing plug 7. Disconnect pipe 2 at the master cylinder. Plug the open ends of pipes to prevent the entry of dirt. Remove bolt 3 to detach pushrod 6 from clutch pedal, then remove nuts 4 and 5 and remove the master cylinder assembly.

Servicing:

Carefully pull back the rubber boot then remove the circlip from the master cylinder bore. Withdraw the pushrod and washer, then extract the internal parts. Gentle air pressure may be used at the outlet port to remove the internal parts, but take care to avoid damage due to parts being ejected at high speed. Remove the rubber seal from the piston.

Examine the rubber boot and feed pipe seal and renew if not in perfect condition. Always renew piston seals. Wash the remaining parts in the correct grade of brake fluid or methylated spirits only. Examine the parts,

checking the piston and cylinder bore for scoring, damage or corrosion. Renew any faulty parts.

Observe absolute cleanliness during assembly to prevent oil or dirt from contacting internal parts. Dip piston and seals into clean brake fluid when installing. Fit the secondary seal over the piston using the fingers only, making sure that it is correctly seated. Insert the spring small end first, making sure that the retainer is in place. Insert the main seal with the lip first, taking care not to turn back the lip. Press the seal down the bore on to the spring retainer. Fit the washer followed by the piston, then install pushrod dished washer and circlip followed by the rubber boot.

Refitting:

This is a reversal of the removal procedure. Make sure that the sealing plug 7 is installed correctly so that no air can enter the system (see **FIG 5:13**). Lubricate pivot bolt 3 with Molykote Longterm 2. When master cylinder is installed and connected, check clutch pedal travel **A**. This should be 160mm (6.3in) for models with external clutch release lever, or 155mm (6.1in) for models with internal clutch release lever. If pedal travel is incorrect,

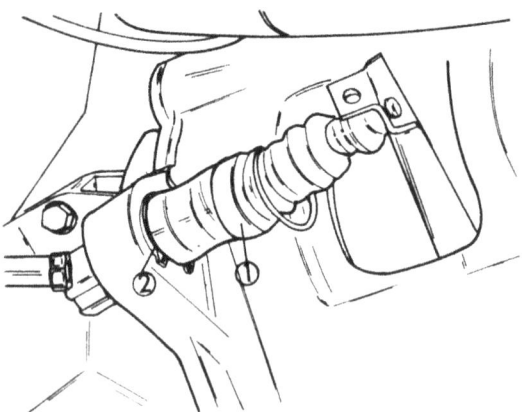

FIG 5:14 Slave cylinder used with external release lever

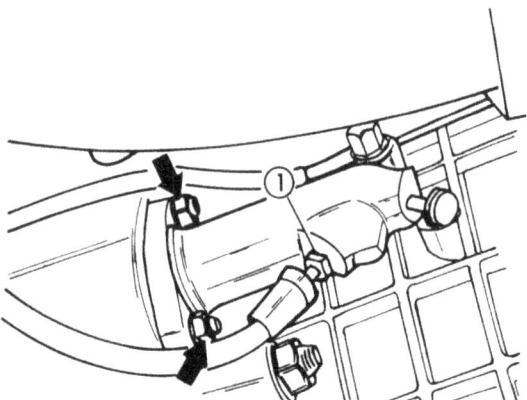

FIG 5:15 Slave cylinder used with internal release lever

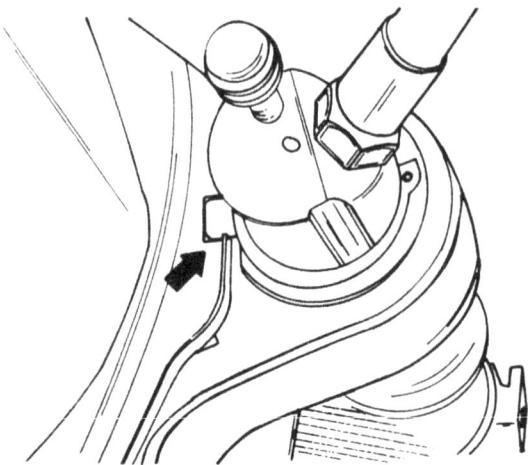

FIG 5:16 Location of anti-rotation lock

slacken the locknut then turn the sleeve which is threaded to pushrod 6. When correct travel is obtained, tighten locknut and recheck.

On completion, refill the fluid reservoir to the correct level and bleed the system as described later.

Slave cylinder:

Removal:

If the slave cylinder is to be removed for access to other components only, the fluid hose can be left connected and the assembly wired to the underbody to prevent strain on the hose. As the hose remains connected it will not be necessary to bleed the system when the slave cylinder is refitted.

If the slave cylinder is to be removed for servicing, siphon fluid from the supply reservoir as described previously for master cylinder removal.

On models with external clutch release lever, refer to **FIG 5:14**. Remove the spring clip and pull back rubber boot 1. Remove circlip 2 and remove slave cylinder towards the front of the car. If necessary, disconnect the fluid pipe to remove the cylinder completely.

On models with internal clutch release lever, refer to **FIG 5:15** and remove the two securing nuts arrowed. If necessary, disconnect hose union 1 to detach the slave cylinder completely.

Servicing:

Remove the rubber boot, if fitted. Remove the circlip from the bore and extract the internal components. Remove the piston seal and discard. Clean all internal parts with approved brake fluid or methylated spirits only. Examine all parts for wear or damage and renew as necessary. Always fit a new piston seal.

Carefully ease the new seal on to the piston and insert the assembly into the bore, taking care not to turn back the seal lip. Refit the remaining components in the reverse order of removal, taking care to avoid dirt or oil contamination.

Refitting:

This is a reversal of the removal procedure. On models with external clutch release lever, make sure that the anti-rotation lock is correctly located as shown by the arrow in **FIG 5:16**. In all cases, lubricate the ball end of the slave cylinder pushrod which contacts the clutch release lever using Molykote Longterm 2.

If the fluid hose was disconnected, reconnect and carefully tighten, then fill the reservoir with fluid to the correct level and bleed the hydraulic system as described next.

Bleeding the system:

This operation is necessary to remove any air which may have entered the system, due to the removal of components, or if the fluid level in the supply tank has been allowed to drop too low and air has entered through the fluid supply passage.

A need for bleeding can be indicated if the clutch drags and cannot be fully released with the pedal pushed to the floor.

Remove the rubber dust cap from the bleed screw on the clutch slave cylinder. Attach a length of rubber or plastic tubing to the bleed screw and lead the free end of the tube into a clean glass jar, into which sufficient fluid of the correct type has been added to cover the end of the tube. Have an assistant operate the clutch pedal through a full stroke approximately 10 times, holding the pedal to the floor at the end of a down stroke. With the pedal held down, open the bleed screw about half a turn and allow fluid to flow into the jar. When the flow stops, tighten the bleed screw and allow the pedal to return. Repeat this operation until no air bubbles are seen in the fluid entering the jar. Replenish the fluid in the supply tank frequently during this operation. If the level falls too low, air may be drawn into the system and the operation will have to be restarted.

On completion, top up the fluid to the correct level. It is not advisable to use fluid drained from the system for refilling purposes, unless it is new and perfectly clean. If so, allow it to stand for at least 24hr before re-use to ensure that it is free from air bubbles. Always store fluid in clean, sealed containers.

5:6 Fault diagnosis

(a) Drag or spin

1 Oil or grease on driven plate linings
2 Misalignment between engine and splined shaft
3 Driven plate hub binding on splined shaft
4 Distorted driven plate
5 Warped or damaged pressure plate or clutch cover
6 Broken driven plate linings
7 Dirt or foreign matter in the clutch
8 Air in hydraulic system

(b) Fierceness or snatch

1 Check 1, 2 and 3 in (a)
2 Worn driven plate linings

(c) Slip

1 Check 1 and 2 in (a) and 2 in (b)
2 Weak diaphragm spring
3 Seized piston in master or slave cylinder

(d) Judder

1 Check 1 and 2 in (a)
2 Pressure plate not parallel with flywheel face
3 Contact area of driven plate linings unevenly worn
4 Bent or worn splined shaft
5 Badly worn splines in driven plate hub
6 Buckled driven plate
7 Faulty engine or gearbox mountings

(e) Tick or knock

1 Badly worn driven plate hub splines
2 Worn release bearing
3 Bent or worn splined shaft
4 Loose flywheel

NOTES

CHAPTER 6

MANUAL TRANSMISSION

6:1 Description

The four-speed gearbox has synchromesh on all forward speeds and is operated by a centrally mounted remote control gearlever. The transmission casing is in three main parts, the clutch bellhousing, the gearbox case and the rear cover. All gears are of helical tooth formation except those in the reverse train which are straight-toothed spur gears.

The rear end of the input shaft and main drive pinion unit runs in a ballbearing in the gearbox front cover, while its front end engages in the pilot bearing in the rear of the engine crankshaft.

The mainshaft is supported at the front end by needle rollers in the main drive pinion, and by a ballbearing in the rear cover. The mainshaft gears run directly on the shaft journals.

Those maintenance and repair operations which can be carried out by a reasonably competent owner/mechanic are detailed in this chapter, but it is not recommended that any attempt be made to dismantle the gearbox and remove internal components. Special tools and hydraulic press equipment are needed to remove and install bearings and gear assemblies, and accurately calibrated heating equipment is necessary to heat certain components so that the correct degree of thermal expansion is obtained. For these reasons, it is recommended that all repair and overhaul procedures involving partial or complete dismantling of the gearbox be entrusted to a fully equipped BMW service station.

6:2 Routine maintenance

Interim topping up procedures and periodic changing of the transmission oil should be carried out at the intervals specified in the manufacturer's service schedule. The transmission oil filler and level plug on the side of the unit and the drain plug beneath the unit must be turned with an Allen key of the correct size. When checking the oil level, clean away all dirt from the filler and level plug before removing it. The oil level should be at the bottom of the threaded hole. Add an approved grade of gearbox oil if necessary, then allow excess oil to drain away fully before refitting and tightening the plug. To change the oil, remove the drain plug and allow the old oil to drain into a suitable container. Refit and firmly tighten the drain plug, then fill the gearbox to the correct level as described previously.

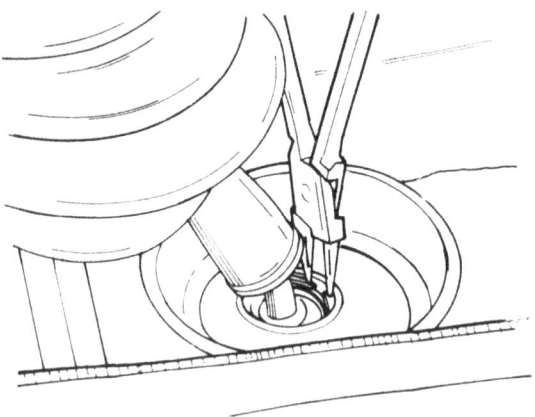

FIG 6:1 Removing gearlever retaining circlip

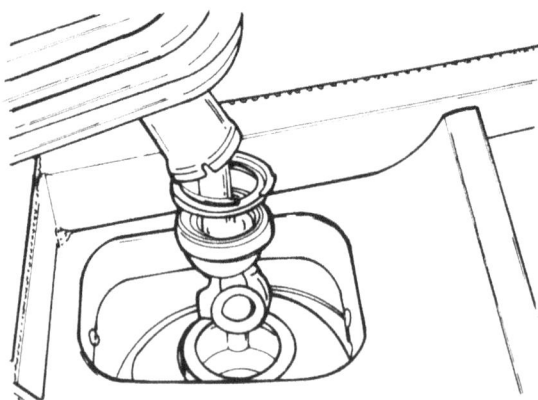

FIG 6:4 Gearlever removal, Getrag gearbox

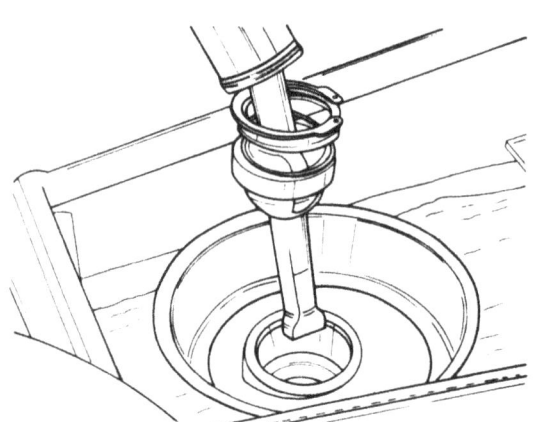

FIG 6:2 Gearlever removal, ZF gearbox

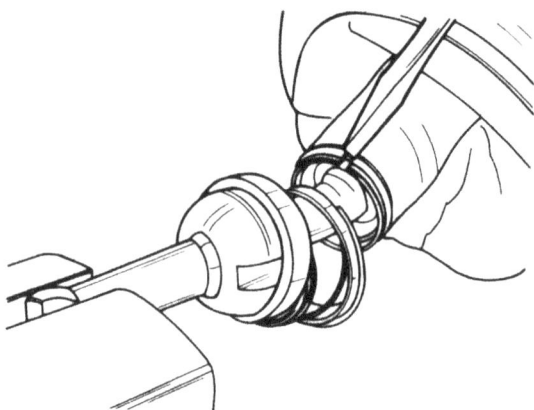

FIG 6:5 Dismantling gearlever components

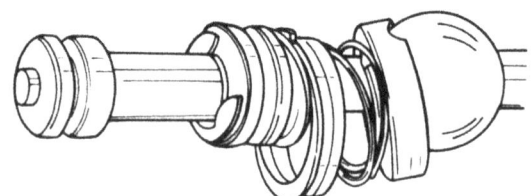

FIG 6:6 Removing gearlever rubber rings

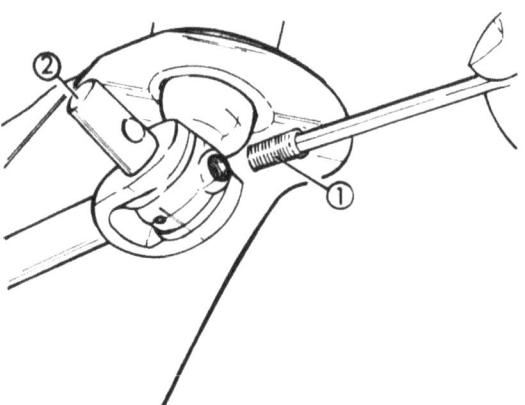

FIG 6:3 Disconnecting linkage, Getrag gearbox

FIG 6:7 Gearlever ball cup renewal

6:3 Gearlever removal and refitting

ZF gearbox:

Push up the rubber gaiter with foam insert and remove the circlip as shown in **FIG 6:1**, then lift out the gearlever assembly as shown in **FIG 6:2**. Refit in the reverse order of removal, lubricating the gearlever ball with Longterm 2 grease.

Getrag gearbox:

Push up the bellows with foam insert and remove the circlip as shown in **FIG 6:1**, then refer to **FIG 6:3** and unscrew setscrew 1 and press out pivot pin 2. Pull out the gearlever assembly as shown in **FIG 6:4**. Refit in the reverse order of removal, making sure that the pivot pin 2 is secured in its bore by means of setscrew 1 (see **FIG 6:3**). Lubricate the gearlever ball with Longterm 2 grease.

Renewing gearlever rubber rings:

Remove the gearlever as described previously, then refer to **FIG 6:5** and detach the wire circlip to release the gearlever. Refer to **FIG 6:6**. Pull off the rubber ring and remove the circlip, then remove the rubber rings. Refit in the reverse order of removal, using new rubber rings.

Renewing gearlever ball cups:

Dismantle the gearlever as described previously, then refer to **FIG 6:7** and remove circlip 1, spacer 2, pressure spring 3, ball cups 4 and 5 and washer 6. Reassemble in the reverse order of dismantling, using new ball cups. Lubricate the ball cups with Longterm 2 grease.

6:4 Speedometer drive pinion

If the car is raised for better access to the underside, support safely on floor stands. Disconnect the speedometer cable from the pinion housing, then remove the bolt shown in **FIG 6:8** and detach the drive pinion assembly from the gearbox. Check the seal fitted to the assembly and renew if not in perfect condition. Refitting is a reversal of the removal procedure.

6:5 Gearbox removal and refitting

Removal:

Remove the gearlever as described in **Section 6:3**. Disconnect the exhaust pipes at the exhaust manifolds, noting that the mounting studs must be smeared with Molykote paste G when the pipes are refitted and gaskets renewed.

Refer to **FIG 6:9** and detach the exhaust bracket from the gearbox. When the bracket is refitted, note that the pipe clip must be tightened first, followed by the exhaust bracket to gearbox mounting nuts. Refer to **Chapter 8** and detach the propeller shaft rubber coupling from the transmission flange and the centre bearing support from the underbody. Pull the propeller shaft from the transmission. Note that the centre bearing support must be properly tensioned when the propeller shaft is refitted.

Disconnect the speedometer cable from the gearbox and pull the cable from the reversing light switch. Refer to **FIG 6:10** and disconnect the gearbox from the clutch bellhousing. Use a suitable jack to support the engine

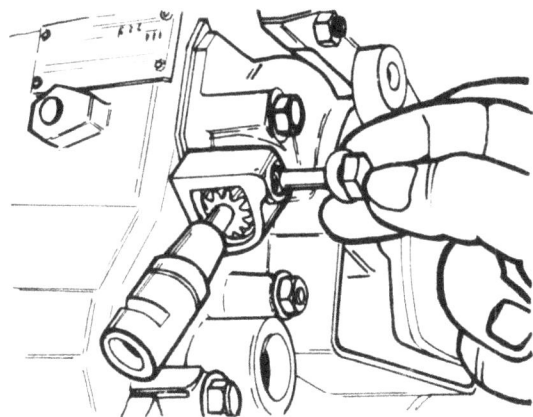

FIG 6:8 Removing speedometer drive pinion

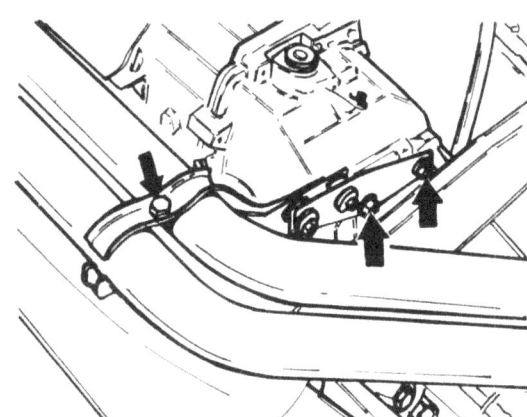

FIG 6:9 Detaching exhaust bracket

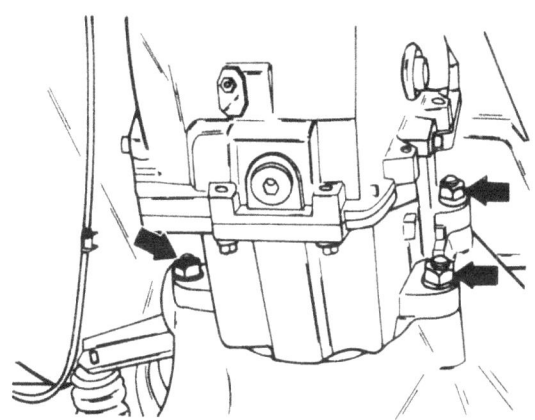

FIG 6:10 Disconnecting gearbox from bellhousing

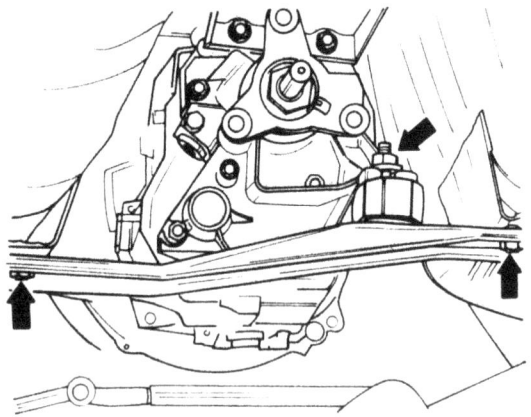

FIG 6:11 Detaching gearbox crossmember

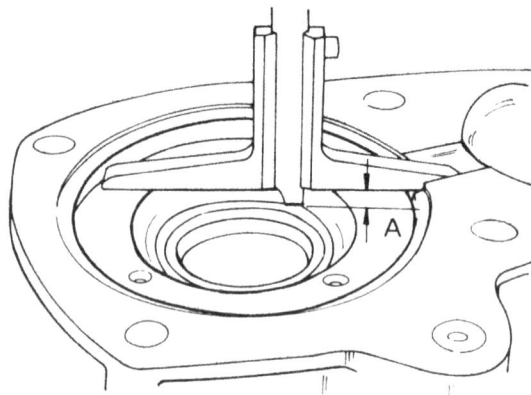

FIG 6:14 Guide flange seal installation

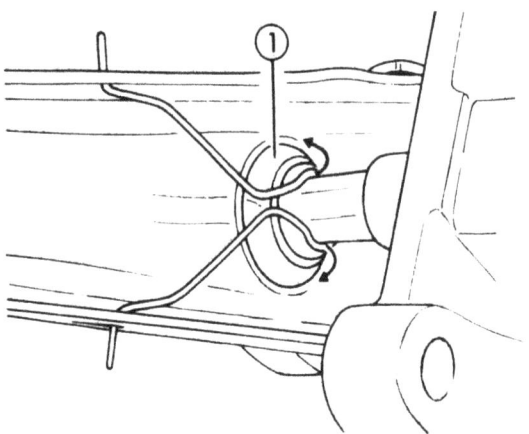

FIG 6:12 Angle seal 1 and retaining spring

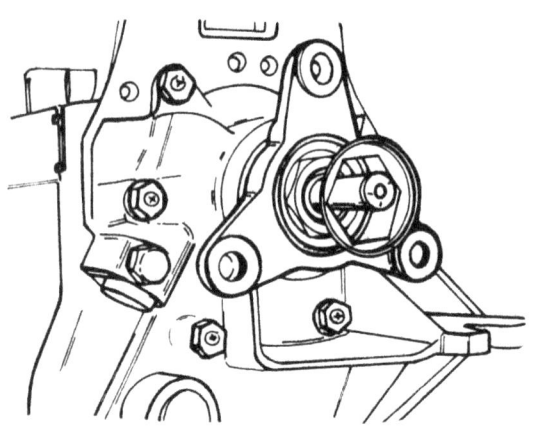

FIG 6:15 Drive flange removal

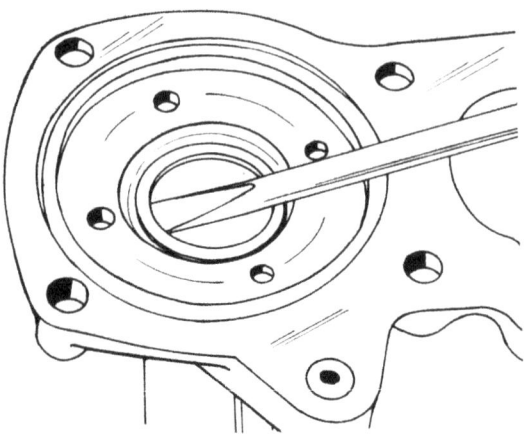

FIG 6:13 Guide flange seal removal

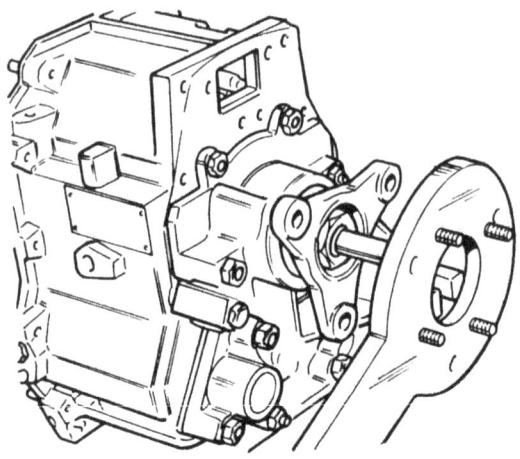

FIG 6:16 Output flange retaining tool

between the front axle brackets. Refer to **FIG 6 : 11**.
Slacken the rubber mountings at the gearbox and detach
the crossmember. Using a suitable jack or with the help
of an assistant, carefully move the gearbox rearward.
Lift the spring over the ballpin flange as shown in
FIG 6 : 12. Note that the angle seal 1 must be between
the ballpin and clutch release lever when refitting. The
transmission must be carefully removed rearwards until
the splined shaft is clear of the clutch hub, then the
assembly removed from beneath the car. **Do not allow
the weight of the gearbox to rest on the splined
shaft while it is still in the clutch hub, otherwise
severe damage to clutch components may occur.**

Refitting :

This is a reversal of the removal procedure. Check the
condition of gearbox rubber mountings and renew if
damaged or perished. When tightening the mounting and
crossmember fixings, make sure that the rubber components are not twisted or distorted. On completion,
check and if necessary top up gearbox oil as described in
Section 6 : 2.

6 : 6 Oil seal renewal

Input shaft seal :

Remove the gearbox as described in **Section 6 : 5**.
Remove the guide flange from the front of the gearbox,
noting the shims fitted between guide flange and
transmission ballbearings. These shims must be installed
in their original positions during reassembly. Carefully
prise out the seal from the guide flange as shown in
FIG 6 : 13. Carefully clean the seal bore, then install the
new seal, open side towards the gearbox, until the fitted
depth **A** shown in **FIG 6 : 14** is 4.5mm (0.177in). Refit
the guide flange to the gearbox, using a new gasket if
the original is not in good condition. Refit the transmission as described in **Section 6 : 5**.

Output shaft seal :

Disconnect the propeller shaft from the gearbox
output shaft flange as described in **Chapter 8**. Release
the staking and remove the locking plate from the
flange retaining nut as shown in **FIG 6 : 15**. It is recommended that the locking plate is always discarded and a
new one used during reassembly.

Lock the output flange against rotation using tool 604
as shown in **FIG 6 : 16** or by other suitable means, then
remove the retaining nut and pull the flange from the
shaft. Carefully lever out the old seal and discard.

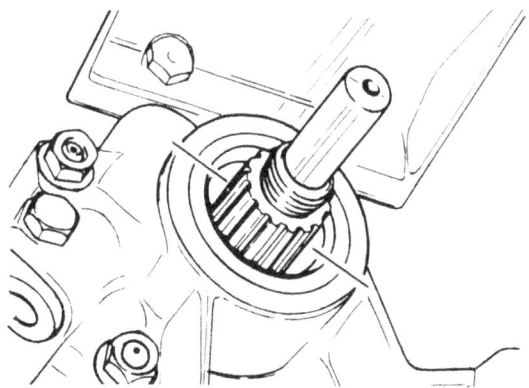

FIG 6 : 17   Output shaft seal installation

Carefully clean the bore, then install the new seal and
drive squarely into place until it is flush with the housing
as shown in **FIG 6 : 17**.

Refit the remaining components in the reverse order
of removal. When the output flange securing nut has
been tightened to the specified torque, fit the locking plate
and use a suitable punch to drive the outer ring of the
locking plate into the groove provided in the housing.

6 : 7 Fault diagnosis

(a) Jumping out of gear

1 Weak or broken detent plunger spring
2 Worn synchromesh unit
3 Loose or worn selector fork
4 Excessively worn selector shaft

(b) Noisy gearbox

1 Insufficient or dirty oil
2 Incorrect clearances between internal components
3 Worn or damaged bearings
4 Worn or damaged gear teeth

(c) Difficulty in engaging gear

1 Clutch not releasing properly
2 Worn synchromesh unit
3 Worn selector shafts or forks
4 Worn gearlever mechanism

(d) Oil leaks

1 Faulty gaskets
2 Leaking oil filler or drain plug
3 Worn or damaged oil seals
4 Faulty joint faces on gearbox case components

NOTES

CHAPTER 7

AUTOMATIC TRANSMISSION

7:1 Description

Automatic transmission is supplied as an optional extra to take the place of the usual clutch and gearbox. The assembly is shown in **FIG 7:1** and consists of a torque converter and hydraulically controlled automatic epicyclic gearbox with three forward speeds and one reverse. In all gears the drive is through the torque converter which results in maximum flexibility, especially in top gear. The gears are selected automatically as the hydraulic control system engages clutches in various combinations. The hydraulic control system and the torque converter assembly are supplied with pressure fluid from a pump mounted within the transmission case. A manually controlled mechanical parking pawl is incorporated so that the transmission output shaft can be locked when the vehicle is stationary.

The torque converter consists of an impeller connected through a drive plate to the engine crankshaft, a turbine which is splined to the transmission input shaft and a stator connected to the unit by a one-way clutch. The impeller, driven by the engine, transmits torque by means of the transmission fluid to the turbine which drives the automatic gearbox. The stator redirects the flow of fluid as it leaves the turbine so that it re-enters the impeller at the most effective angle.

When the engine is idling, the converter impeller is being driven slowly and the energy of the fluid leaving it is low, so little torque is imparted to the turbine. As the throttle is opened impeller speed increases and the process of torque multiplication begins. As the turbine picks up speed and the slip between it and the impeller reduces, the torque multiplication reduces progressively until, when their speeds become substantially equal, the unit acts as a fluid coupling. In this condition, the stator is no longer required to redirect the fluid flow and the one-way clutch permits it to rotate with the impeller and turbine.

The maintenance and adjustment procedures which can be carried out by a reasonably competent owner are given in this chapter. More serious performance faults which require special equipment for correct analysis, adjustment of the governor or clutches, partial or complete dismantling to replace worn or failed internal components dictate that the services of a fully equipped specialist should be enlisted. Quite apart from the specialised knowledge which is required, test equipment and a large number of special tools are essential. It should be noted that the torque converter is supplied as an assembly only, no internal parts being available separately.

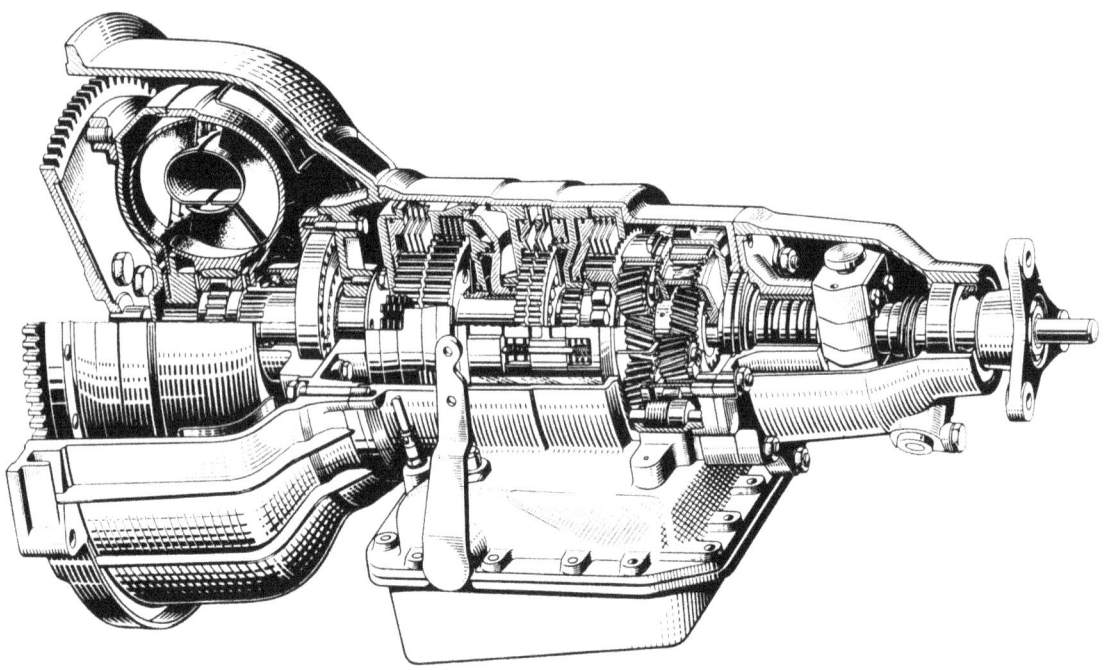

FIG 7:1   Cut-away view of automatic transmission assembly

7:2 Routine maintenance

Checking of the automatic transmission fluid level and the periodic changing of the fluid in the system should be carried out at the intervals recommended in the manufacturer's service schedule. Gearchange linkage and accelerator cable adjustments should be carried out whenever dictated by faulty performance, and after any servicing operation involving the detachment of any part of the linkage system. The procedures are described in **Section 7:3**.

Checking fluid level:

The fluid level must be checked either when the transmission is cold or when it is at normal operating temperature after a run of some miles.

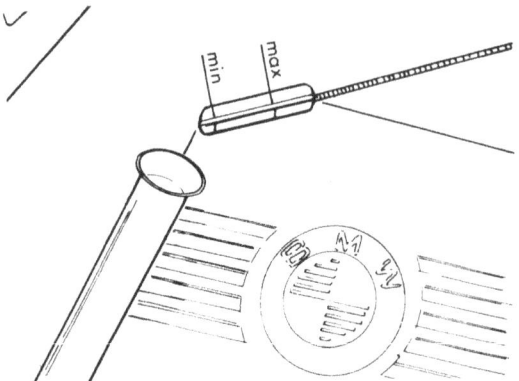

FIG 7:2   Transmission fluid dipstick markings

Apply the handbrake, start the engine, then move the selector lever through all gear ranges then leave it in the **P** (Park) position. Leave the engine idling while the fluid level is checked. Remove the automatic transmission dipstick, wipe it clean on a non-fluffy cloth and refit it fully. Remove the dipstick again and check the level of fluid against the appropriate marks shown typically in **FIG 7:2**. Top up through the dipstick tube if necessary to bring the fluid to the appropriate upper mark on the dipstick, according to fluid temperature. If the dipstick is not provided with two sets of markings, the fluid level should be at the MAX mark when the transmission is warm or approximately $\frac{1}{4}$in above the MIN mark when the transmission is cold. In such cases, if topping up is carried out with the transmission cold it is recommended that a further check be made when the transmission is at normal operating temperature, as this provides a more accurate reading.

Do not overfill the transmission. Use Dexron Automatic Transmission Fluid. **Never use anything but the recommended fluid in the automatic transmission.**

Changing transmission fluid:

Place a suitable container beneath the transmission, then remove the drain plug and washer which may be located either at the lower rear or lower side of the transmission. Allow the oil to drain fully, then wipe clean and refit the drain plug and washer. Renew the washer if it is damaged in any way.

Examine the drained fluid to check for possible transmission internal faults. If the fluid has a burnt smell and black discolouration, burnt clutch friction linings

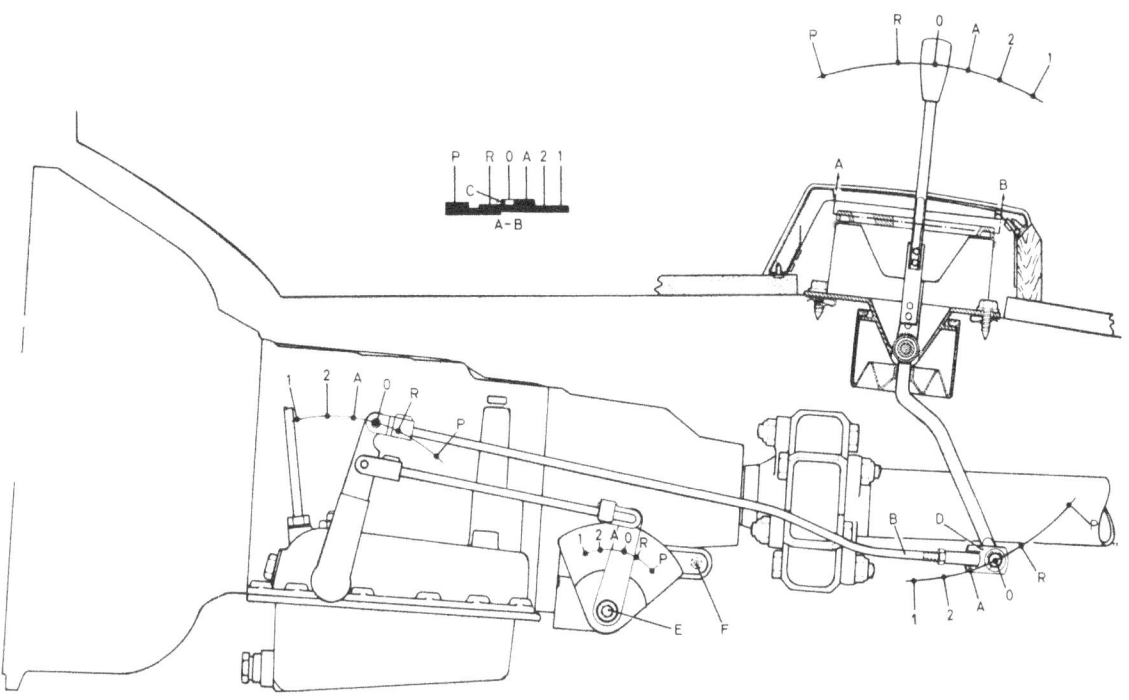

FIG 7:3   Selector linkage adjustment, ZF-3HP-20 transmission

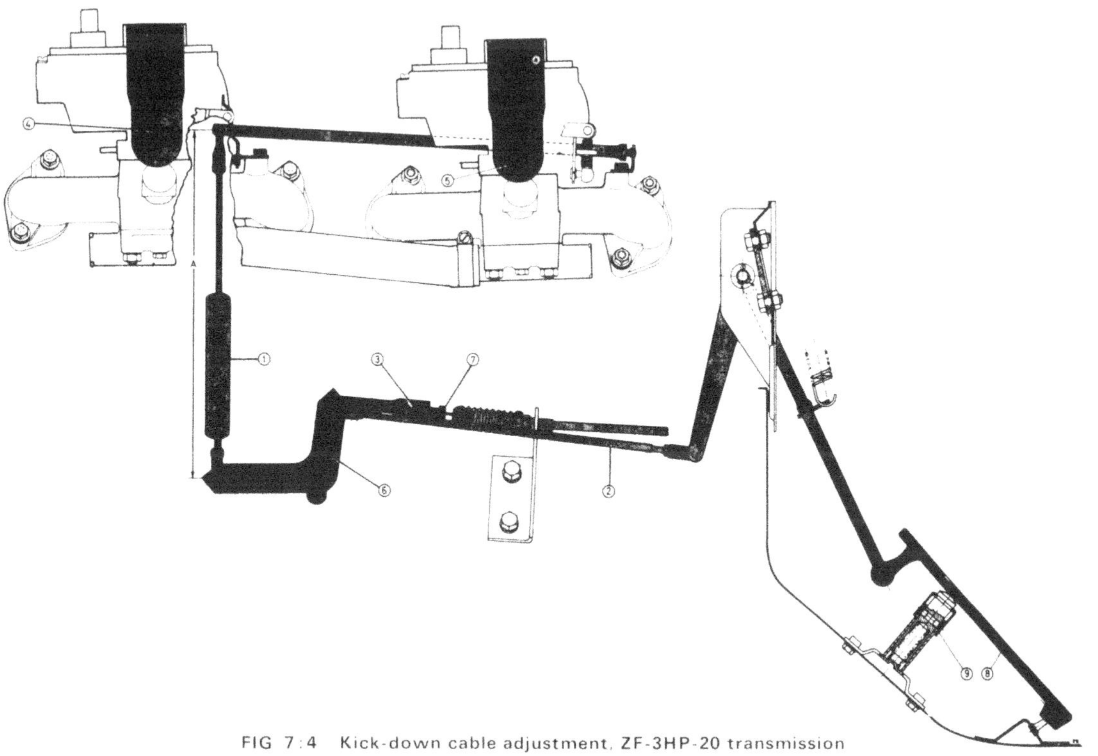

FIG 7:4   Kick-down cable adjustment, ZF-3HP-20 transmission

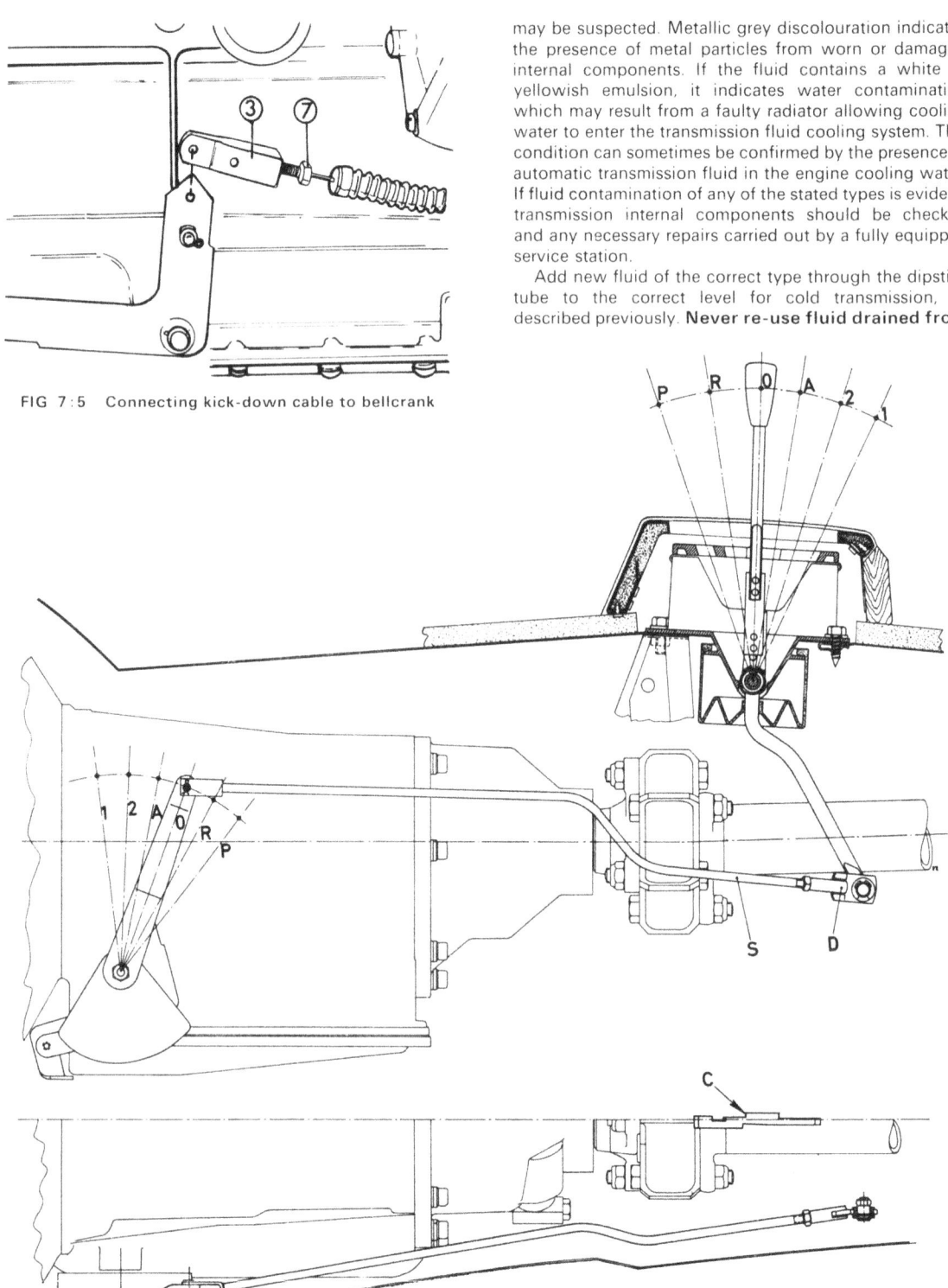

FIG 7:5 Connecting kick-down cable to bellcrank

may be suspected. Metallic grey discolouration indicates the presence of metal particles from worn or damaged internal components. If the fluid contains a white or yellowish emulsion, it indicates water contamination which may result from a faulty radiator allowing cooling water to enter the transmission fluid cooling system. This condition can sometimes be confirmed by the presence of automatic transmission fluid in the engine cooling water. If fluid contamination of any of the stated types is evident, transmission internal components should be checked and any necessary repairs carried out by a fully equipped service station.

Add new fluid of the correct type through the dipstick tube to the correct level for cold transmission, as described previously. **Never re-use fluid drained from**

FIG 7:6 Selector linkage adjustment, ZF-BW 65 transmission

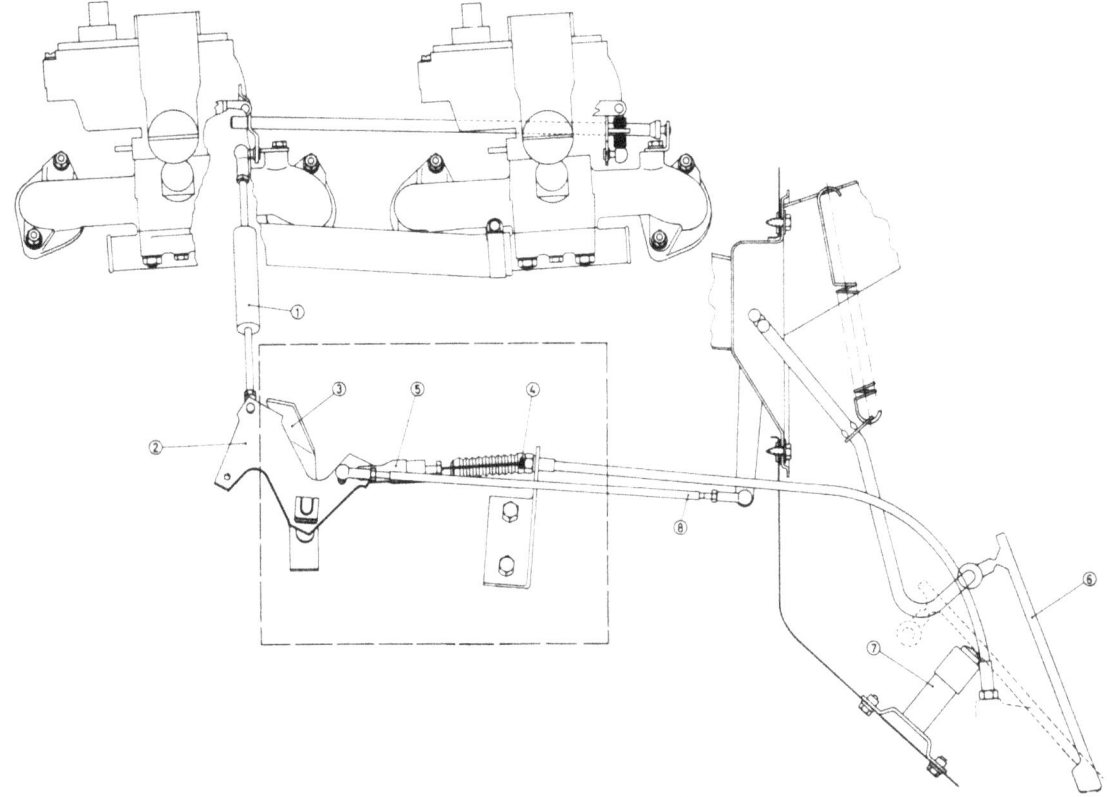

FIG 7:7 Kick-down cable adjustment. ZF-BW 65 transmission

the transmission. Always make sure that any containers or funnels used to handle transmission fluid are completely clean and dry before use

7:3 Gear selector linkages

ZF-3HP-20 transmission:

Selector linkage adjustment:

The selector linkage, which incorporates a selector lever position indicating switch, is shown in **FIG 7:3**. Apply the handbrake and place the selector lever in the car to the **O** (Neutral) position. Working beneath the car, disconnect eye bolt **D** from the lower end of the selector lever. Slacken the securing locknut and turn the eye bolt until, when it is refitted to the end of the selector lever, the selector lever is moved to just touch stop **C** on the gate. From this position, shorten the overall length of selector rod **B** by turning eye bolt **D** by three complete turns. Tighten the locknut to secure this position, then reconnect the eye bolt to the lower end of the selector lever. This done, loosen screws **E** and **F** and move the selector lever position indicating switch forwards or back as necessary until the operating lever is centralised at the **O** (Neutral) position without strain. Without moving the switch from this position, tighten screws **E** and **F**. On completion, check the operation of selector mechanism through all lever positions.

Kick-down cable adjustment:

Refer to **Chapter 2** and remove the air cleaner assembly. Refer to **FIG 7:4**. Slacken the connector locknuts and rotate tension element 1 until a total length (**A**) of 275 mm (10.83in) is achieved. Detach thrust rod 2 with kick-down cable 3. Have an assistant depress the throttle pedal 8 until it lightly contacts kick-down stop 9. Operate bellcrank 6 to fully open carburetter throttles 4 and 5. When doing this, make sure that tension element 1, which is spring-loaded, is not extended to the kick-down position. With the throttle linkage and accelerator pedal held in the correct positions, refer to **FIG 7:5** and pull kick-down cable 3 to the full throttle position. The full throttle position occurs before the cable is pulled as far as possible to the kick-down position, and can be clearly determined by pulling the cable repeatedly. When in the full throttle position, the hole in the connector must align exactly with the hole in the bellcrank as shown. If not, adjust position by turning connector while holding bolt 7. When correct, attach the cable connector to the bellcrank

With the throttle pedal and carburetter throttle valves still in the set positions previously described, refer to **FIG 7:4** and slacken the locknut securing connector on thrust rod 2. Rotate the connector until thrust rod can be reconnected to bellcrank 6 without moving either bellcrank or throttle lever. Tighten the locknut to secure the

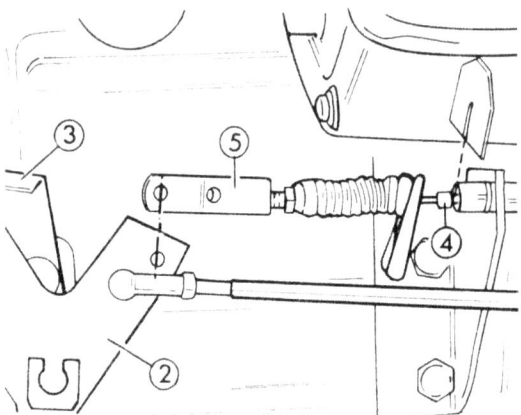

FIG 7:8 Detail of linkage framed by broken line in FIG 7:7

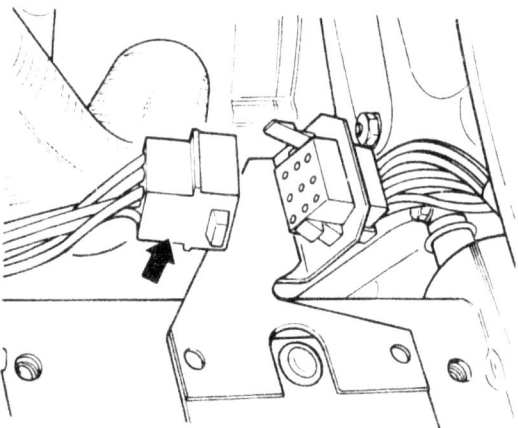

FIG 7:9 Wiring connector plug

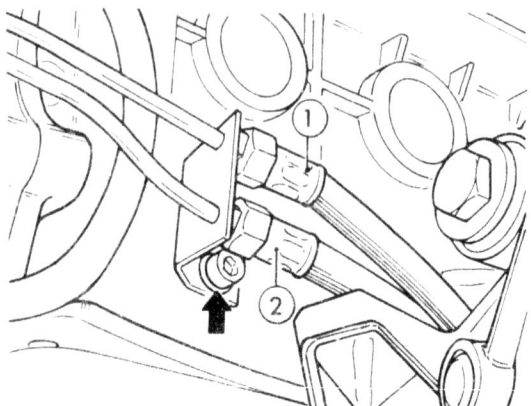

FIG 7:10 Fluid cooler pipe connections with mounting bracket

adjustment. The linkage should now be correctly adjusted. To check, press accelerator pedal 8 gently against kick-down stop 9. In this position, carburetter throttle valves 4 and 5 should be fully open, but the spring-loaded tension element 1 should not be extended at all. From this position, full pressure of the accelerator pedal against stop 9 will cause tension element 1 to extend and kick-down cable to move the mechanism in transmission case to the kick-down position. Road test the car and check that when driving with light throttle pressure a kick-down change from top to second, and from second to first, can be obtained when the throttle pedal is pushed fully to the floor into the kick-down position.

ZF-BW 65 transmission:

Selector linkage adjustment:

Refer to FIG 7:6. Apply the handbrake and place selector lever in position O (Neutral). Working from beneath the car, disconnect eye bolt D from lower end of selector lever. With the transmission selector lever properly engaged in the O position, slacken the locknut and turn eye bolt D until length of selector rod S is such that it moves the selector lever in the car to a position where it is just touching stop C on the gate. From this position, turn eye bolt D two or two-and-a-half turns inwards to shorten the overall length of rod S. The higher or lower number of turns is selected as necessary to ensure that the eye bolt is correctly angled when connected finally to the selector lever. Tighten the locknut to secure eye bolt adjustment and reconnect to selector lever.

Kick-down cable adjustment:

Run the engine until it reaches normal operating temperature. Refer to FIG 7:7 and disconnect upper ball end of tension element 1 from carburetter linkage. Check that idle speed is correct with carburetters properly synchronised as described in Chapter 2, then switch off engine. Disconnect kick-down cable clevis 5 from bellcrank 2. Slacken the locknuts and rotate the ball end connectors for tension element 1 until its overall length is such that when properly reconnected it pulls bellcrank 2 firmly into contact with the stop 3. Note that the tension element, which is spring-loaded, must not be extended at all under these conditions.

Refer to FIG 7:8. Pull back the rubber cover and retain in this position using a crocodile clip or similar. Clearance between cable nipple 4 and cable sleeve end must now be set to 0.25 to 0.50mm (0.0098 to 0.0197in). To do this, pull the cable away from the sleeve end and insert a slotted shim of the correct thickness as shown in the illustration. Under these conditions, the fixing hole in clevis 5 must be exactly aligned with the hole in bellcrank 2. If not, hold the hexagon on the cable and rotate the clevis as necessary. Note that there must be no slack in the kick-down cable. When correct, reconnect clevis to bellcrank and remove the shim.

Have an assistant depress throttle pedal 6 until it gently contacts kick-down stop 7 (see FIG 7:7). With this position held, slacken the locknuts and rotate thrust rod 8 until its length is such that the distance between cable nipple 4 and cable sleeve end is 37mm (1.4567in).

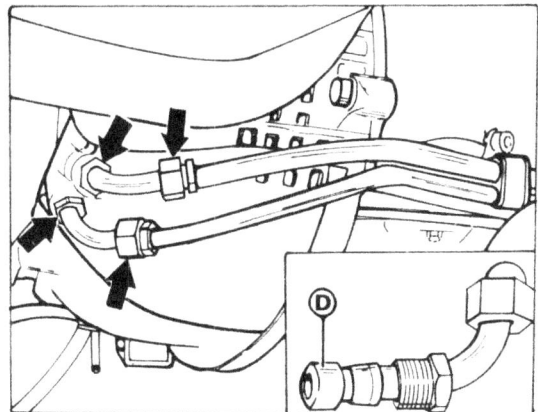

FIG 7:11 Fluid cooler pipe connections with sealing elements D

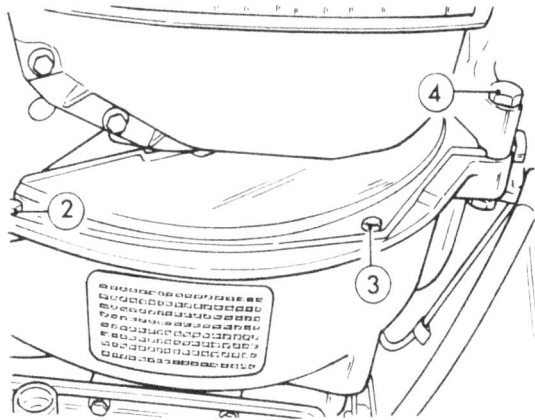

FIG 7:12 Detaching coverplate

Tighten the locknuts to secure the adjustment. Have the accelerator pedal pressed fully down to the kick-down position and check that nipple 4 is moved away from the cable sleeve end by a minimum of 43mm (1.6929in). On completion, remove the clip and reposition the rubber cover over the kick-down cable.

7:4 Transmission removal and refitting

Removal:

Raise and safely support the car on floor stands for access to the underside. Disconnect the battery negative cable. Disconnect the wiring connector plug shown in **FIG 7:9**. Refer to **FIG 7:8** and disconnect kick-down cable clevis 5 from bellcrank 2. Disconnect the outer cable sleeve from the mounting bracket. Drain transmission fluid as described in **Section 7:2**.

Disconnect the fluid filler pipe bracket from the exhaust manifold then pull the filler pipe from the mounting hole in the transmission or unscrew the filler pipe from the transmission fluid pan, according to type. On the press-in type, check the 'O' ring in the housing and renew if necessary during reassembly.

Remove the entire exhaust system by disconnecting the front pipes at the exhaust manifold connections, detaching the pipe clip and removing the retaining rings from the rear silencer.

If fluid cooler hoses are attached at a mounting bracket as shown in **FIG 7:10**, detach feed hose 1 and return hose 2, then unscrew the bolt arrowed to detach the bracket. If fluid cooler pipes are connected as shown in **FIG 7:11**, disconnect the elbows at the points arrowed. Note that, from transmission number 16676 the holes for connecting the fluid pipes are cylindrical. Make certain that sealing elements D are in place, as if these are missing fluid will leak from the transmission.

Refer to **FIG 7:12**. Remove mounting bolts 2 and 3, then slacken bolt 4 and swing the cover plate downwards. Detach the protective screen if fitted, then remove the four bolts (see arrow in **FIG 7:13**) to separate torque converter from drive plate, turning the assembly for access to each bolt in turn.

Refer to **FIG 7:6** and detach the selector rod from lower end of selector lever. Refer to **Chapter 8** and

FIG 7:13 Torque converter mounting bolt

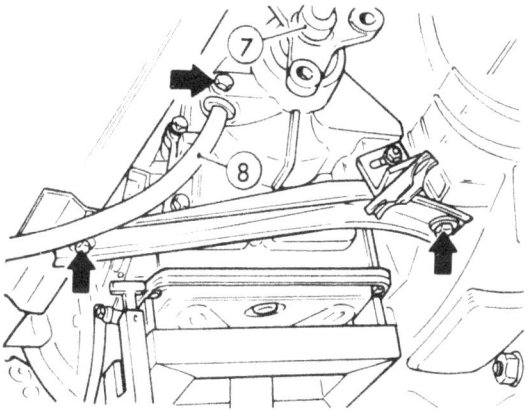

FIG 7:14 Removing components from rear of transmission

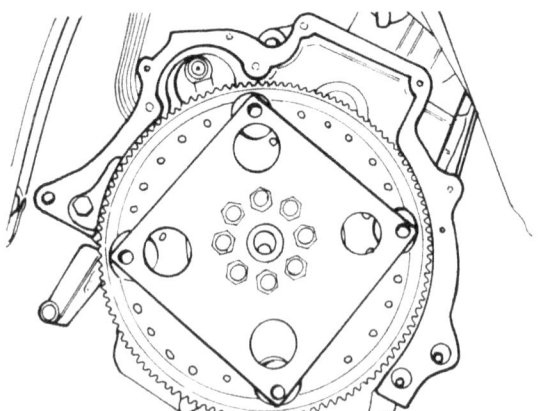

FIG 7:15   Drive plate and flywheel

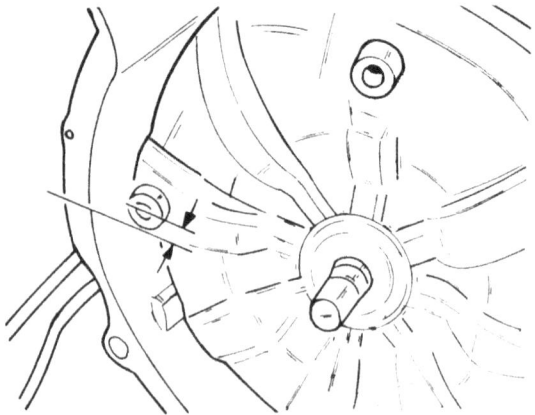

FIG 7:16   Torque converter installation

disconnect the propeller shaft from the rear of the transmission and the centre bearing from the underbody. Swing the propeller shaft clear of the work area and support carefully to prevent damage.

Support the weight of the transmission with a suitable jack and a support tool such as 7060-1 as shown in **FIG 7:14**. Pull off buffer 7, remove speedometer cable 8 and detach mounting crossmember from transmission and underbody. Lower the transmission slowly until the engine oil sump contacts the front axle crossmember. Remove all bolts securing transmission to engine crankcase noting the locations of cable and hose retainers which may be secured by some of the bolts. Pull the breather line from the transmission.

Raise the transmission, place a suitable piece of wood between the engine oil sump and front axle crossmember, then lower the transmission until the sump contacts the piece of wood. Carefully remove the transmission from the engine, pressing the torque converter into its housing at the same time to prevent it from falling.

Check the drive plate on the engine flywheel for cracking or other damage and renew if necessary. When removing the drive plate, the flywheel should be locked against rotation by using tool 7007 or similar as shown in **FIG 7:15**.

Refitting:

This is a reversal of the removal procedure, noting the following points:

Check that the torque converter is in the correct installed position, as shown in **FIG 7:16**. The position is correct when the drive plate mounting is below the edge of the housing. If not, insert both converter dogs into slots of the primary pump while turning the torque converter slightly. Make sure that the torque converter is firmly held in place as the transmission is installed to the engine crankcase. On completion, refill the transmission with fluid as described in **Section 7:2**, then adjust the gear selector and kick-down cable linkages as described in **Section 7:3**.

7:5 Fault diagnosis

As indicated earlier in this chapter, serious automatic transmission faults will require expert diagnosis and rectification. But the checks and adjustments described in this chapter can be used as a first step. Always begin by checking that the fluid level is correct. Drive faults may be cured by adjusting the selector linkage and kick-down cable. Remember also that the fuel and ignition systems must be correctly adjusted so that engine pick-up is smooth and progressive. If no improvement results from these measures, expert advice should be sought.

CHAPTER 8

PROPELLER SHAFT, REAR AXLE
AND REAR SUSPENSION

8:1 Description

The layout of the independent rear suspension, rear axle and drive shafts is shown in **FIG 8:1**. The main suspension crossmember and the differential carrier assembly are attached to the underbody by rubber cushioned mountings. The trailing arms are attached to the crossmember by means of rubber bushed pivots. The suspension struts which control vertical suspension travel consist of coil springs controlled by double acting hydraulic dampers. On some models, an anti-roll bar is fitted between the trailing arms (see **Section 8:7**).

Power is transmitted from the transmission output shaft to the differential unit pinion shaft by a two-piece propeller shaft provided with universal joints and an intermediate ballbearing attached to the underbody by a flexible rubber mounting. The front end of the propeller shaft is provided with a rubber coupling to cushion the drive.

Power is transmitted from the differential assembly to the rear wheels by drive shafts having flanged connections to the differential side gears and stub axles. On some models, a limited slip differential assembly is available as an optional extra.

The items of maintenance and overhaul which can be carried out by a reasonably competent owner/mechanic are given in this chapter. but it is not advised that any further operations be attempted. Special tools and equipment are essential to overhaul the differential components and set the necessary preloads, so, for this reason, the components should be dismantled and serviced only by a BMW service station having the necessary special equipment and trained personnel.

8:2 Routine maintenance

Checking of the oil level in the differential carrier and periodic changing of the oil should be carried out at the intervals specified in the manufacturer's service schedule. To check the oil level, make sure that the vehicle is standing on level ground, then remove the combined filler and level plug from the differential carrier. If necessary, add an approved grade of oil through the hole until the level is at the bottom of the hole. Allow excess oil to drain away fully, then refit the plug. To drain the oil, remove the filler and level plug and also the drain plug beneath the differential carrier. Allow the old oil to drain

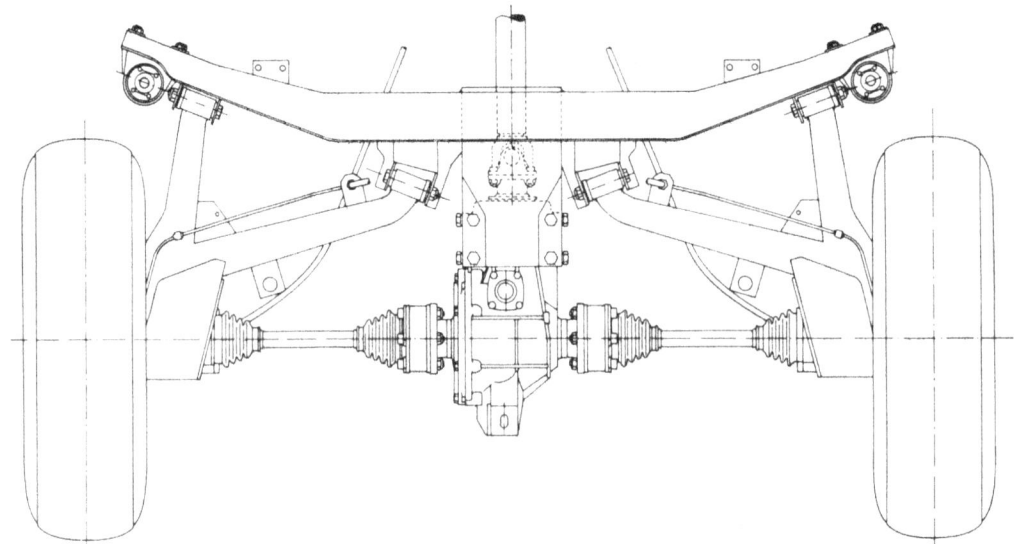

FIG 8:1   Layout of rear suspension, rear axle and drive shafts

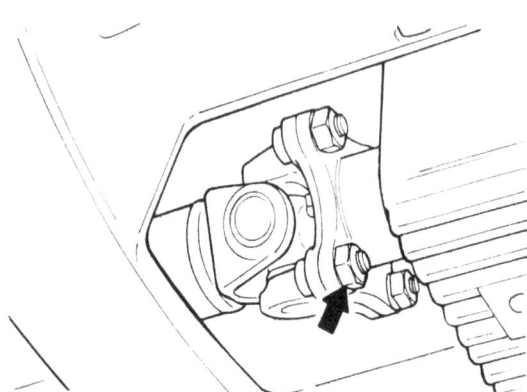

FIG 8:2   Propeller shaft to differential flange connection

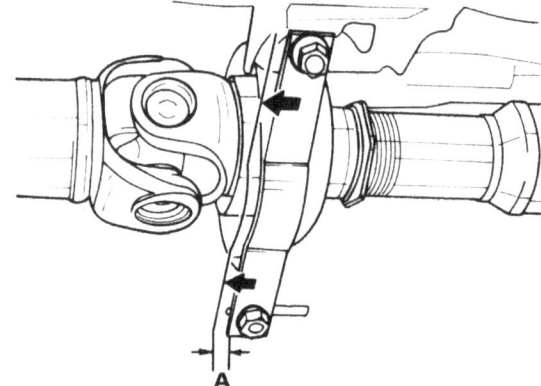

FIG 8:4   Centre bearing attachments

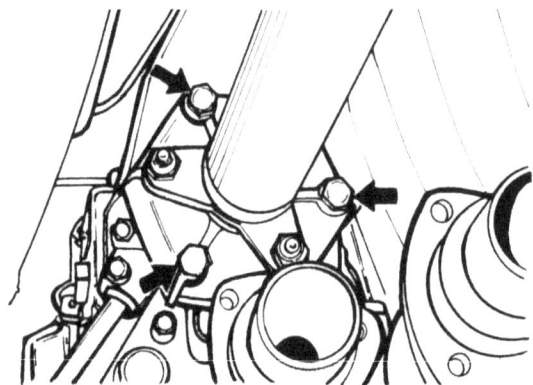

FIG 8:3   Disconnecting propeller shaft at rubber coupling

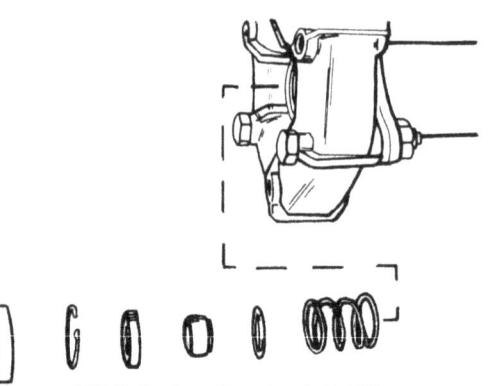

FIG 8:5   Locating ring assembly

fully into a suitable container, then refit the drain plug and add new oil to the correct level as described previously.

8:3 Propeller shaft

Removal:

Remove the rear exhaust pipes and silencers to gain the necessary access to the propeller shaft. Disconnect the rear end of the propeller shaft from the differential flange as shown in **FIG 8:2**. Disconnect the front end of the propeller shaft from the transmission output shaft by disconnecting the rubber coupling at the points arrowed in **FIG 8:3**. Do not remove the rubber coupling from the propeller shaft unless it is to be renewed, as it is pretensioned and therefore may be difficult to refit correctly. Refer to **FIG 8:4** and remove the two nuts to detach the centre bearing from the underbody. Bend the propeller shaft downwards at the centre and remove from beneath the car. If the propeller shaft is defective in any way it must be renewed complete, as the front and rear parts are matched and balanced as an assembly.

Locating ring and rubber coupling:

To remove the locating ring, refer to **FIG 8:5** and press off the sealing cap. Remove the circlip then extract ball cup, locating ring, washer and spring. Refitting is a reversal of the removal procedure, packing the locating unit with approximately 6g (0.212oz) of Molykote Longterm 2.

To renew the rubber coupling, remove the fixing bolts and discard the old unit. New rubber couplings are supplied complete with a tensioning strap to retain the unit suitably compressed for installation (see **FIG 8:6**). Install the unit and tighten the fixing bolts to the specified torque, then carefully cut free the strap and discard.

Centre bearing assembly:

Before removing the centre bearing, mark the two parts of the propeller shaft as shown by the arrows in **FIG 8:7**, so that the original balance of the assembly can be retained when the parts are reassembled. Slacken the screw bush and pull the shaft from the splines.

Refer to **FIG 8:8** and remove the circlip and dust cap. Press the bearing support from the propeller shaft, then press the bearing from the support as shown in **FIG 8:9**. Check the bearing for wear or damage and renew if necessary. Reassemble in the reverse order of dismantling, smearing the mounting socket for the ballbearing with plain water before pressing the bearing into place.

Refitting:

This is a reversal of the removal procedure, tightening the component fixings to the specified torque figures. When installing the central bearing support bracket, refer to **FIG 8:4** and press the assembly 2mm (0.079in) in the direction of the arrows and hold in this position while firmly tightening the mounting nuts. To prevent strain on the rubber coupling, tighten the nuts only, holding the bolts against rotation with a second spanner.

8:4 Drive shafts

Note that drive shafts must not be deflected beyond an angle of 18° or damage to the universal joints may

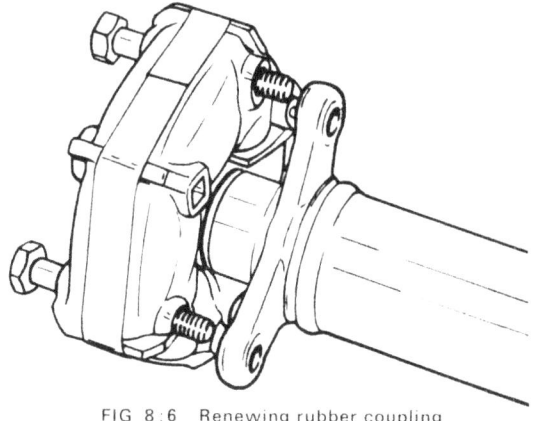

FIG 8:6   Renewing rubber coupling

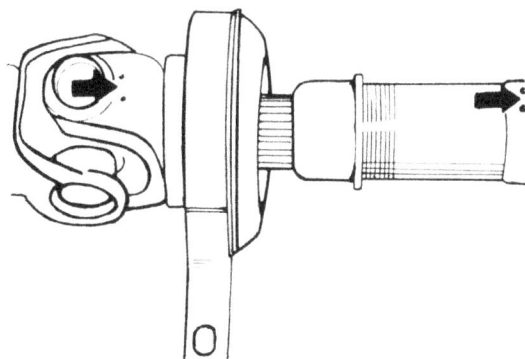

FIG 8:7   Marking propeller shaft for correct reassembly

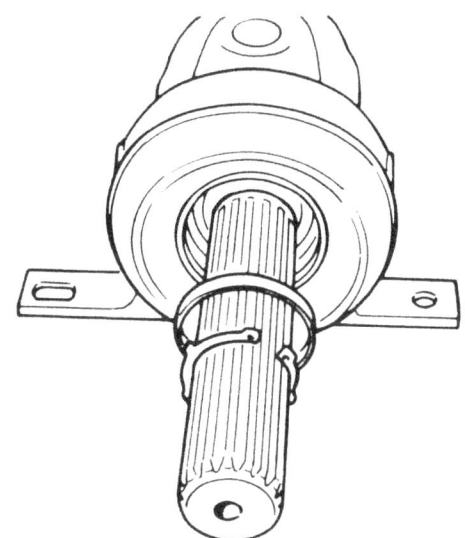

FIG 8:8   Removing circlip and dust cap

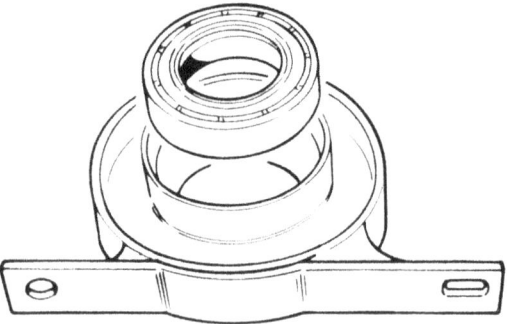

FIG 8:9   Centre bearing removal

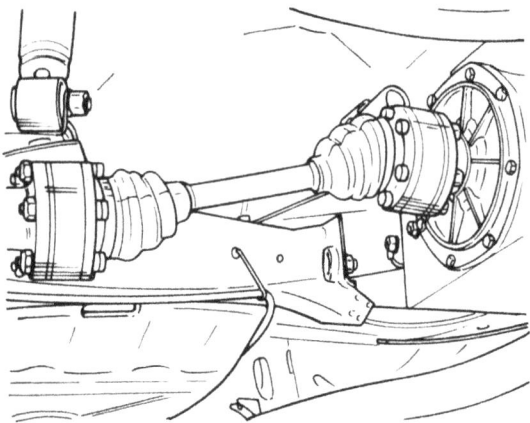

FIG 8:10   Drive shaft installation

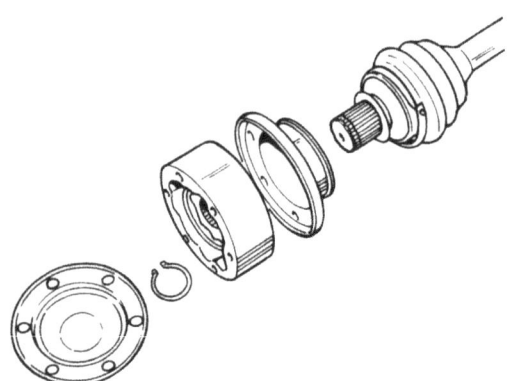

FIG 8:11   Drive shaft components

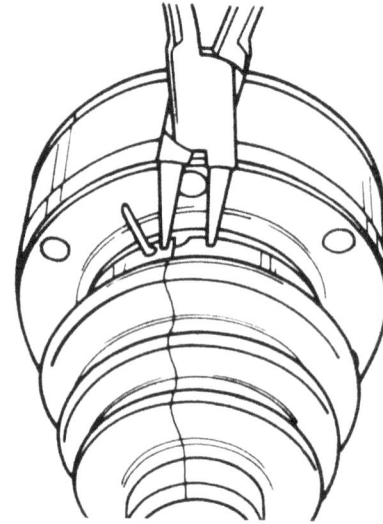

FIG 8:12   Tightening retaining clip

occur. To prevent this, always make sure that the drive shaft is properly supported when disconnected at either end.

Removal:

Raise and safely support the rear of the car on floor stands. Refer to **FIG 8:10** and remove the bolts securing the drive shaft flanges to the differential and stub axle flanges. Carefully remove the drive shaft from beneath the car.

Examine the drive shaft for wear or damage. If the rubber gaiter is damaged in any way, it must be renewed without delay otherwise the ingress of dirt and grit will cause rapid wear of the universal joint. If the shaft or either of the universal joints are faulty in any way, components must be renewed as necessary.

Renewing rubber gaiter:

Refer to **FIG 8:11**. Tap off the sealing cover then remove the circlip. Remove the gaiter securing clip then press off the universal joint and pull off the gaiter. Note that the axial clamp ring which fits over the drive shaft splines is installed with the internal dishing towards the universal joint.

Discard the old gaiter and retaining clips and thoroughly degrease the remaining parts. Pack the universal joint and inside of gaiter with 120g (4.2oz) of approved grease. Clean all traces of grease from the gaiter sealing surface and the universal joint flange. Smear the gaiter sealing surface with sealing compound EC750M-2G51 or similar. To facilitate tightening of the new retaining clips, drill two holes 2mm (0.078in) in diameter so that the ends of the clip can be squeezed together with circlip pliers as shown in **FIG 8:12**. Bend the tab to secure the clip.

Refitting:

Refit the drive shaft in the reverse order of removal, tightening the fixing bolts alternately and evenly to the specified torque.

8:5 Stub axles and wheel bearings

Removal:

Raise the rear of the car and support safely on floor stands. Remove the road wheel. Refer to **Section 8:4** and detach the outer end of the drive shaft from the stub axle flange. Tie the end of the drive shaft away from the work area so that the universal joint is not strained. Refer to **FIG 8:13** and lift out the locking plate, remove the flanged nut and pull off the drive flange.

On models fitted with disc rear brakes, detach the caliper without disconnecting the fluid pipe and support safely by wiring to the suspension. On models fitted with drum brakes, remove the brake drum. Detailed instructions concerning brake system components are given in **Chapter 11**.

To remove the stub axle, refer to **FIG 8:14**. Screw the flanged nut back on to the axle until it is flush with the end to protect the threads, then drive out the stub axle using a soft-faced hammer. Remove the nut and detach the stub axle completely. Check the stub axle spacer ring shown arrowed in **FIG 8:15** for wear or damage and renew if necessary.

If the wheel bearings are to be removed, take great care to avoid dirt or oil contamination of brake system components. **FIG 8:16** shows a section through the wheel hub and bearings. Use a suitable drift to drive out the outer bearing and seal, working evenly around the circumference to prevent jamming. Remove the spacer sleeve, then drive out the inner bearing and seal in a similar manner. Remove the spacer ring indicated by measurement **C**. Carefully degrease hub, bearings and spacer components. Discard the seals. Both wheel bearings must be renewed if either is found worn or damaged, but note the recommendation that bearings are renewed regardless of apparent condition at approximately 60,000 mile (100,000km) intervals. Only use replacement bearings which are marked C3 on the outer race.

Refitting:

When installing wheel bearings, the required thickness **C** for the inner bearing spacer must be determined, and a spacer of the correct thickness installed (see **FIG 8:16**). Drive the outer bearing fully into place first, then determine distance between bearing and hub shoulder, as shown at **B** in **FIG 8:17**. The length of the spacer sleeve must now be measured to determine length **A**, as shown in **FIG 8:18**. The difference between the two measurements must now be calculated and a standard figure **D** of 0.1mm (0.004in) deducted from the result to give required thickness **C**. Measurement **D** is deducted to give the required hub end float of 0.05 to 0.10mm (0.002 to 0.004in).

For example, if **A** equals 63.5mm (2.5in) and **B** equals 58.6mm (2.307in), the difference of 4.9mm (0.192in) less measurement **D** of 0.1mm (0.004in) will give a required spacer thickness **C** of 4.8mm (0.188in).

Remove the outer wheel bearing again. Pack each wheel bearing with 35g (1.2oz) of approved grease, then install outer bearing, spacer sleeve, spacer ring of correct thickness and inner bearing. Note that the space between each wheel bearing and grease seal must be free of grease, but that the space between the lips of each

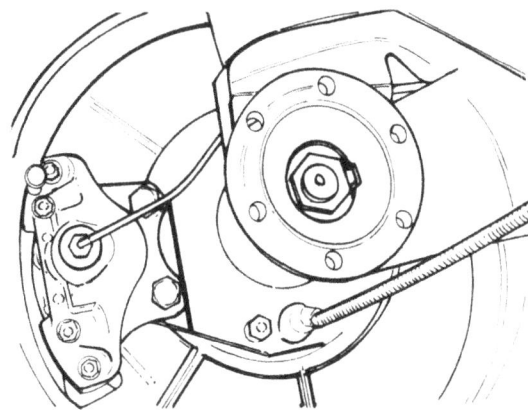

FIG 8:13   Drive flange retaining nut and locking plate

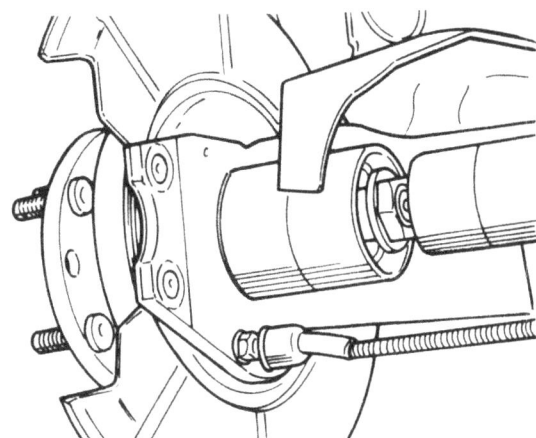

FIG 8:14   Stub axle removal

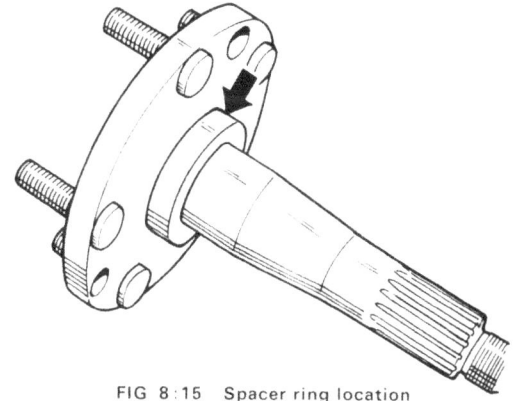

FIG 8:15   Spacer ring location

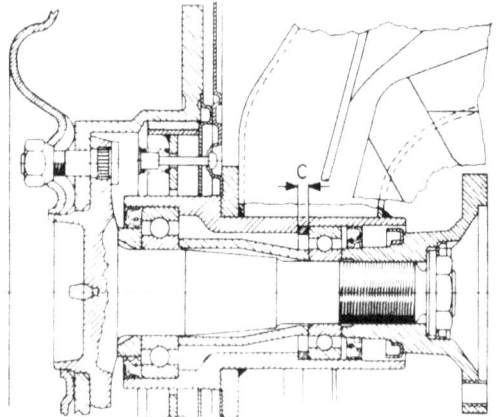

FIG 8:16 Section through wheel hub and bearings

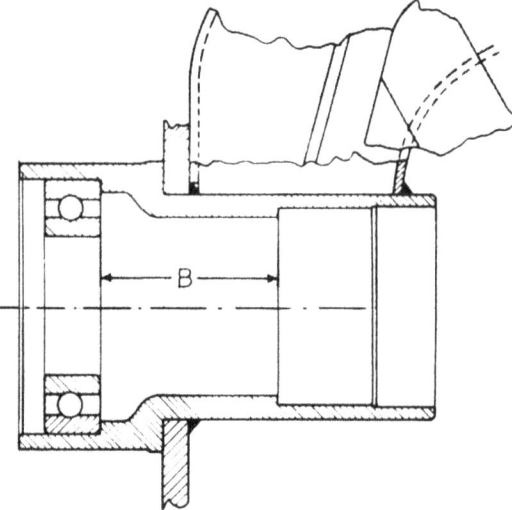

FIG 8:17 Distance between outer bearing and hub shoulder

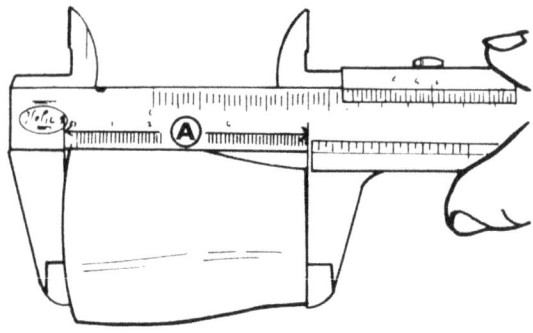

FIG 8:18 Measuring length of spacer sleeve

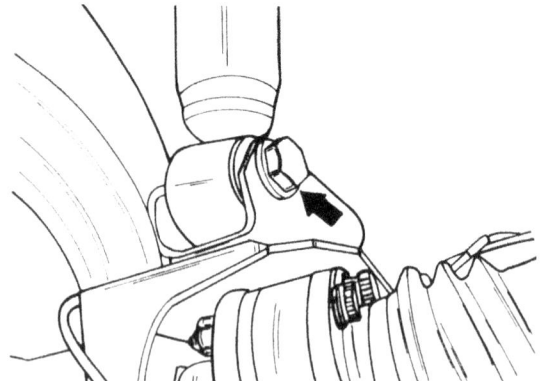

FIG 8:19 Suspension strut lower mounting bolt

seal should be packed with approved grease. Install the new seals, driving them fully and squarely home. Take care to avoid grease contamination of braking system components.

Refit the stub axle, taking care not to displace the bearings and seals. Correct locations of bearings are finalised when the drive flange is secured to the stub axle. Fit the drive flange, taking care not to damage the seal, then tighten the flanged nut to the specified torque. Tighten the nut a fraction further if necessary to ensure correct alignment of locking plate, then fit locking plate over nut and into drive flange groove (see **FIG 8:13**). Refit braking system components as described in **Chapter 11**, then reconnect the drive shaft and install the road wheel.

8:6 Suspension struts

Either Nivomat self-levelling units or conventional coil spring and damper units may be fitted, it being possible to convert the former type to the latter specification if desired as described later in this section. Other modifications also described are the installation of additional damper rings and rubber discs to the suspension strut assemblies on older models to improve ride comfort.

Note that suspension strut assemblies must be renewed in pairs, never on one side of the car only. As several modifications have been introduced over the period of production, particularly to the suspension strut lower mounting, it is advisable to take the old units to the spares department so that they can be properly matched with the replacements.

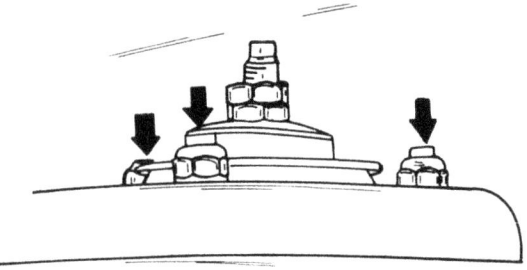

FIG 8:20 Suspension strut upper mounting nuts

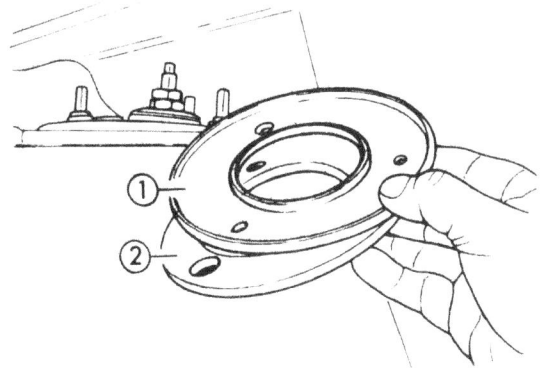

FIG 8:21 Cover ring 1 and damper plate 2

FIG 8:22 Spacer ring locations

If faulty operation of Nivomat units is suspected, the car should be taken to a BMW service station so that their operation can be checked using special equipment.

Removal:

Raise the rear of the car and support the body safely on floor stands so that the suspension hangs free, then raise a suitable jack beneath the trailing arm to take the weight of the unit from the suspension strut assembly. The strut controls downward movement of the suspension, so if the strut is disconnected without support beneath the trailing arm, the resultant drive shaft deflection may be sufficient to damage the universal joints (see also **Section 8:4**).

Remove the nut from the bolt arrowed in **FIG 8:19**, then lower the trailing arm until the bolt can be released to disconnect the suspension strut from the bracket. Do not lower the trailing arm any further than necessary. From inside the luggage compartment, remove the three nuts arrowed in **FIG 8:20** to release the suspension strut upper centring bush from the wheelarch. On later versions, remove cover ring 1 and damper plate 2 as shown in **FIG 8:21**. Manoeuvre the lower end of the suspension strut from the trailing arm bracket and detach the unit from beneath the car.

Refitting:

This is a reversal of the removal procedure, making sure that the spacer rings, where fitted, are properly installed as shown by the arrows in **FIG 8:22**. The suspension strut must be installed so that the rubber protrusions on damper plate 3 face to the front and rear of the car respectively.

Dismantling:

Remove the suspension strut assembly as described previously. Note that it is essential to use compressor tool 6035 or similar when dismantling the unit. Never attempt to remove damper upper components without the use of such a tool.

Compress the coil spring with the special tool until it is clear of the upper damper plate (see **FIG 8:23**), then hold the lower nut on the damper rod with one spanner while slackening the locknut with a second spanner. Remove the nuts then detach the plate, damper plate

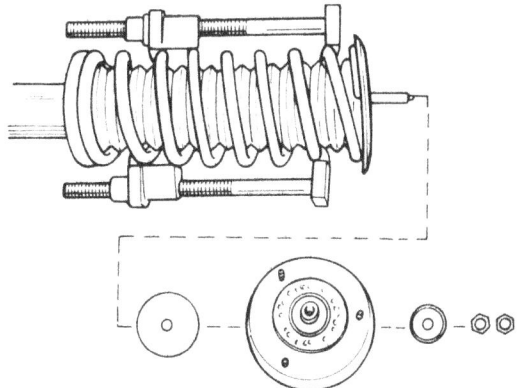

FIG 8:23 Compressing spring and removing damper upper components

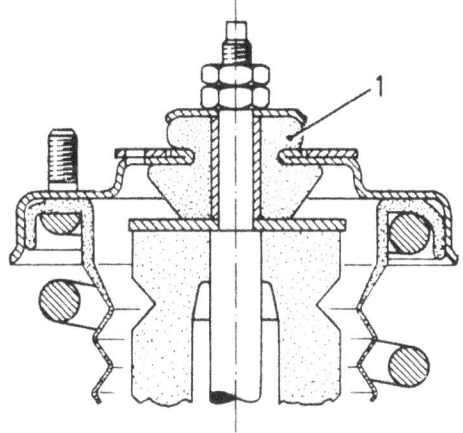

FIG 8:24 Rubber bush 1 on early models

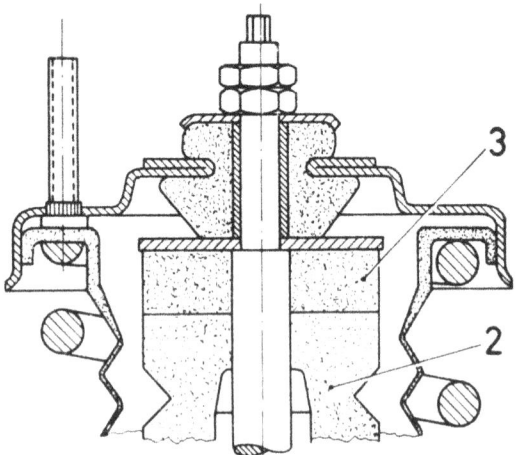

FIG 8:25 Additional rubber ring 3 above auxiliary spring 2 on later models

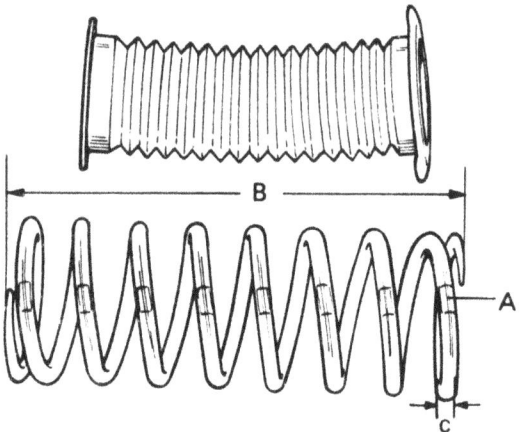

FIG 8:26 Checking coil spring specifications

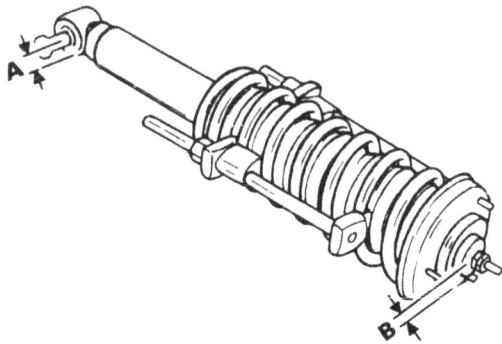

FIG 8:27 Suspension strut alignment

and supporting ring. Check the rubber bush in the damper plate and renew if damaged or perished. Rubber bush installation on early models is shown at 1 in **FIG 8:24**. Later models are fitted with an additional rubber disc 15mm (0.6in) thick, as shown at 3 in **FIG 8:25**, the disc being placed on top of auxiliary spring 2. The purpose of this additional disc is to provide additional stiffening of the suspension when the car is heavily laden. This disc can be subsequently fitted to earlier models not so equipped, if desired, without modifying any of the remaining parts.

Slacken the spring compressor until all spring pressure is released, then remove the coil spring and detach the inner rubber components. Replace any rubber component which is worn, perished or split. If a coil spring is to be renewed, the new spring must comply with the original in respect of identification mark **A**, overall length **B** and thickness **C** as shown in **FIG 8:26**. It is recommended that the rubber gaiter also shown in the illustration is renewed at the same time as the coil spring, regardless of its apparent condition.

Reassembly:

This is a reversal of the dismantling procedure. Before finally releasing the spring compressor, make sure that the suspension strut assembly is correctly aligned as shown in **FIG 8:27**. Dimension **A** must be the same on both sides and dimension **B** must be 43mm (1.6929in). Make sure that the locknut is firmly tightened against the upper securing nut. Remove the spring compressor tool, then refit the assembly to the vehicle as described previously.

Installation of later type damper rings:

The later type damper rings may be fitted to earlier models not so equipped, if desired. To do this, remove each strut assembly in turn, compress the coil spring and remove the upper damper plate and rubber gaiter all as described previously. Carefully tap the upper mounting studs from the damper plate and discard them. In their place, install longer (8 × 35mm) knurled head studs of the correct type (see **FIG 8:25**). Discard the original rubber gaiter and install a replacement of the correct type having the appropriate recesses for the knurled head bolts.

Enlarge the strut upper mounting holes in the car bodywork from the original 9mm (0.3543in) diameter to 16mm (0.6299in), using a special Turatol type drill as shown in **FIG 8:28**. Drill shaft length should be 110mm (4.3307in).

Fit three spacer rings of the correct type to the studs, as shown by the arrows in **FIG 8:22**, then install the suspension strut assembly to the vehicle as described previously.

Modifying Nivomat units to spring strut type:

If desired, the Nivomat self-levelling suspension strut assemblies can be modified to convert them to the spring strut type. Note that, if this work is carried out, the anti-roll bar, if fitted, should be removed completely as it is not used with the modified type of suspension strut (see **Section 8:7**).

Remove and dismantle the suspension strut assemblies as described previously. The original components and those components required to carry out the modifications are shown in **FIG 8:29**. The new parts required are damper assembly 1, rubber ring 2, support ring 3, coil spring 4, spacer tube 5, upper plate 6 and upper nut and locknut 7. Original parts from the Nivomat units for fitting to the modified units are rubber gaiter 8, auxiliary spring 9, damping ring 10 and upper damper plate 11. The remaining original parts must be discarded. Reassemble and install the modified unit as described previously.

8:7 Anti-roll bar

Some models may be fitted with an anti-roll bar which is mounted to the rear suspension crossmember by means of rubber bushes and to the trailing arms on each side by means of rubber bushed links (see **FIG 8:30**). Removal and installation of the anti-roll bar are straightforward operations. Renew the rubber bushes if worn or perished. Make sure that the rubber bushes are installed free of dirt and grease.

8:8 Trailing arms and thrust stays

Trailing arm removal:

Refer to **Chapter 11** and disconnect the handbrake cables from the handbrake lever, then plug the fluid outlets from the master cylinder reservoir with pointed wooden sticks.

Raise and safely support the rear of the car so that the rear suspension hangs free, then remove the road wheel. Disconnect the anti-roll bar, if fitted. Pull the handbrake cable from the protective tube and disconnect the brake hoses. Refer to **Section 8:4** and remove the drive shaft completely, then disconnect the lower end of the suspension strut from the trailing arm as described in **Section 8:6**. Refer to **FIG 8:31** and disconnect the trailing arm from the mountings on the crossmember.

If the rubber mounting bushes in the trailing arm bores are worn, damaged or perished, they should be renewed. Press the old bushes out with a suitable drift and coat the new bushes with poly-glycol before forcing them into position. Always make sure that the collar end of the bush is towards the outer side of the trailing arm. If it is suspected that the trailing arm assembly is distorted, it should be taken to a BMW service station so that it can be checked using special equipment.

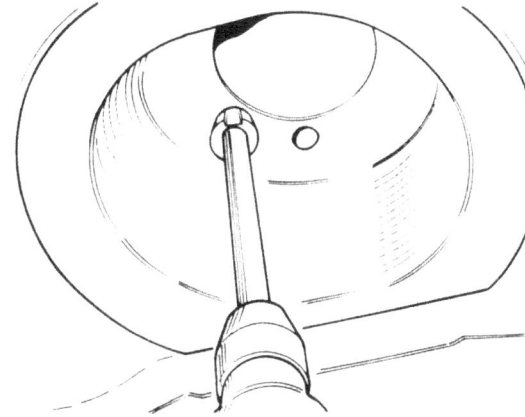

FIG 8:28   Drilling out mounting holes to accept modified suspension strut

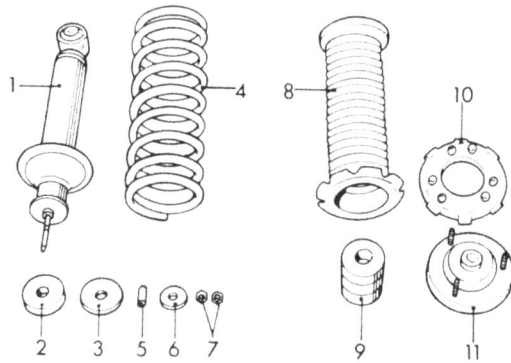

FIG 8:29   Parts required to modify suspension struts to later type

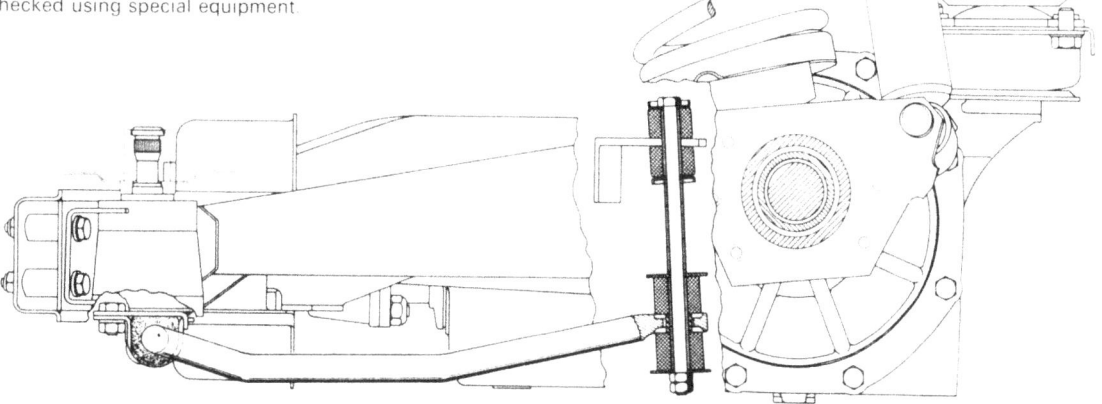

FIG 8:30   Anti-roll bar installation

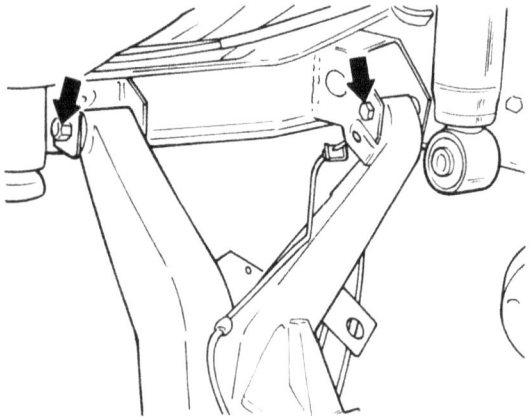

FIG 8:31 Trailing arm to crossmember mountings

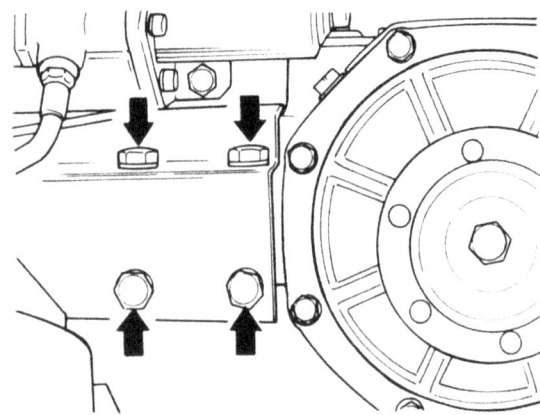

FIG 8:34 Differential carrier to crossmember attachments

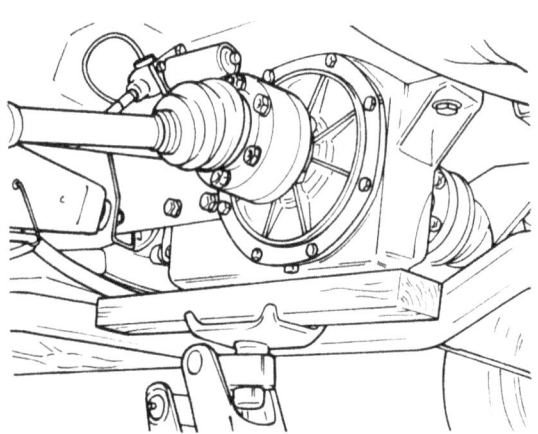

FIG 8:32 Supporting differential carrier

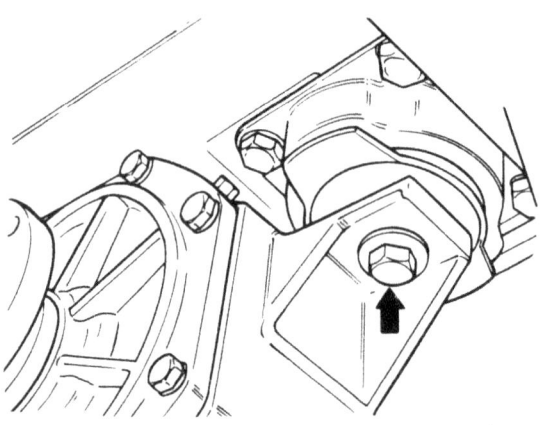

FIG 8:35 Bolt securing carrier to rubber mounting

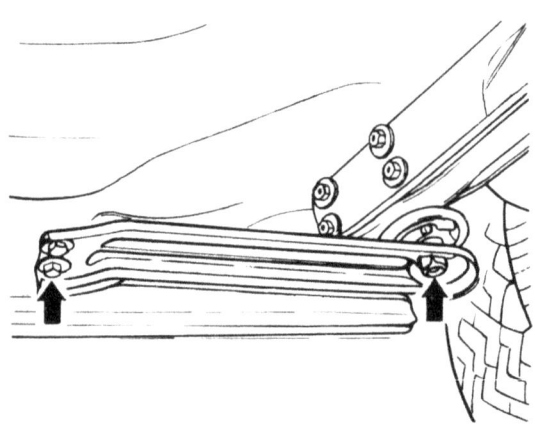

FIG 8:33 Thrust stay attachment points

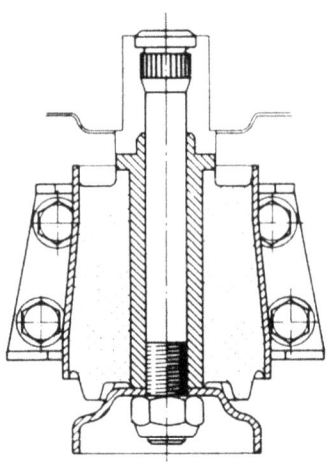

FIG 8:36 Section through crossmember rubber mounting

Refitting:

This is a reversal of the removal procedure, but note that the trailing arm to crossmember attachments must not be fully tightened during assembly. Reconnect the brake hoses and bleed the braking system, then reconnect the handbrake cables and adjust, referring to **Chapter 11** for full instructions. When all other work is complete, the trailing arm to crossmember fixings must be tightened to the specified torque with the car correctly loaded, the appropriate details being given in **Chapter 9, Section 9:4**.

Thrust stay removal:

Raise and safely support the rear of the car on floor stands. Raise a jack beneath the differential carrier to support the weight of the unit, fitting a piece of wood between the carrier and jack to prevent damage as shown in **FIG 8:32**. Remove the nut and bolts arrowed in **FIG 8:33** and detach the thrust stay from beneath the car.

Refitting is a reversal of the removal procedure.

8:9 Differential carrier

Removal:

Raise and safely support the rear of the car on floor stands, then disconnect the rear end of the propeller shaft from the differential flange as described in **Section 8:3** and remove both drive shafts as described in **Section 8:4**. Support the weight of the differential carrier with a suitable jack acting against a wooden insulator, as shown in **FIG 8:32**. Refer to **FIG 8:34** and remove the four bolts on each side securing the differential carrier to the rear axle crossmember. Remove the fixing bolt arrowed in **FIG 8:35** securing the rear of the carrier to the rubber mounting.

Refitting:

This is a reversal of the removal procedure. On completion, check oil level in differential carrier as described in **Section 8:2**.

8:10 Differential and crossmember mountings

Differential mounting removal:

Raise and safely support the rear of the car on floor stands, then use a suitable jack and wooden insulator to support the differential carrier as shown in **FIG 8:32**. Remove the carrier to mounting attachment bolt arrowed in **FIG 8:35**, then remove the four attachment bolts and remove the rubber mounting assembly from the car body.

Refitting is a reversal of the removal procedure.

Crossmember mounting removal:

Raise and safely support the rear of the car on floor stands, then use a suitable jack and wooden insulator to support the weight of the differential carrier as shown in **FIG 8:32**. Remove the rear seat squab from inside the car. Refer to **Section 8:8** and remove the thrust stay for access to the crossmember mounting. A section through the mounting is shown in **FIG 8:36**. Use a soft-faced hammer to drive out the knurled head bolt, then remove the rubber bush from the crossmember.

Refitting is a reversal of the removal procedure.

8:11 Rear wheel alignment

Due to the need for accurate results, the checking of rear wheel toe-in and camber angles should be carried out with optical measuring equipment. If rear wheel alignment is incorrect the rear suspension system must be examined for faulty, damaged or distorted components, including the wheel rims. Checks should also be made for correct location of the rear suspension crossmember on the underbody, and for possible distortion of the underbody itself. All checks should be carried out by a BMW service station having the necessary special equipment.

8:12 Fault diagnosis

(a) Noisy axle

1 Insufficient or incorrect lubricant
2 Worn bearings or gears

(b) Excessive backlash

1 Worn gears or bearings
2 Worn propeller shaft joints
3 Worn drive shaft joints

(c) Oil leakage

1 Defective seals
2 Damaged gaskets or joint faces

(d) Vibration

1 Propeller shaft out of balance
2 Worn universal joints

(e) Rattles

1 Worn universal joints
2 Worn suspension component bushes
3 Worn or damaged rubber mountings
4 Worn suspension strut mountings

NOTES

CHAPTER 9

FRONT SUSPENSION AND HUBS

9:1 Description

Independent front wheel suspension is by means of MacPherson struts. These suspension struts incorporate helically coiled springs controlled by double-acting hydraulic telescopic dampers. The damper units also act as pivots for the front wheel hub assemblies to accommodate steering movement. The suspension springs are fitted coaxially to the damper struts between two pressed steel support cups.

The upper ends of the suspension struts are attached to the undersides of the wheel arches, the lower ends being located by means of control arms and trailing links. Some models are additionally equipped with an anti-roll bar fitted between the outer ends of the control arms. An anti-roll bar can be fitted to models not so equipped, if desired, using the mounting points provided at the control arms and on the underbody. Layout of the front suspension components, without anti-roll bar, is shown in **FIG 9:1**.

The suspension ball joints are packed with lubricant on assembly and sealed for life, so apart from a periodic check on the general condition of all suspension components, no routine maintenance is required.

Note that certain special tools will be needed in order to carry out some of the overhaul work described in this chapter and the owner would be well advised to check on the availability of these tools or suitable substitutes before tackling the items involved.

9:2 Front hubs

The front hubs are mounted on taper roller bearings and the wheel bolts are splined and pressed into the hub flange. A spring-loaded lip-type seal is incorporated in the hub at the inner end and the hub is retained on the stub axle by a special washer, slotted nut and splitpin. **FIG 9:2** shows a section through the front hub assembly.

Checking hub bearings:

Jack up the front of the car so that the road wheels are clear of the ground. Spin the wheels and check that they rotate freely without bearing noise, taking care not to confuse noise from the brake with that from a defective bearing. Grasp the tyre at the top and bottom of the wheel and attempt to rock the top of the wheel in and out while noting the play. Repeat the test with the tyre gripped at each side of the wheel. If excessive play is evident, the wheel bearings should be adjusted first and, if roughness is still apparent, the bearings should be dismantled for inspection.

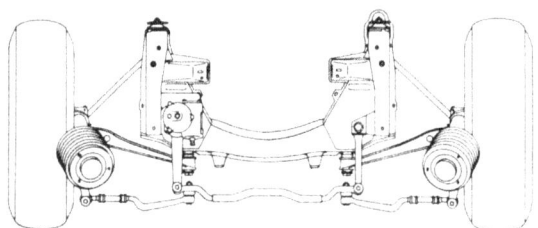

FIG 9:1 Layout of front suspension and steering gear

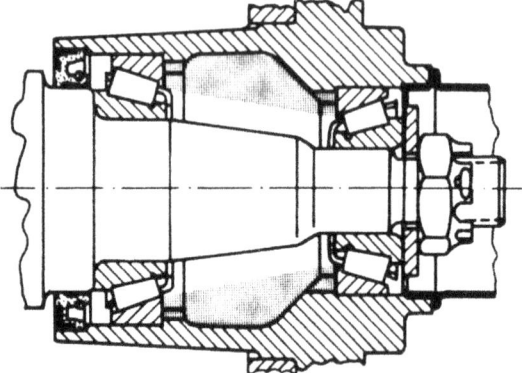

FIG 9:2 Section through front hub assembly

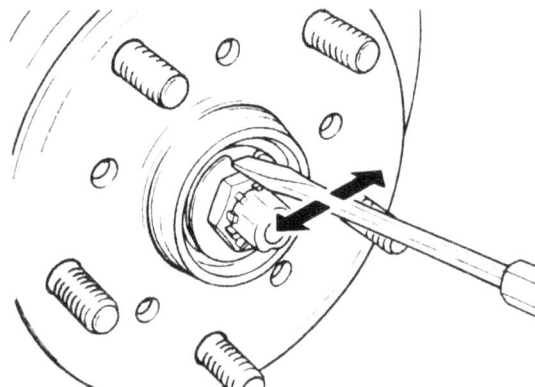

FIG 9:3 Checking movement of special washer

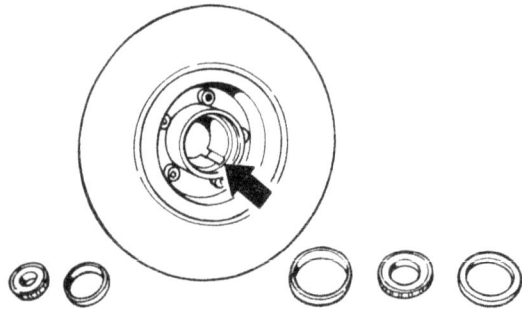

FIG 9:4 Hub and wheel bearing components

Adjustment:

Jack up the front of the car and remove the road wheel. Carefully pull the grease cap from the centre of the hub. Remove the splitpin and tighten the nut to a torque of 1kgm (7.23lb ft) while turning the wheel hub. This aligns the bearing rollers and inner races and presses out any grease which might cause play. Now loosen the nut by approximately a quarter turn and check that the special washer can be moved in each direction without excessive force, using a screwdriver as shown in **FIG 9:3**. Hub end float should be between 0.02 and 0.06mm (0.0008 and 0.0024in), aiming to obtain the minimum value. End float is best measured using a dial gauge assembly. When the bearings are correctly adjusted, slacken the nut a fraction more if necessary to align the splitpin hole, then insert and lock a new splitpin. 20g (0.7oz) of approved grease should be placed inside the cleaned grease cap, which should then be carefully tapped into position.

Removal:

Slacken the wheel nuts and raise the front of the car on to stands. Remove the road wheel. Remove the brake caliper as described in **Chapter 11** and wire it to the suspension to avoid straining the hoses.

Remove the grease cap from the hub. Remove the splitpin, hub nut and special washer. Remove the hub and brake disc assembly from the stub axle. Collect the inner race of the outer bearing as it comes free. Remove the grease seal from the hub and remove the inner race of the inner bearing.

Servicing:

Wipe the old grease from the hub, bearings and grease cap, then thoroughly degrease the parts in paraffin or a similar solvent. Wash the bearing races separately by rotating them in a bowl of clean solvent. The brake disc must be thoroughly washed with solvent to remove all traces of grease or dirt.

Examine the operating face of the stub axle on which the grease seal operates for scoring or nicks. Light damage can be smoothed with fine grade emerycloth. Check the stub axle for hairline cracks or other damage, which would dictate renewal.

Check the outer races of the bearings in the hub for fretting, scoring or wear. If damage is found, both outer races must be driven out evenly with a suitable copper drift, working through the access slots provided in the hub (see arrow in **FIG 9:4**). Both bearings must then be renewed complete.

Lubricate the inner races with light oil. Press each inner race firmly back into its outer and rotate the bearing to check for any roughness in operation. Dirt can be a cause of roughness, so wash the bearing again thoroughly before repeating the test. If an air-line is used to dry the bearings, do not allow them to spin in the air blast as this chips the faces. If a bearing is defective, both bearings must be completely renewed, including the outer races in the hub.

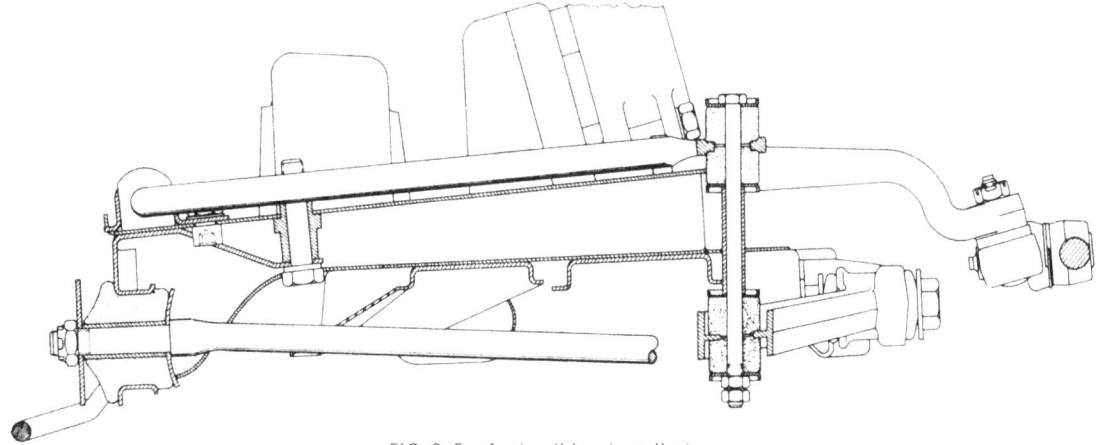

FIG 9:5 Anti-roll bar installation

Reassembly:

If the outer races of the hubs have been removed, they or the new components should be driven back evenly and fully using a suitable drift.

The wheel bearings must be lubricated with approved grease. Evenly pack the inside of the hub between the bearing positions using 50g (1.8oz) of grease. Liberally pack the inner race of the inner bearing, working the grease well into the rollers. Install this bearing into the hub and press a new grease seal into the hub to retain the race in position.

Slide the hub assembly back on to the stub axle, taking care not to damage the seal. Pack the inner race of the outer bearing with grease and fit it back into place, followed by the special washer and nut. Adjust the wheel bearing as described previously. Apply 20g (0.7oz) of grease to the inside of the grease cap, then refit to the wheel hub. Refit the brake caliper as described in **Chapter 11**, then pump the brake pedal hard several times to make sure that the brake is correctly adjusted. Refit the road wheel and lower the car to the ground.

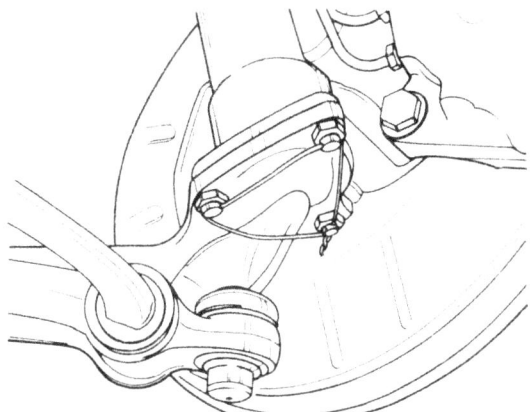

FIG 9:6 Steering arm to suspension strut attachments

9:3 Anti-roll bar

The anti-roll bar, if fitted, is attached to the underbody by rubber bushed mountings and to the outer ends of the control arms by means of rubber bushed links (see **FIG 9:5**). Removal and installation of the anti-roll bar are straightforward operations. Examine the condition of the rubber bushes and renew any found perished, worn or otherwise damaged. Make sure that the rubber parts are free from grease and dirt.

9:4 Control arms and trailing links

Removal:

Raise the front of the car and support safely on floor stands so that the front suspension is allowed to hang free. If an anti-roll bar is fitted, it must be disconnected on each side of the car by detaching the lower ends of the links from the control arms (see **FIG 9:5**).

Refer to **FIG 9:6**. Remove the securing wire and detach the three nuts to disconnect the steering arm from the suspension strut. Remove the securing nut,

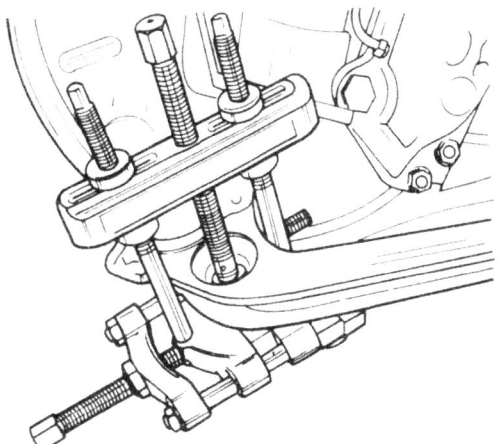

FIG 9:7 Pressing control arm ball joint from steering arm

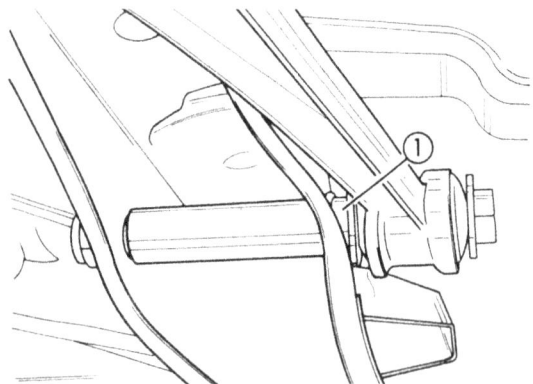

FIG 9:8 Control arm to crossmember mounting

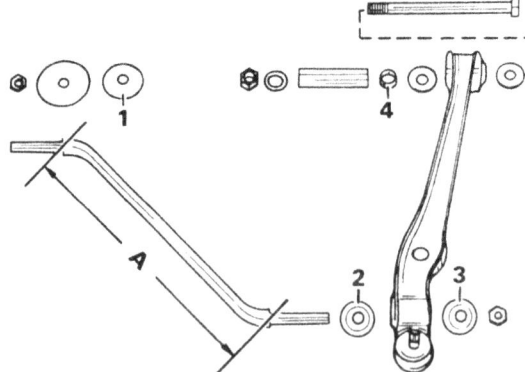

FIG 9:11 Control arm and trailing link components

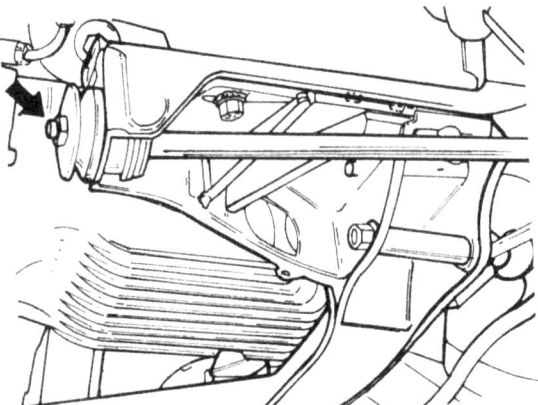

FIG 9:9 Trailing link connection to underbody

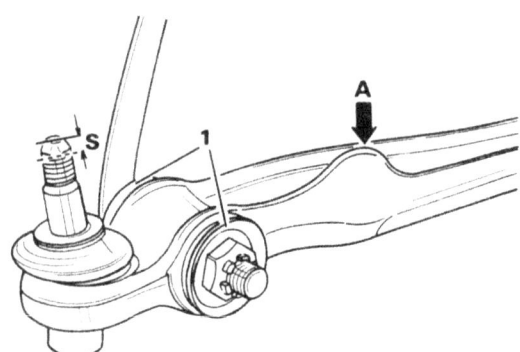

FIG 9:10 Trailing link connection to control arm

then press the control arm ball joint from the steering arm using the Kukko extractor or other suitable tool as shown in **FIG 9:7**.

Refer to **FIG 9:8** and disconnect the control arm from the front axle crossmember, noting the position of spacer ring 1. Unlock and remove the slotted nut arrowed in **FIG 9:9** to detach the front end of the trailing link from the underbody. Remove the control arm and trailing link complete. If necessary, unlock and remove the slotted nut to detach trailing link from control arm (see **FIG 9:10**). Note that convex outer radius of washers 1 must face the rubber bush.

Servicing:

Check the axial play of control arm ball joint as shown at **S** in **FIG 9:10**. If play exceeds 2.4mm (0.0945in), the ball joint or, possibly the complete control arm assembly, must be renewed. A control arm with a stop as shown at **A** may be installed in conjunction with a steering arm without a stop, but a control arm without a stop must never be installed in conjunction with a steering arm having a stop (see also **Chapter 10**).

Examine all trailing link and control arm components, which are shown in **FIG 9:11**, for wear or damage and renew as necessary. If the trailing link is renewed, note that dimension **A** must be 355mm (13.977in).

Check the rubber bushes in front axle carrier and control arm for wear, perishing or other damage. To renew the front axle carrier bush, use a suitable bolt, nut, washer, metal plate and tube (see **FIG 9:12**). Tube internal diameter should be 68mm (2.677in). Use the same tools to install the new bush from the opposite direction, smearing the front edge of the bush with soft soap before pulling into position. In this case, the tube should have an internal diameter of 60mm (2.362in) and 1mm (0.0394in) wall thickness. The control arm rubber bush is renewed in a similar manner to that just described, using a tube with 35mm (1.378in) inside diameter (see **FIG 9:13**). Smear the front edge of the new rubber bush with soft soap to facilitate installation.

Reassembly:

This is a reversal of the removal procedure, noting the following points.

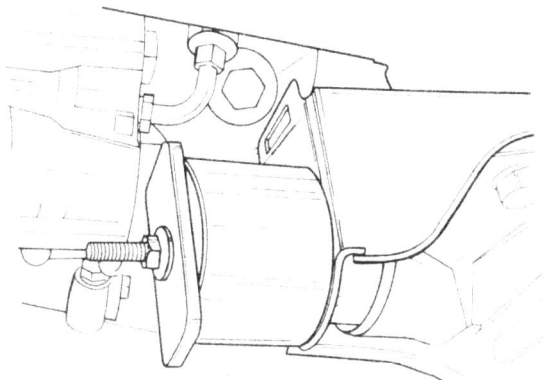

FIG 9:12 Removing front axle carrier bush

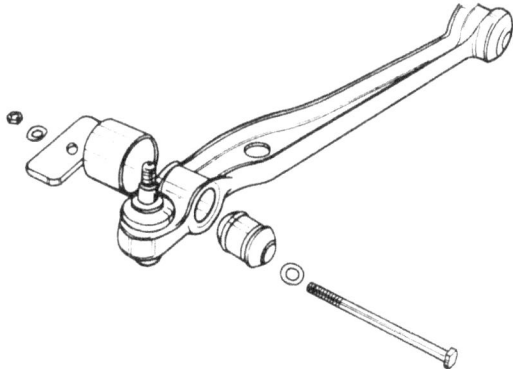

FIG 9:13 Removing control arm bush

The convex outer sides of washers 1, 2 and 3 shown in **FIG 9:11** must face the rubber bushes. Note the correct position of spacer ring 4, which is also shown at 1 in **FIG 9:8**. Tighten the fixings of the control arm to front axle crossmember and trailing link to underbody loosely at first, then fully tighten to the specified torque with the car resting on its road wheels under the correct static load. For these purposes, static load is with a weight of 2 × 65kg (2 × 143lb) on front seats, 1 × 65kg (1 × 143lb) on rear seat, and 30kg (66lb) in luggage compartment on the lefthand side. Additionally, the fuel tank must be full. Lock the slotted nut securing the trailing link to the underbody with a new splitpin. Use a new piece of soft wire to lock the nuts securing the steering arm to suspension strut (see **FIG 9:6**).

9:5 Suspension struts

Removal:

Raise the front of the car and safely support on floor stands so that the suspension hangs free. Remove the road wheel. Refer to **Chapter 11** and detach the brake caliper, without disconnecting the fluid pipes. Wire the caliper to the underbody to prevent strain on the brake hoses.

Disconnect the outer end of the control arm from the suspension strut as described in **Section 9:4**. Remove the three nuts securing the upper end of the suspension strut to the wheel arch (see **FIG 9:14**), then remove the suspension strut assembly from the car.

Dismantling:

Note that suspension strut assemblies or damper units must only be installed in pairs, so that the components are correctly matched on each side of the car. If necessary, remove the brake disc and wheel hub components as described in **Section 9:2**

To remove and refit a coil spring it is essential to use a spring compressor tool, as shown in **FIG 9:15**. Never attempt dismantling procedures without the use of such a tool. Tighten the compressor tool until all spring pressure is removed from the upper spring seat, then refer to **FIG 9:16** and remove sealing cap 1 and unscrew locknut 2. Lock the piston rod and remove suspension strut thrust bearing 3. If the bearing is faulty in any way, it must be

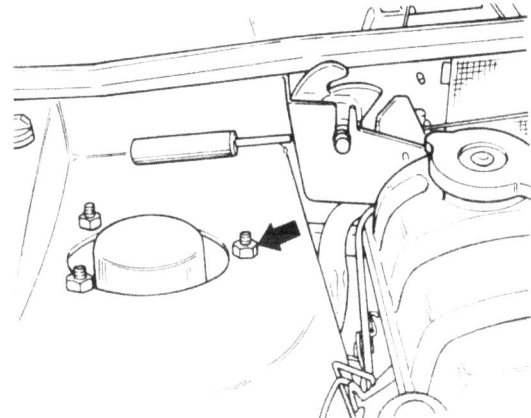

FIG 9:14 Suspension strut upper mounting nuts

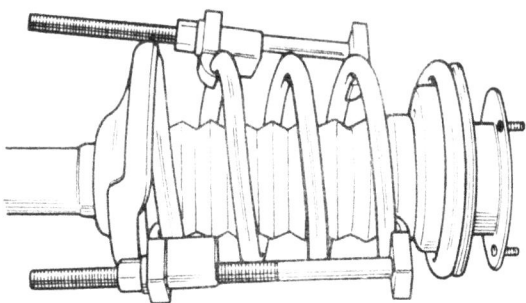

FIG 9:15 Compressing coil spring

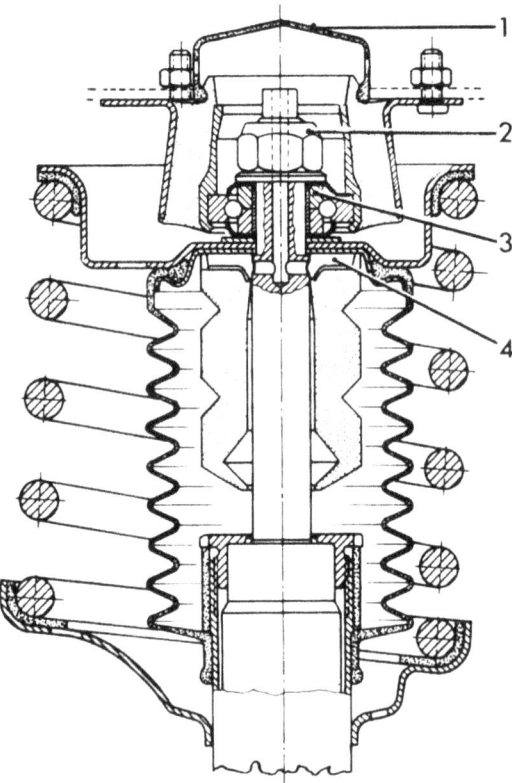

FIG 9:16 Section through suspension strut upper components

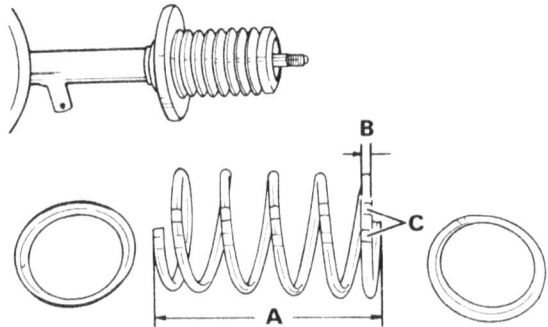

FIG 9:17 Checking coil spring specifications

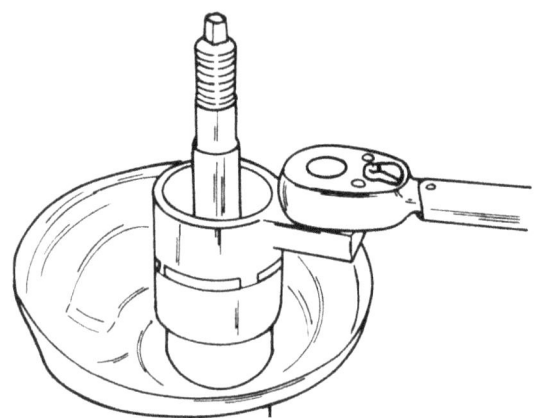

FIG 9:18 Removing threaded ring

renewed complete. Release the spring compressor tool, then remove the coil spring and upper spring seat. If a coil spring is to be renewed, make sure that the springs on each side of the car are properly matched, according to the information given in **FIG 9:17**. Spring length **A** must be correct according to model type. Spring thickness **B** and spring strength according to markings **C** must be uniform on each side of the car. During installation, the spring ends must be correctly wound into the upper and lower seats.

If the dampers are to be removed, pull the sleeve and auxiliary spring assembly from the suspension strut, then use special tool 6016 or similar to remove the threaded ring, as shown in **FIG 9:18**. The damper unit can then be lifted from the suspension strut assembly. Note that, before installing a damper to the suspension strut, 50cc of SAE 30 engine oil must be poured into the suspension strut tube. The purpose of this oil is to conduct heat away from the damper unit.

Reassembly:

This is a reversal of the dismantling procedure. Make sure that the bleeder plate is correctly fitted as shown at 4 in **FIG 9:16**. Ensure that the dished sealing washer then flat washer are installed above the thrust bearing before fitting the locknut, noting that the concave side of the sealing washer must face towards the thrust bearing.

Refitting:

This is a reversal of the removal procedure. Use a new piece of soft wire to lock the nuts securing the steering arm to suspension strut assembly (see **FIG 9:6**). If the wheel hub assembly was dismantled, reassemble and adjust as described in **Section 9:2**. Refit the brake caliper as described in **Chapter 11**, not forgetting to pump the brake pedal several times afterwards to correctly adjust the brake.

9:6 Front axle crossmember

Removal:

Refer to **Section 9:4** and disconnect the trailing links and control arms from the underbody, supporting the components when detached to prevent strain on the suspension ball joints. Refer to **Chapter 10** and detach the steering box from front axle support and tie the unit to the brake servo to prevent damage. Remove the steering idler arm.

Attach suitable lifting equipment to the engine assembly and raise sufficiently to take the weight of the engine from the mountings on the crossmember. Disconnect the crossmember from the underbody at the fixing points arrowed in **FIG 9:19** while supporting the weight of the assembly, then remove from beneath the car.

Refitting:

This is a reversal of the removal procedure. Note that the trailing link and control arm attachments must be finally tightened with the car properly loaded, as described in **Section 9:4**

9:7 Front wheel geometry

Due to the need for special optical measuring equipment for accurate results, the checking and adjusting of front wheel caster and camber angles should be carried out by a fully equipped service station. Correct specifications are given in **Technical Data**. No means of adjustment is provided to compensate for incorrect front wheel geometry, so if faults are found a check should be made for damaged, distorted or incorrectly assembled front suspension components.

The method for setting the correct toe-in of the front wheels is described in **Chapter 10**.

9:8 Fault diagnosis

(a) Wheel wobble

1 Worn hub bearings
2 Broken or weak front spring
3 Uneven tyre wear
4 Worn suspension linkage
5 Loose wheel fixings
6 Incorrect front wheel alignment

(b) Car pulls to one side

1 Unequal tyre pressures
2 Incorrect suspension geometry
3 Defective suspension bushes or damaged parts
4 Weak spring on one side
5 Fault in steering system

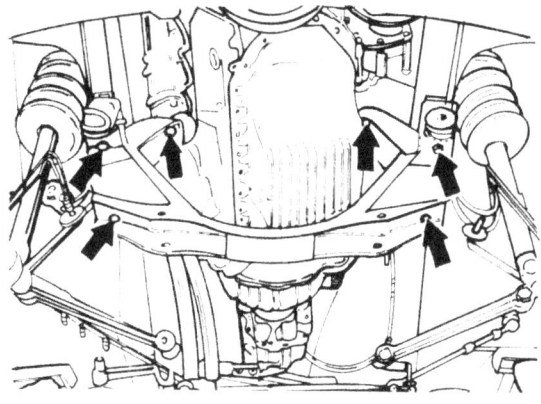

FIG 9:19   Crossmember attachment points

(c) Bottoming of suspension

1 Auxiliary suspension units worn or damaged
2 Broken or weak coil spring
3 Defective damper
4 Car overloaded

(d) Excessive body roll

1 Check 2 and 3 in (c)
2 Defective anti-roll bar (if fitted)

(e) Rattles

1 Check 2 and 4 in (a); 2 and 3 in (c)
2 Defective mounting bushes
3 Loose component fixings

(f) Suspension hard

1 Tyre pressures too high
2 Springs of wrong specification installed
3 Dampers faulty

NOTES

CHAPTER 10

THE STEERING GEAR

10:1 Description

Worm and roller steering gear is fitted to all models covered by this manual. Motion from the steering column assembly is transmitted to the worm shaft in the steering gear through a lower shaft equipped with two universal joints. The roller is moved up or down the worm according to the amount and direction of steering wheel movement, the roller turning a shaft to which is attached the steering Pitman arm. The Pitman arm operates the steering linkage. This linkage consists of the centre tie rod to which the Pitman arm and idler arm are connected and the outer tie rods which connect between the centre tie rod and the steering arms at the wheel hubs. Ball joints are used at the tie rod connections. Threaded adjusters are provided on each outer tie rod, to allow for adjustment of front wheel toe-in settings. The layout of the steering gear and front suspension components are shown in **Chapter 9, FIG 9:1**

Some models are equipped with power assisted steering gear, a belt driven pump supplying fluid under pressure to the steering gear assembly to assist the effort applied by the driver to the steering wheel.

A steering damper unit may be installed between the steering linkage and the bodywork on some models, and can be installed on standard models not so equipped if

desired. However, as the damper assembly operates to progressively resist movement of the steering linkage, it should not be installed on models equipped with power assisted steering gear

10:2 Routine maintenance

The necessary items of routine maintenance should be carried out at the intervals specified in the manufacturer's service schedule. On models fitted with standard steering gear, the oil level should be maintained at the edge of the filler plug hole, using an approved grade of lubricant. On models fitted with power assisted steering gear, the fluid level in the system should be checked and topped up as necessary and frequent checks on the tension of the pump drive belt should be made and adjustments carried out as necessary. Instructions concerning the last two items will be found in **Section 10:6**

In all cases, the ball joints in the steering linkage are sealed for life and no routine maintenance is required

Steering gear adjustment:

If the steering gear is stiff to operate, or if excessive slackness is noted, the checks and adjustments described in this section should be carried out. Note, however,

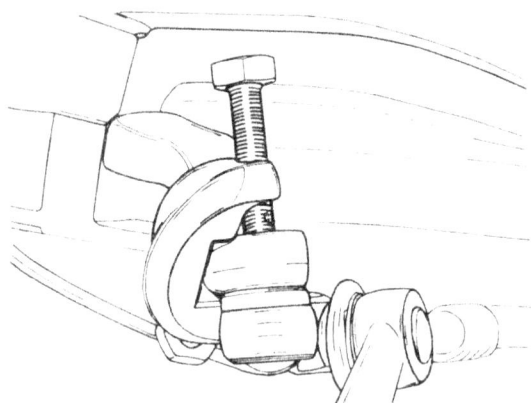

FIG 10:1   Detaching ball joint from Pitman arm

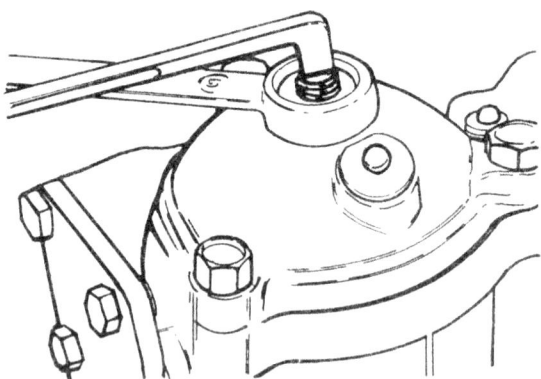

FIG 10:4   Steering gear adjustment

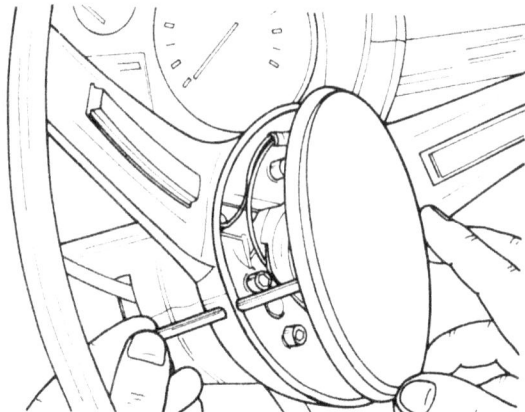

FIG 10:2   Removing steering wheel pad

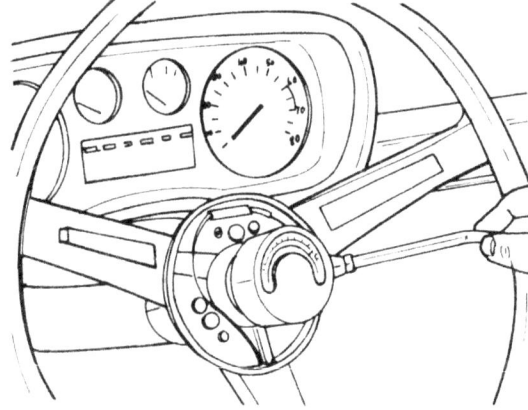

FIG 10:3   Checking turning torque

that heavy steering on models fitted with power assisted steering gear can be caused by a slack drive belt, air in the fluid system or possibly more serious faults in the system components. In order to check steering gear adjustment the use of a special tool is necessary. If this is not available, the work should be carried out by a service station.

Raise the front of the car and support safely on floor stands. From beneath the car, remove the splitpin and slotted nut securing the ball joint to the steering Pitman arm, then press out the ball joint using tool 7009 or other suitable puller, as shown in **FIG 10:1**. Use a thin rod to push off the steering wheel central pad as shown in **FIG 10:2**. Turn the steering wheel fully in one direction, then turn fully to the opposite lock while counting the number of turns and part turns taken to do so. Do this gently, as rapid movement to the lock stops may damage the steering gear. Calculate the exact centre point of the steering gear by halving the total number of turns, then move the steering gear to this position. Now turn the steering wheel one complete turn to the left and fit the friction meter over the steering wheel retaining nut as shown in **FIG 10:3**. Move the arm on the meter to turn the steering gear to the right through the central position and read the effort needed to do this on the meter. The correct reading is 8 to 12kgcm for all 2500, 2800 and 2800A models, or 10 to 12 kgcm for other 2800 models, 3.0 and 3.3 models. If incorrect, turn the steering gear back to the central position then slacken the locknut on the steering gear housing with a ring spanner and turn the adjuster with a suitable screwdriver as shown in **FIG 10:4**. The illustration shows standard steering gear components, but that for power assisted assemblies is very similar. Turn the adjusting screw a little at a time until the meter reading is correct under the conditions stated. Tighten the locknut and recheck.

On completion, press the steering wheel central pad back into position and reconnect the steering linkage to the Pitman arm. Tighten the slotted nut to the specified torque, then tighten a little more if necessary to align the splitpin holes and lock using a new splitpin.

10:3 Steering linkage

Checking ball joint assemblies:

If the front of the car is raised for access, support safely on floor stands. Grasp each ball joint in turn while having an assistant turn one of the front wheels gently in and out in the steering directions. If excessive free play is noted at any ball joint position, the appropriate tie rod or tie rod end should be renewed. Take care not to confuse front wheel bearing play with play in ball joint assemblies. Wheel bearing play will be felt by rocking the front wheel both horizontally and vertically, ball joint play will be evident only when rocking the wheel horizontally. Front wheel bearing adjustment is described in **Chapter 9 Section 9:2**

Outer track rods:

Remove the splitpin and slotted nut, then press the outer ball joint from the steering arm using tool 6056 or other suitable puller as shown in **FIG 10:5**. If the outer ball joint only is to be renewed, slacken the clamp on the tie rod sleeve and unscrew the ball joint assembly, carefully counting the number of turns taken to do so. Screw the new ball joint assembly into the sleeve by the number of turns previously counted, then temporarily tighten the clamp to secure. Tighten the ball joint securing nut to the specified torque, then tighten a little more if necessary to align the splitpin holes and lock with a new splitpin. Check front wheel alignment as described in **Section 10:7**. If the entire outer tie rod is to be removed, remove the splitpin and slotted nut and press the inner ball joint from the centre tie rod. When installing an outer tie rod, screw the inner part and the outer ball joint into the threaded sleeve by equal amounts, until dimension **A** shown in **FIG 10:6** is 330mm (13in). Temporarily tighten the sleeve clamps and refit the ball joint assemblies to the centre tie rod and steering arm. Tighten the slotted nuts to the specified torque, plus a little more if necessary to align the splitpin holes, then lock with new splitpins. Check front wheel alignment as described in **Section 10:7**.

Centre tie rod:

Detach the outer tie rods from the centre tie rod as described previously. Disconnect the steering damper, if fitted. Disconnect the centre tie rod from the Pitman arm as described in **Section 10:2**, then disconnect the centre tie rod from the idler arm in a similar manner. When installing, soak the sealing ring shown at 1 in **FIG 10:7** with oil to prevent premature failure of the joint due to the ingress of water. Note that the installed length **A** should be 574 ± 1mm (22.60 ± 0.04in). Install in the reverse order, tightening the slotted nuts to the specified torque plus a little more if necessary to align the splitpin holes. Lock with new splitpins. Reconnect the steering damper, if fitted. Note that the shim 3 shown in **FIG 10:8** must always be properly installed. The steering damper mounting bolt must be in a vertical position. The clamping piece must be attached to the tie rod so that there is sufficient distance **a** between the clamp and dust cover to allow for free movement of the steering linkage over its full travel. The clamping piece attachment must be tightened to 2kgm (14.5lb ft). On completion, check front wheel alignment as described in **Section 10:7**.

Idler arm:

To remove the idler arm assembly, disconnect the centre tie rod ball joint as described previously. Remove

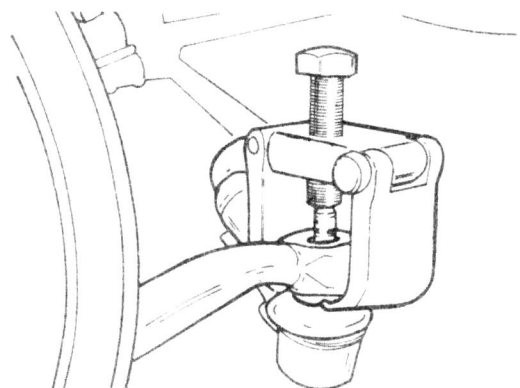

FIG 10:5 Disconnecting outer tie rod from centre tie rod

FIG 10:6 Outer tie rod installed length A is 330mm (13in)

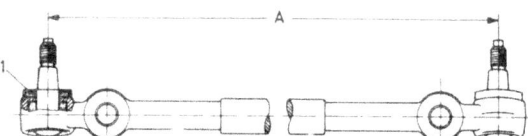

FIG 10:7 Centre tie rod showing location of sealing ring 1

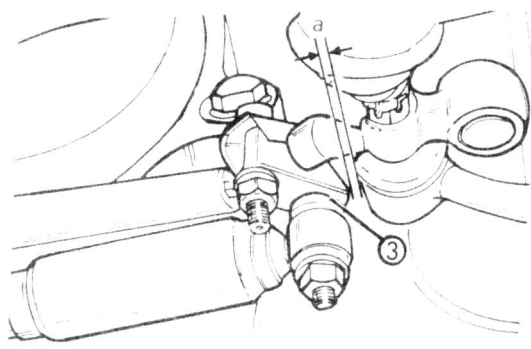

FIG 10:8 Steering damper installation

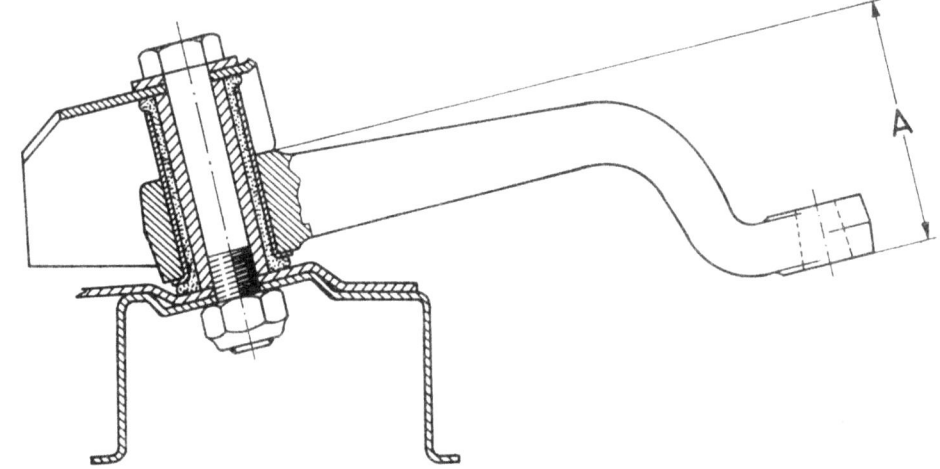

FIG 10:9   Section through idler arm assembly

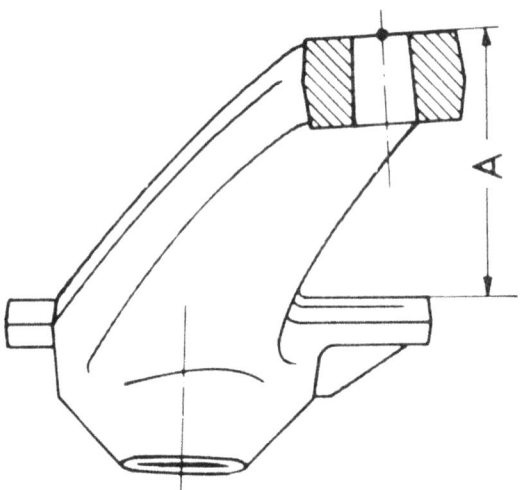

FIG 10:10   Checking steering arm for distortion

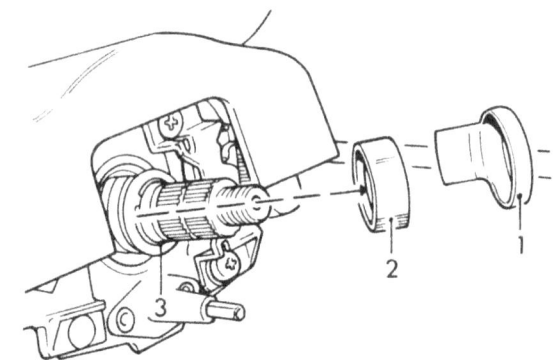

FIG 10:12   Cancelling cam 1 and collar 2

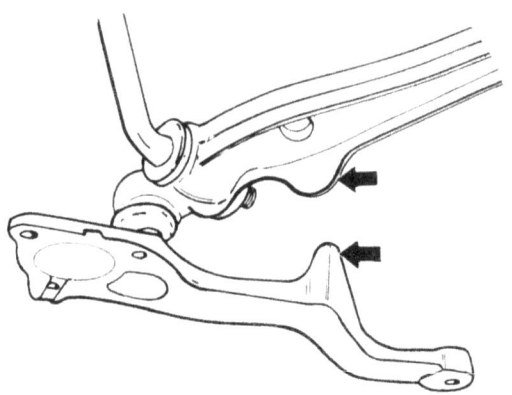

FIG 10:11   Boss locations on steering arm and control arm

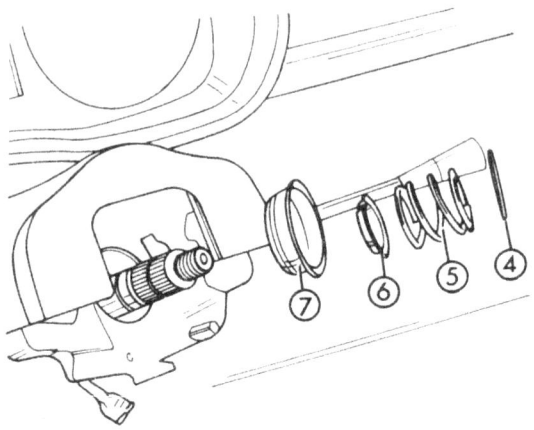

FIG 10:13   Column upper bearing removal

the fixing nut and detach the idler arm assembly from the crossmember. Check the idler arm and bearing assembly for wear or damage and renew if necessary. The arm must also be renewed if it is distorted. Check by measuring dimension **A** as shown in **FIG 10:9**. This should be 42 to 42.5mm (1.6535 to 1.6732in). Refit the idler arm assembly in the reverse order of removal.

Steering arms:

To remove a steering arm, disconnect the outer tie rod ball joint from the arm then detach the arm from the suspension strut assembly as described in **Chapter 9, Section 9:5**. Check the steering arm for faults and renew if necessary. Check for distortion by measuring dimension **A** shown in **FIG 10:10**. This should be 53.5mm (2.1063in). If the suspension control arm has a boss as shown in **FIG 10:11**, only steering arms with a corresponding boss may be installed. Never use a steering arm with a boss together with a control arm without a boss. However, a steering arm without a boss may be used if the control arm has a boss.

Refit the steering arm in the reverse order of removal.

10:4 Column bearings and universal joints

Renewing upper column bearing:

Remove the pad from the centre of the steering wheel as shown in **FIG 10:2**. Disconnect the wiring for the horn pushes in the steering wheel. Make sure that the steering gear is in the straightahead position, then remove the retaining nut and pull the steering wheel from the shaft. Remove the lower part of the steering column housing.

Refer to **FIG 10:12** and pull off cancelling cam 1 and collar 2. Carefully prise circlip 3 from the groove and remove from the column. Refer to **FIG 10:13** and remove washer 4, coil spring 5 and ring 6. Drive upper bearing 7 from the housing.

Drive the new bearing into position, then fit the ring with shank towards the bearing, spring and washer. Fit the circlip over the shaft splines. Fit the collar shown in **FIG 10:12** the wrong way round, and use it to press the circlip down against the spring until it snaps into its groove. Remove the collar and refit the correct way round making sure that the recess in the collar locates over the circlip. Make sure that the turn indicator switch is in the central position, then install the cancelling cam as shown in **FIG 10:14**. Check that the distance shown is approximately 0.3mm (0.012in). If necessary, adjust at the turn indicator switch. Locate the steering wheel in the straightahead position and press on to the shaft splines. Fit and tighten the retaining nut then reconnect the wiring. Refit the column lower housing and the steering wheel central pad.

Renewing column lower bearing:

Detach the steering column housing for access to the bearing. Pull the cable from the rear fog lamp warning light switch and swing the housing to the right. Mark the relationship of the universal joint coupling to steering shaft, then loosen the clamp bolt on the upper part of the universal joint. Detach the upper section of the housing from the instrument panel, then pull the steering column upwards to disconnect the steering shaft from the universal joint.

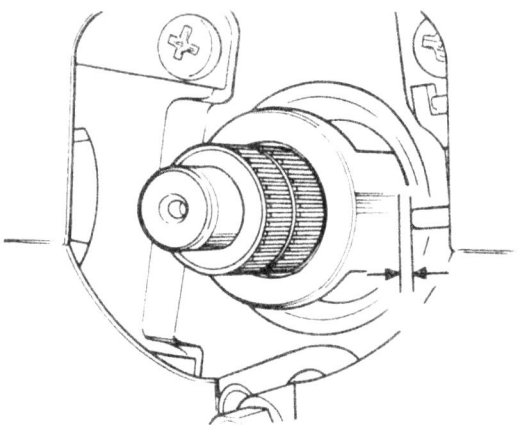

FIG 10:14   Cancelling cam installation

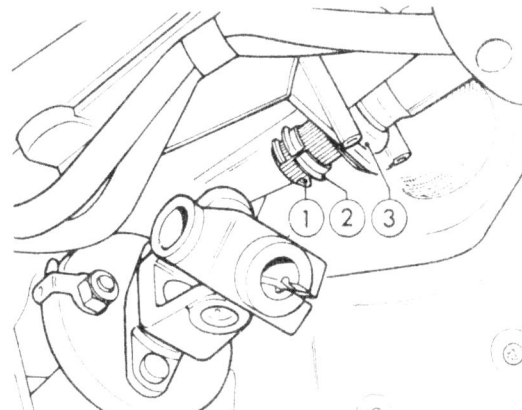

FIG 10:15   Removing steering column lower bearing

FIG 10:16   Upper universal joint removal

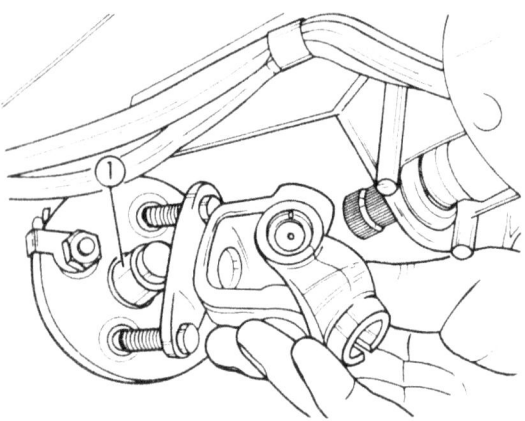

FIG 10:17   Location of plastic bush

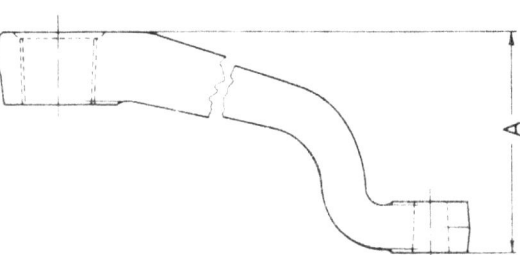

FIG 10:19   Checking Pitman arm for distortion

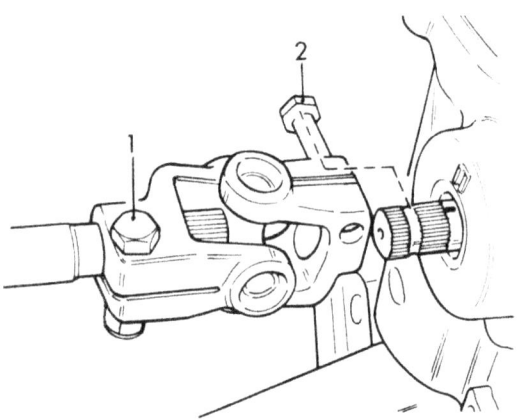

FIG 10:18   Lower universal joint removal

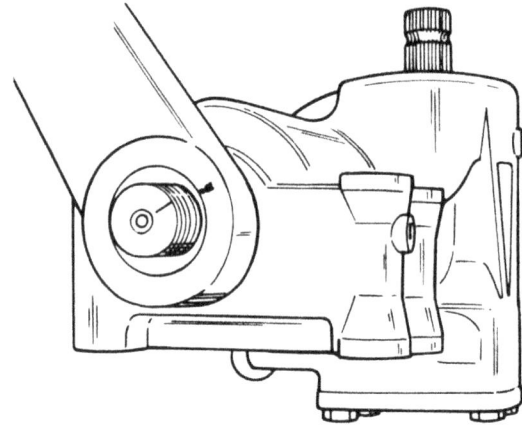

FIG 10:20   Pitman arm installation

Loosely attach the upper section of the housing with two screws, then press down on the steering wheel to expose circlip 1 (see **FIG 10:15**). Remove the circlip and collar 2, then drive out bearing 3.

Drive the new bearing into position, then install collar 2 with shank towards bearing and retain with circlip 1. Refit the remaining components in the reverse order of removal, using the marks made previously to align universal joint and steering shaft. Fog lamp warning light switch connections are + yellow/white, **S** grey/violet and 31 brown.

Renewing upper universal joint:

Detach the steering column housing, then pull the cable from the rear fog lamp warning light switch and swing the housing to the right. Refer to **FIG 10:16**. Remove the clamp screw and unscrew the stop nuts, then detach the upper section of the housing from the pedal pivot bracket. Pull the universal joint away from the steering shaft and out of the joint disc. Avoid turning the steering wheel or shaft, so that the original relationship of shaft to universal joint will be maintained.

Check condition of plastic bush 1 (see **FIG 10:17**) and renew if worn or damaged. Install the new universal joint and refit the remaining parts in the reverse order of removal. Reconnect the wiring to the warning switch as described previously.

Renewing lower universal joint:

Remove the housing and disconnect the warning light switch as described previously. Make sure that the steering gear is in the straightahead position. Detach the upper section of the housing from the pedal pivot bracket.

Refer to **FIG 10:18**. Remove clamp bolt 1 and pull the steering shaft from the universal joint. Remove clamp bolt 2 and disconnect universal joint from steering gear.

Make sure that the mark on the steering gear shaft is aligned between the marks on the steering gear housing. Fit the new universal joint to the steering gear and tighten clamp bolt 2. Make sure that the steering wheel is centralised, then fit the steering shaft to the universal joint and tighten clamp bolt 1. Make sure that the clamp bolts are correctly engaged in the shaft grooves. Note

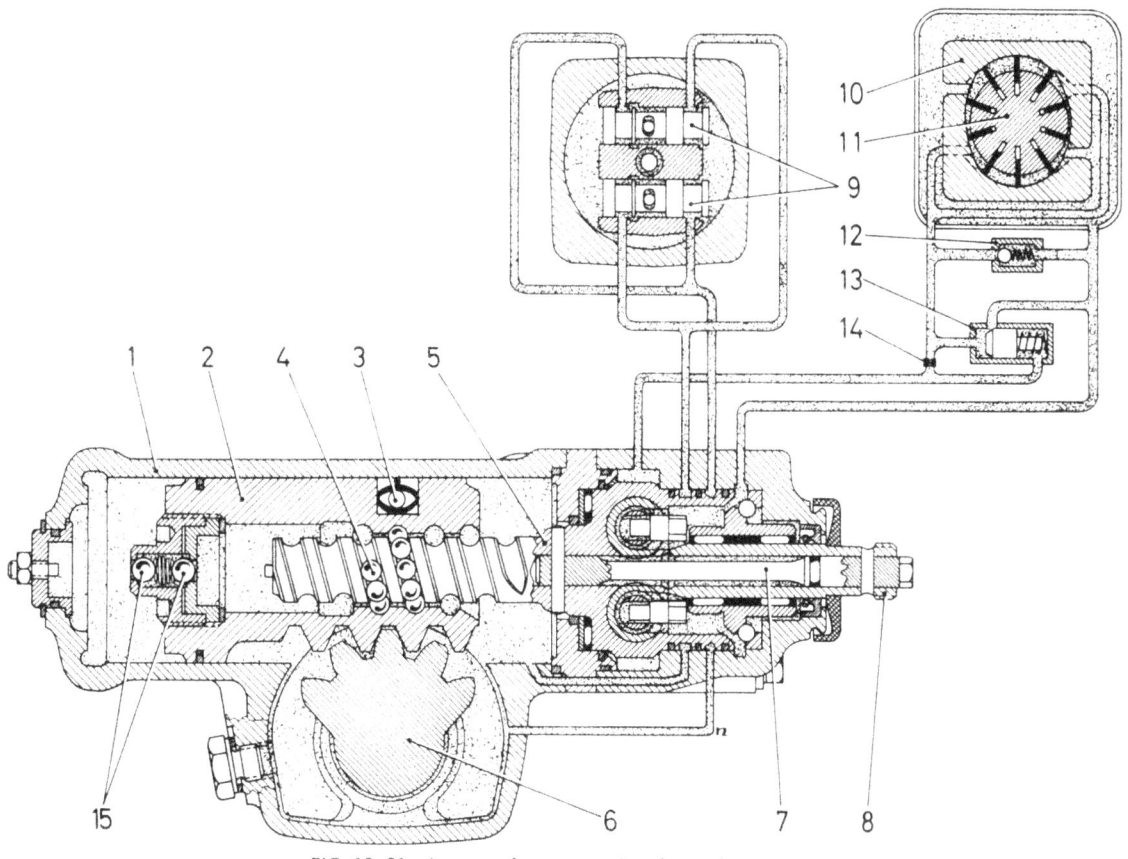

FIG 10:21 Layout of power assisted steering system

Key to Fig 10:21   1 Housing   2 Piston   3 Circulation tube   4 Balls   5 Worm   6 Steering worm sector shaft   7 Torsion
bar   8 Steering shaft   9 Valve piston   10 Curved ring   11 Impeller   12 Pressure relief valve   13 Pressure check valve
14 Throttle element   15 Locking valve

that the longer yoke of the universal joint must face
towards the steering column. Refit the remaining parts in
the reverse order of removal, connecting the warning
switch wiring as described previously.

10:5 Steering gear

Instructions for the removal and installation of the
steering box are given in this section, but it is not
recommended that the owner attempt to dismantle the
unit. Special tools are needed to remove and install
certain internal components and for setting the necessary
friction values and preloads. For these reasons, it is
recommended that steering box overhaul procedures are
carried out only by a fully equipped service station.

Removal:

Make sure that the steering is in the straightahead
position. Refer to **FIG 10:18**. Loosen clamp bolt 1 and
remove clamp bolt 2, then push the universal joint
upwards as far as possible to disconnect from the shaft.
Disconnect the centre tie rod from the Pitman arm on the
steering gear as described in **Section 10:3**. Remove the

three bolts securing the steering box to the front crossmember then remove the steering box downwards.

Refitting:

This is a reversal of the removal procedure. Before
connecting the universal joint to the steering box splined
shaft, make sure that the mark on the shaft is aligned
between the two marks on the housing as shown in
FIG 10:18. Check that the steering wheel is in the central
position then reconnect the universal joint to the shaft and
install the lower clamp bolt, making sure that it aligns
correctly in the locating groove. Tighten both clamp
bolts.

Pitman arm removal:

Disconnect the centre tie rod from the steering gear
Pitman arm as described in **Section 10:3**. Release the
tab washer and remove the nut, then pull the Pitman arm
from the steering shaft using a suitable puller tool.

If the Pitman arm is damaged or distorted it must be
renewed. Check for distortion as shown in **FIG 10:19**.
Dimension **A** should be 89.5 + 0.5mm (3.524 + 0.020in).

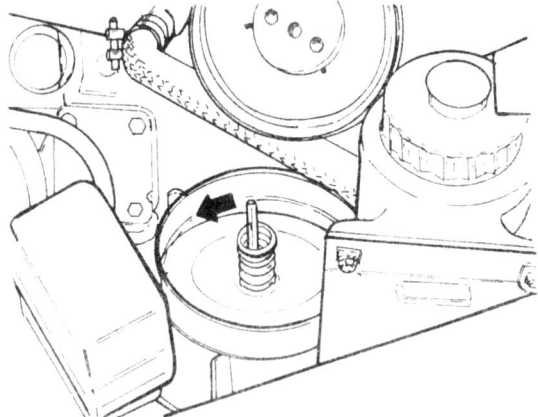

FIG 10:22   Correct level of fluid in reservoir

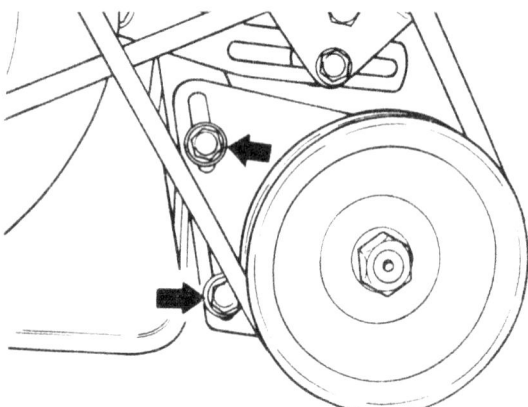

FIG 10:23   Pressure pump front mounting bolts

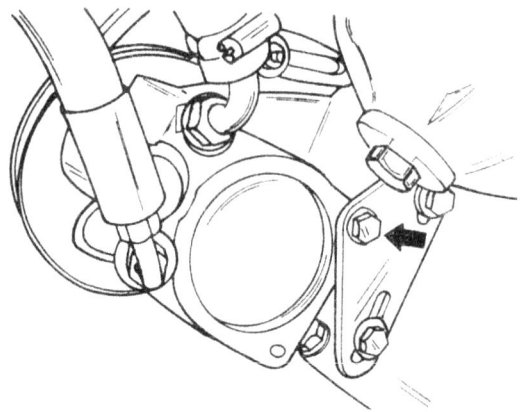

FIG 10:24   Pressure pump rear mounting bolt

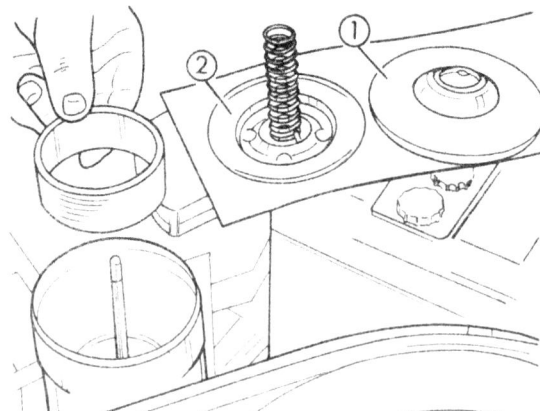

FIG 10:25   Reservoir fluid filter renewal

Refitting:

This is a reversal of the removal procedure, using a new tab washer. Make sure that the arrow on the Pitman arm is aligned with the mark on the steering shaft as shown in **FIG 10:20**. Tighten the securing nut to the specified torque and lock with the tab washer.

10:6 Power assisted steering

Layout of the recirculating cam and ball nut steering gear and hydraulic pressure system is shown in **FIG 10:21**. The items of maintenance and adjustment which can be carried out by a reasonably competent owner/mechanic are given in this section, but due to the complexity of the system and the need for special tools and equipment to carry out repairs and overhaul, it is recommended that any work requiring partial or complete dismantling of system components be carried out only by a fully equipped service station.

Checking fluid level:

Remove the filler cap from the fluid reservoir, wiping dirt from around the cap before doing so. The fluid level should be at the mark arrowed in **FIG 10:22**. Top up if necessary using an approved grade of automatic transmission fluid, then refit the cap.

Bleeding the system:

The system will require bleeding only if the fluid level has been allowed to drop so low that air has been drawn into the system, or if hoses have been disconnected.

Remove the reservoir filler cap and top up with an approved grade of automatic transmission fluid to the level shown in **FIG 10:22**. Disconnect the central HT lead from the ignition coil to prevent the engine from starting, then have an assistant operate the ignition key to crank the engine on the starter motor. Continue to add fluid to maintain the correct level in the reservoir. When the level no longer drops, reconnect the ignition lead and start the engine. With the engine running at idle speed, turn the steering wheel rapidly from one full lock position to the other and back until no further air bubbles can be seen rising through the fluid in the reservoir. During this operation, continue to add fluid as necessary to maintain the correct level. Refit the filler cap.

Drive belt tensioning:

The tension of the belt driving the high pressure pump for the system is correct when the belt can be deflected by 5 to 10mm (0.2 to 0.4in) when firm thumb pressure is applied in the centre of the longest belt run. If tension is incorrect, slacken the two front mounting bolts shown in **FIG 10:23** and slacken the two mounting bolts which are in similar positions at the rear of the unit. Push the pump assembly downwards until belt tension is correct, then firmly tighten all mounting bolts. To remove the belt, slacken all mounting bolts and push the pump unit upwards as far as possible. Remove the belt from the pulleys. Refit in the reverse order, tensioning the belt correctly as described previously.

Pressure pump removal:

Place a suitable container beneath the pump to collect any spillage of fluid, noting that any fluid drained from the system must be discarded and new fluid only used for topping up later. Slacken and remove the drive belt as described previously. Remove the single fixing bolt arrowed in **FIG 10:24** and the two fixing bolts arrowed in **FIG 10:23**, then lift the pump unit from the engine. Do not disconnect the fluid pipes unless pump renewal or overhaul is necessary. Instead, wire the pump unit to an adjacent component so that the hoses are not strained.

Refitting:

This is a reversal of the removal procedure. On completion, tension the drive belt and bleed the hydraulic system as described previously.

Reservoir filter renewal:

Remove the filler cap from the reservoir, then refer to **FIG 10:25** and remove end cap 1, filter cover 2 and the filter element. Discard the element. If the fluid in the reservoir is not absolutely clean, it should be siphoned from the reservoir and discarded. Install the new filter in the reverse order of removal, then refill and bleed the hydraulic system as described previously.

10:7 Front wheel alignment

The front wheels should be set so that the distance between the rear of the wheels is 1 ± 1mm (0.04 ± 0.04in) more than the distance between the front of the wheels, when the car is correctly loaded as described in **Chapter 9, Section 9:4**. Adjustment is carried out by slackening the tie rod clamps on each side of the car (see **FIG 10:6**), then rotating the sleeves by equal amounts until the toe-in setting is correct. It is not recommended that owners attempt this work themselves, as great accuracy is essential. Instead, the work should be entrusted to a BMW service station or a wheel and tyre specialist having optical setting equipment, the complete procedure taking only a short time under these conditions.

10:8 Fault diagnosis

(a) Wheel wobble

1 Unbalanced wheels and tyres
2 Slack steering connections
3 Incorrect steering geometry
4 Excessive play in steering gear
5 Faulty suspension
6 Worn or loose hub bearings

(b) Wander

1 Check 2, 3 and 4 in (a)
2 Uneven tyre pressures
3 Ineffective dampers
4 Uneven tyre wear

(c) Heavy steering

1 Check 3 in (a)
2 Very low tyre pressures
3 Lack of lubrication
4 Wheels out of track
5 Steering gear adjustment too tight
6 Tight or damaged bearings
7 Faults in power assisted steering system

(d) Lost motion

1 Loose steering wheel connection
2 Worn steering gear
3 Worn steering ball joints
4 Worn suspension ball joints
5 Worn steering gear bearings
6 Steering gear out of adjustment

NOTES

CHAPTER 11

THE BRAKING SYSTEM

11:1 Description

The brake units on all four wheels are hydraulically operated from the footbrake pedal. Front disc brakes are standard on all models, but either disc or drum brakes may be fitted at the rear according to model type and year of manufacture. The handbrake mechanism is cable operated. If rear drum brakes are fitted, these are operated both by the footbrake system and by the handbrake mechanism, but if disc rear brakes are fitted the handbrake operates on a separate set of brake shoes against a small drum incorporated in the disc brake hubs.

The hydraulic system has two separate circuits, one chamber in the master cylinder providing pressure to all four brake units, the other chamber providing pressure to the front disc brakes only. Thus if the system is damaged and a brake fluid leak results, braking power can only be lost on the rear brakes, the front pair being unaffected. A leak can be detected by abnormally long pedal travel and reduced braking efficiency.

A vacuum servo unit to assist the pressure applied at the brake pedal is a standard fitment. A brake pressure regulating valve fitted in the circuit reduces hydraulic pressure supplied to the rear brakes according to the load on the pedal, to minimise the possibility of the rear wheels locking under heavy braking.

The master cylinder which draws fluid from twin reservoirs is operated from the brake pedal via the servo unit by a short pushrod and coupling. Fluid pressure from the master cylinder is conveyed to the brake units by means of the brake pipes and hoses.

11:2 Routine maintenance

Regularly check the level of fluid in the master cylinder reservoir and replenish if necessary. Wipe dirt from around the cap before removing it and check that the vent hole in the cap is unobstructed. The fluid level should be maintained at the mark on the side of the reservoir. If frequent topping up is required, the system should be checked for leaks, but it should be noted that with disc brake systems the fluid level will drop gradually over a period of time due to the movement of caliper pistons compensating for friction pad wear. The recommended brake fluid is ATE 'S'. **Never use anything but the recommended fluid.** The brake fluid in the system should be completely changed at yearly intervals. This can be carried out by opening all bleed screws and pumping

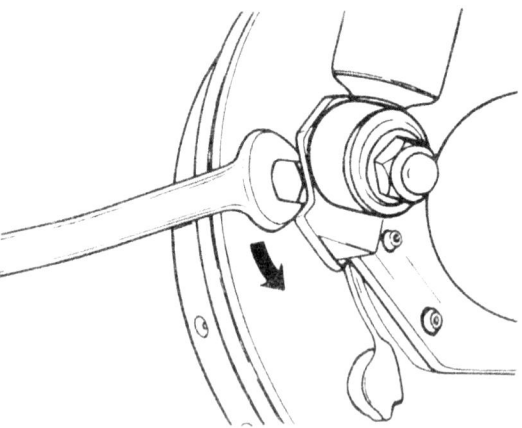

FIG 11:1 Rear drum brake adjustment

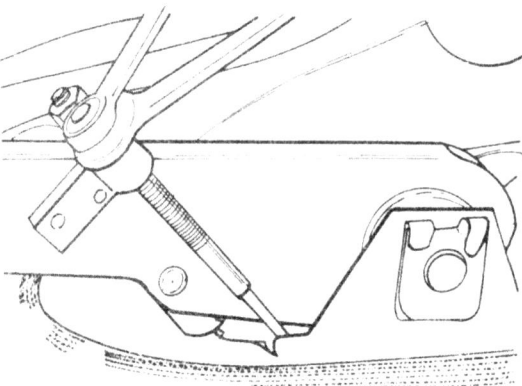

FIG 11:2 Handbrake cable adjustment

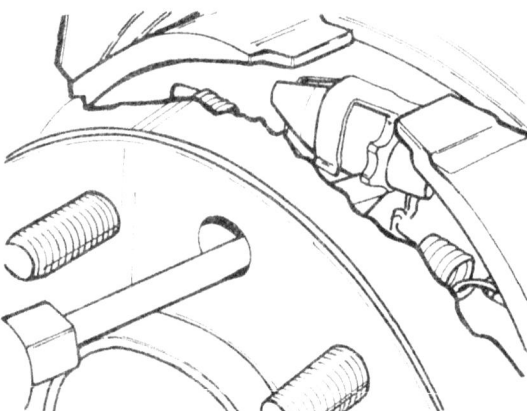

FIG 11:3 Cut-away view showing handbrake shoe adjustment mechanism

out the old brake fluid by operating the brake pedal. The system should then be filled with fresh brake fluid of the correct type and the brakes bled as described in **Section 11:12**. Alternatively, the work can be carried out very quickly by pressure-bleeding at a service station.

Checking brake pads and linings:

Regularly check the thickness of friction lining material on disc brake pads and drum brake shoes.

To check lining wear on disc brake pads, raise and safely support the car then remove the road wheels. Look into the caliper recess and examine the friction lining which is adjacent to the brake disc. If the lining on any pad has worn to a thickness of 2mm (0.08in), or if any lining is cracked or oily, all four friction pads on that axle (front or rear) must be renewed. **Do not renew pads singly or on one side of the car only as uneven braking will result.**

To check the friction linings on models fitted with drum rear brakes, or the linings for the handbrake mechanism on models fitted with drum rear brakes, the brake drum or brake disc must first be removed as described later. If any lining is worn down almost to the rivet heads, or to a thickness of 2mm (0.08in) in the case of bonded linings, or if any lining is damaged or oily, all four rear brake linings should be renewed.

Brake adjustment:

No adjustments are required for any of the disc brakes in the system. The disc brakes are self-adjusting, due to the action of the operating pistons in the calipers. These pistons are returned to the rest position after each brake operation by the piston seals, the seals being slightly stretched during brake application. As the friction pads wear, piston stroke is increased and the pistons will travel further than before and move through the stretched seals a little, the seals returning the pistons to new positions nearer the pads when the brakes are released. In this manner, the piston stroke remains constant regardless of the thickness of friction pads.

Rear drum brakes should be adjusted whenever brake pedal travel becomes excessive. Always check that the linings are not worn to the limit before carrying out the adjustment procedure. On all models, handbrake adjustment procedures should be carried out if the handbrake will not hold the car securely when the lever is pulled up by five clicks on the ratchet.

Drum brake adjustment:

Chock the front wheels against rotation, then raise and safely support the rear of the car and fully release the handbrake. The adjusters are located on the brake backplate as shown in **FIG 11:1**. To take up the adjustment, the adjuster at the rear of the backplate must be turned anticlockwise and at the front clockwise.

Spin the road wheel forwards while turning the adjuster until the wheel is just locked against rotation. Slacken the adjuster until the wheel is just able to spin freely, then apply the handbrake and footbrake several times and recheck the adjustment. Repeat the adjustment procedure at the second adjuster on the same brake unit, then repeat the entire adjustment procedure at the opposite rear wheel.

Handbrake adjustment:

Drum brakes:

On models fitted with drum rear brake units, the adjustment procedure described previously will normally take up excessive slack in the handbrake mechanism. Always carry out this adjustment before attempting to adjust the handbrake cables.

Chock the front wheels against rotation, then raise and safely support the rear of the car and fully release the handbrake. Release the rubber boot from the base of the handbrake lever then push the boot up the lever to expose the cable adjusting nuts (see **FIG 11:2**). Using two spanners as shown, hold the adjusting nut against rotation while slackening the locknut on each cable. Pull the handbrake up by five clicks on the ratchet from the fully released position.

Evenly tighten the adjusting nuts a little at a time until resistance to turning by hand can be felt at one or both of the rear wheels. If resistance is unequal, tighten the appropriate individual adjusting nut until resistance is equal at both wheels. Continue tightening equally until both rear wheels are locked against rotation under heavy hand pressure. Now fully release the handbrake and check that both rear wheels are completely free to turn, with no sign of binding. If necessary, slacken the adjusters a little. On completion, firmly tighten the locknuts to secure the adjustment then refit the rubber boot to the handbrake lever.

Rear disc brakes:

Chock the front wheels, raise and safely support the rear of the car, then remove the rear road wheels and fully release the handbrake. Turn the brake disc until the access hole is aligned with the adjuster wheel in the brake unit, then insert a suitable screwdriver through the hole to engage the adjuster as shown in **FIG 11:3**. Use the screwdriver to turn the adjuster one tooth at a time, removing the screwdriver and rotating the brake disc between each adjustment. Continue until the disc cannot be turned by hand, then slacken the adjuster by two to three teeth. Operate the handbrake several times and recheck the adjustment. Slacken a little further if binding is evident. Repeat the adjustment procedure for the opposite rear brake.

When shoe adjustment is correct as just described, refit the road wheels and carry out the handbrake adjustment procedure as described previously for models with drum rear brakes. Never carry out adjustments at the handbrake cables before carrying out the adjustment procedures at the handbrake shoes.

11:3 Brake pad renewal

Apply the handbrake then raise and safely support the front or rear of the car as necessary. Remove the road wheels.

Refer to **FIG 11:4** and drive out the pad retaining pins towards the centre of the car. Remove the spreader spring and pull out the pads, using a suitable hooked tool as shown in **FIG 11:5** If the pads are being removed only to allow for other servicing operations, they must be marked so that they can be refitted in their original positions. When renewing brake pads, the replacements

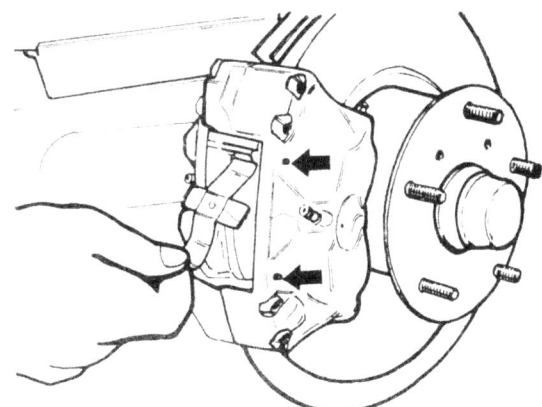

FIG 11:4 Retaining pin and spring removal. Front brake caliper shown

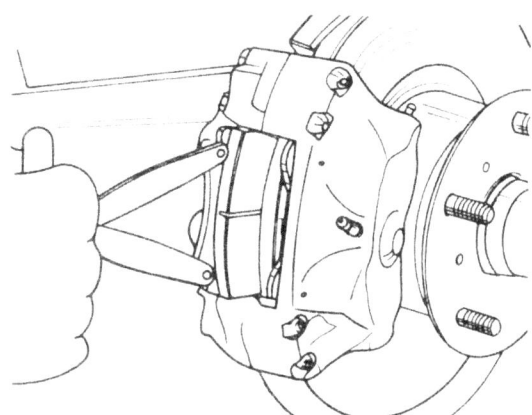

FIG 11:5 Brake pad removal

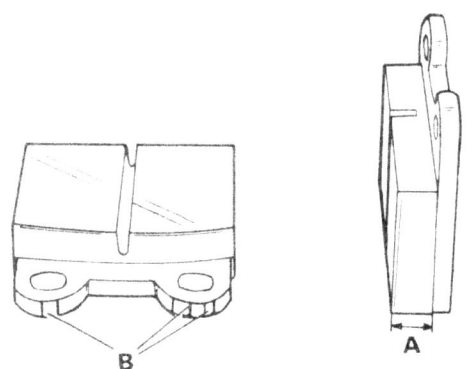

FIG 11:6 Pad lining thickness A and colour code B

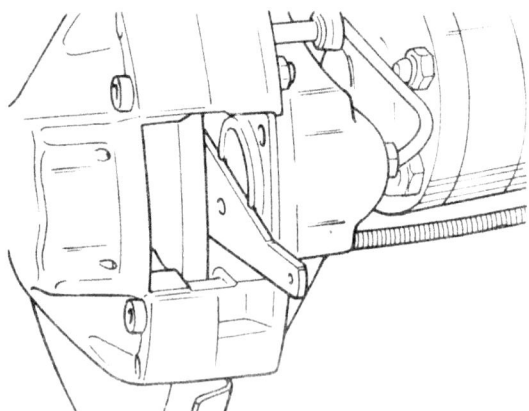

FIG 11:7 Checking piston cut-out position in rear caliper

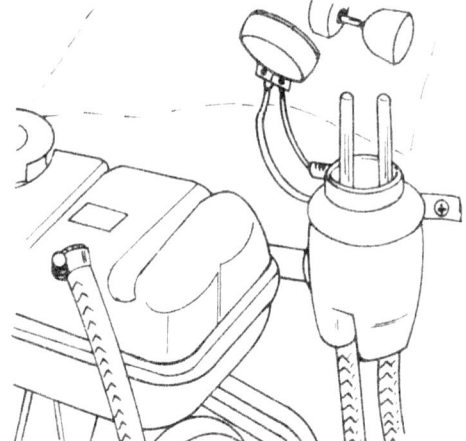

FIG 11:8 Plugging fluid reservoir outlets

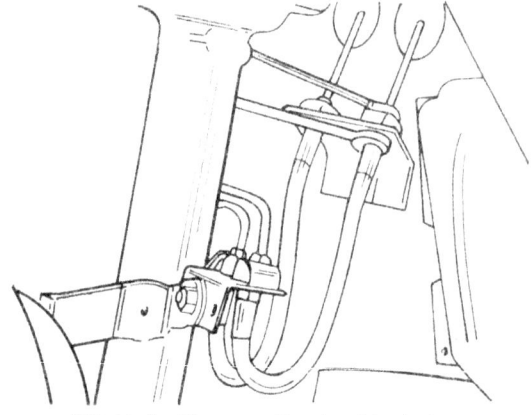

FIG 11:9 Disconnecting front brake hose

must always be of the same type as the originals, as indicated by the colour coding shown at **B** in **FIG 11:6**.

Check that the new pads are of the correct type and that they are free from grease, oil and dirt. Clean dirt and rust from the caliper before fitting the pads. To enable the new pads to be fitted, push the caliper pistons, four on front brake units or two on rear brake units, down into their bores to allow for the extra thickness of the new pads. Note that this operation will cause the level of brake fluid in the master cylinder reservoir to rise, so it may be necessary to siphon off some of the fluid to maintain the fluid at the correct level and prevent overflowing. Note that brake fluid is poisonous and that it can damage paintwork. On rear brake units, the positions of the cut-outs on the pistons must be checked, using the BMW special tool or similar as shown in **FIG 11:7**. The lower part of the tool which seats in the caliper is flat and the upper part which contacts the sides of the cut-out in the piston is at a 20° angle to the lower face. If necessary, the piston must be carefully rotated to the correct position using the special BMW tool or by other suitable means, taking care not to damage the piston or dust seal. If the piston cut-out is incorrectly positioned, brake judder, squealing or excessive pad wear may result.

Make sure that the recesses for the pads in the caliper are free from dirt and rust. Fit the new friction pads and drive one retaining pin through the pads and the caliper up to its stop. Fit the spreader spring beneath the first pin then install the second pin, making sure that the spring is correctly located. Any retaining pin which is not a tight fit in the caliper must be renewed. Check that the pads are free to move slightly in the caliper. If any pad binds in position, it must be removed and the backing plate lightly filed as necessary so that it fits freely in the caliper. When all four brake pads have been installed, operate the brake pedal hard several times to bring the pads close to the disc. If this is not done, the brakes may not function the first time that they are used. Top up the fluid in the master cylinder reservoir to the correct level. Refit the road wheels and lower the car, then carefully road test to check the brakes.

The efficiency and life of new brake pads will be greatly increased if they are allowed to bed-in gradually. To ensure this, heavy braking, except in emergencies, should be avoided until the car has been driven for approximately 600km (375 miles) under normal running conditions.

11:4 Brake hoses

Master cylinder supply hoses:

Before removing the hoses connecting the fluid reservoir to the master cylinder, siphon out the contents of the reservoir into a clean container. Note that brake fluid is poisonous and can damage paintwork. Carefully pull the hoses from the reservoir, then pull the connectors from the rubber plugs in the master cylinder. Always pull the connectors vertically out of the plugs, as if they are tilted they may be fractured. When refitting, make sure that the connectors are seated correctly in the master cylinder sealing plugs. Refill the fluid reservoir to the correct level then bleed the brakes as described in **Section 11:12**.

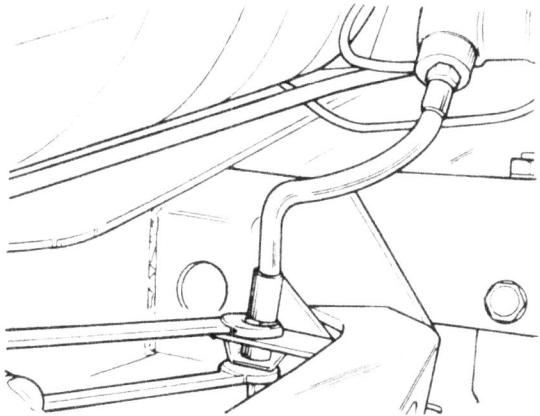

FIG 11 : 10 Disconnecting rear brake hose

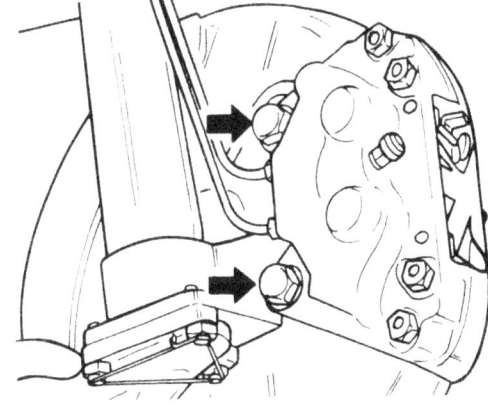

FIG 11 : 11 Front brake caliper mounting bolts

Front and rear brake hoses:

Before disconnecting a hose, plug the fluid reservoir outlets using two pointed wooden dowels as shown in **FIG 11 : 8**. Make sure that the dowels are free of dirt and splinters to avoid contamination of the fluid. Hold the hose connector with one spanner as shown in **FIG 11 : 9** or **11 : 10**, then use a second spanner to unscrew the pipe connector. Detach the hose and collect the retaining spring, then disconnect the other end of the hose in a similar manner. When refitting, allow the hose to adopt a natural sweep so that it is not strained or twisted. Hold the hose connector with one spanner while carefully tightening the pipe connector with a second spanner. Remove the dowels and top up the fluid in the reservoir if necessary. On completion, bleed the brake in question as described in **Section 11 : 12**. Have an assistant apply heavy pressure on the brake pedal, then check for fluid leaks at the hose connections.

11 : 5 Front disc brakes

Caliper removal and refitting:

Raise and safely support the front of the car and remove the road wheel. If the caliper is to be detached for access to other components only, remove the two mounting bolts arrowed in **FIG 11 : 11**, then remove the nut arrowed in **FIG 11 : 12** to disconnect the brake line connector. Carefully lift the caliper with connected brake lines from the mounting on the suspension strut. Wire the caliper by one mounting hole to the inside of the wheel arch so that the brake pipes and hoses are not strained.

If the caliper is to be dismantled, plug the fluid reservoir outlets and remove the brake pads all as described previously. Remove the mounting bolts arrowed in **FIG 11 : 11**, then disconnect the brake pipes from the caliper. Lift the caliper from the suspension.

Refit the caliper in the reverse order of removal. If the brake pipes were disconnected, bleed the brake as described in **Section 11 : 12** on completion.

Caliper overhaul:

Remove dirt and grease from the outside of the caliper before dismantling. If two calipers are to be dismantled

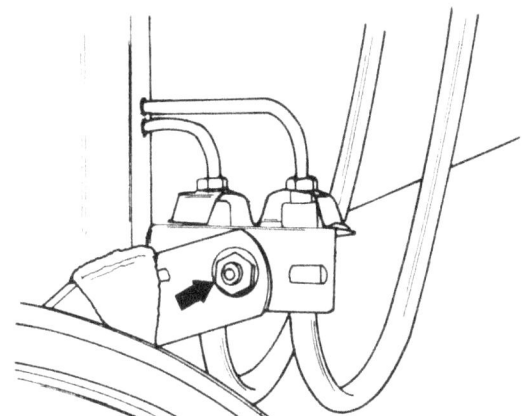

FIG 11 : 12 Brake line connector removal

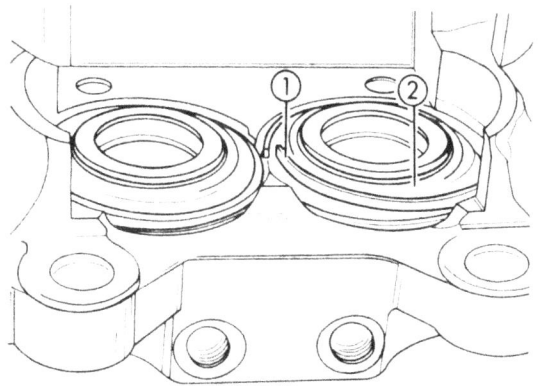

FIG 11 : 13 Clamp ring 1 and dust cover 2

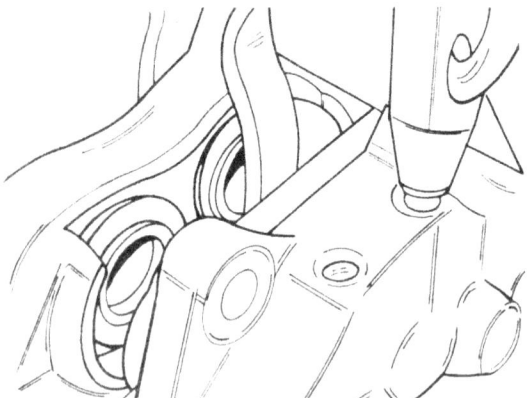

FIG 11:14   Removing a caliper piston

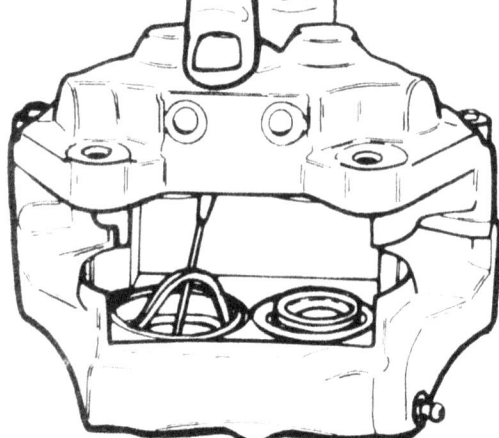

FIG 11:15   Piston seal removal

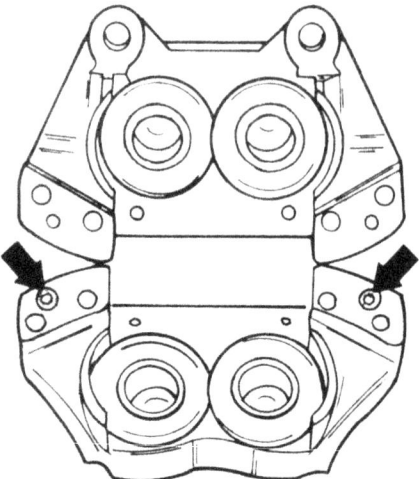

FIG 11:16   Caliper internal seals

at the same time, take care not to mix the parts. **The calipers must not be separated into two halves during servicing, unless leakage from the internal seals is detected.** Otherwise, all work is carried out with the two halves bolted together.

Refer to **FIG 11:13** and remove clamp rings 1 and dust covers 2 from all four pistons. Use a suitable clamp to hold one piston on one side of the caliper in position as shown in **FIG 11:14**, then use low-pressure compressed air applied at the brake pipe connection to eject the opposite piston far enough to be removed with the fingers. Do not use high pressure as the piston may be ejected rapidly causing damage or accidental injury. Move the clamp to the opposite side and use it to retain a suitable wooden or rubber sealing plate against the open end of the cylinder, then repeat the operation to remove the opposite piston. Repeat the entire operation to remove the remaining pair of pistons.

Use a suitable plastic or wooden rod to remove the piston seals from the cylinder bores as shown in **FIG 11:15**, taking care not to damage the bores or seal grooves.

If leaks have been detected from the caliper internal seals, remove the four bolts holding the two caliper halves together, then carefully remove the seals which are arrowed in **FIG 11:16**. Discard the four bolts, as it is essential to fit new ones during reassembly.

Discard all rubber parts and wash the remaining parts in commercial alcohol, methylated spirits or clean approved brake fluid. **Use no other cleaner or solvent on brake components.** Inspect all parts for wear or damage and the pistons and cylinder bores for scoring or pitting. Renew any parts found worn, damaged or corroded, making sure that the correct replacement part is obtained and fitted.

Dip all internal parts in clean brake fluid or smear with ATE brake cylinder paste before installation. Reassemble the caliper using new rubber parts throughout, and new expansion bolts to hold the two halves of the caliper together if they were separated. In the latter case, carefully fit the new internal seals then fit the two caliper halves together and fit the expansion bolts finger tight. Tighten the bolts a little at a time, in the order shown in **FIG 11:17**, to the specified torque figure.

Use the fingers only when fitting new seals to the caliper bores, making sure that they are fully seated in the grooves. Fit the pistons, crown first, taking care not to dislodge the seals. Press the pistons down to the bottom of their bores. Fit the new dust covers and retain with the clamp rings. Install the brake pads after the caliper has been refitted, as described previously.

Brake disc removal:

The brake disc is removed together with the front hub assembly as described in **Chapter 9, Section 9:2**. Using a suitable hexagonal key, remove the fixing bolts and detach the disc from the hub. If the disc is rusted in position or is otherwise difficult to remove, refit the hub assembly to the removed road wheel and tighten the wheel nuts. Lay the wheel down with the disc uppermost, then stand on the wheel and twist and pull the disc from the hub. **Never hammer against the disc in an attempt to remove it, as this will cause damage or distortion.** When refitting, it is permissible to lightly tap

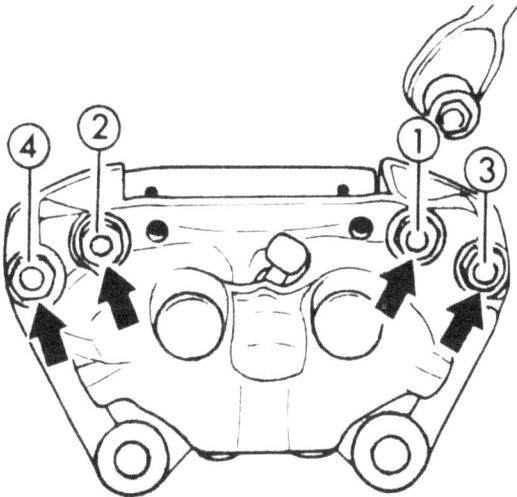

FIG 11:17   Caliper expansion bolt tightening sequence

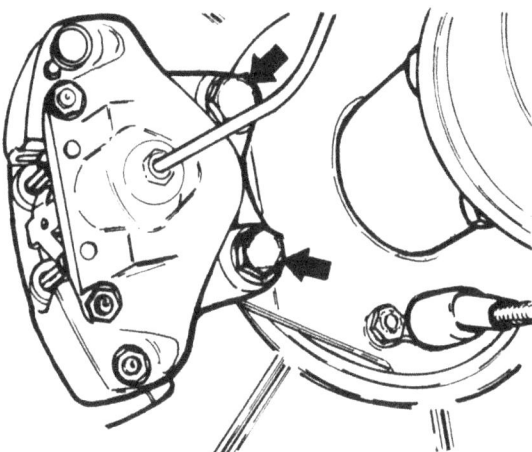

FIG 11:18   Rear brake caliper mounting bolts

the disc on to the hub, using a block of wood placed across the disc to cushion the hammer blows. Tighten the retaining bolts alternately and evenly to the specified torque. Lubricate the hub bearings and refit the assembly as described in **Chapter 9, Section 9:2**.

11:6 Rear disc brakes

Caliper removal and refitting:

Raise and safely support the rear of the car then remove the road wheel. If the caliper is to be removed for access to other components only, remove the two mounting bolts arrowed in **FIG 11:18** and carefully detach the brake caliper and support in such a way that the brake pipe is not strained. If the caliper is to be dismantled, plug the fluid reservoir outlets and remove the brake pads, all as described previously. Remove the mounting bolts and disconnect the brake pipe from the rear of the caliper, plugging the end of the pipe to prevent the entry of dirt. Lift the caliper from the mountings.

Refit in the reverse order of removal. If the brake line was disconnected, bleed the brake as described in **Section 11:12** on completion.

Caliper overhaul:

Apart from having only two pistons instead of four, design and construction of the rear caliper is similar to that of the front, so dismantling and overhaul procedures should be carried out as described in **Section 11:5**. Note however that during reassembly the cut-outs in the piston faces must be properly located as described in **Section 11:3** and shown in **FIG 11:7**.

Brake disc removal:

Detach the rear brake caliper without disconnecting the brake pipe, as described previously. Make sure that the handbrake is fully released, then separate the brake disc from the axle shaft as shown in **FIG 11:19**. Refit in the reverse order of removal, making sure that the holes in the brake disc assembly and the stub axle flange are correctly aligned.

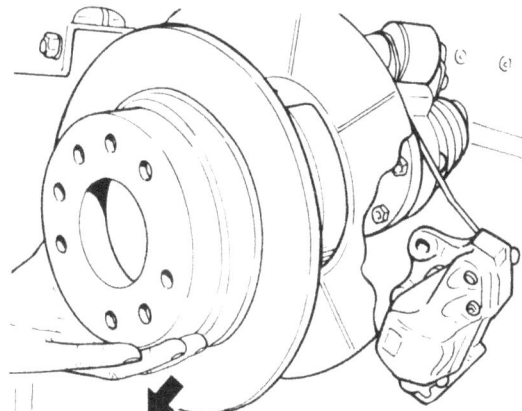

FIG 11:19   Rear brake disc removal

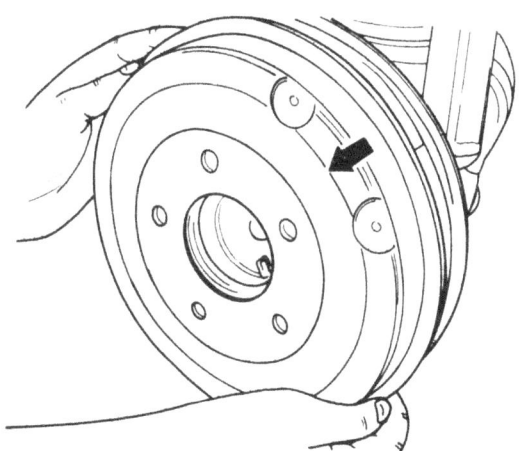

FIG 11:20   Rear brake drum removal

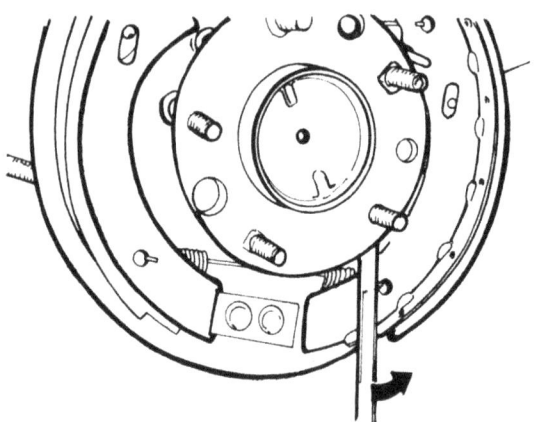

FIG 11:21 Levering out rear shoe to disconnect return spring

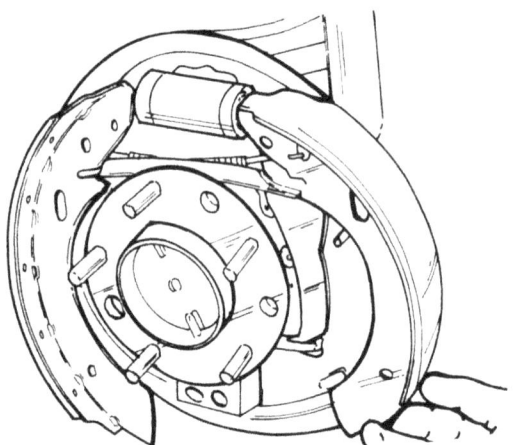

FIG 11:22 Brake shoe removal

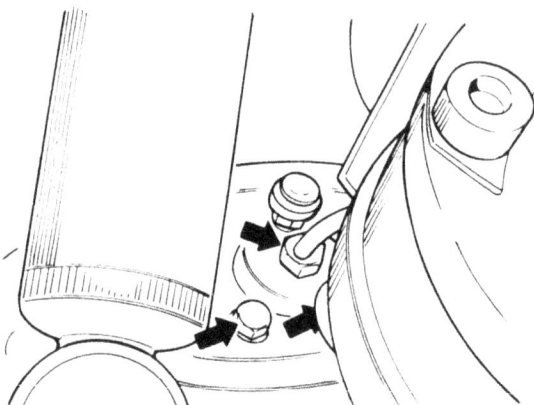

FIG 11:23 Wheel cylinder retaining screws and brake pipe connection

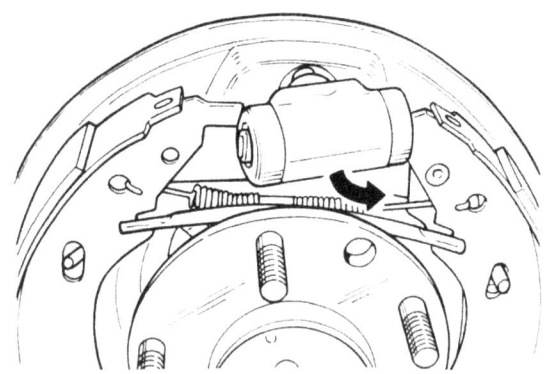

FIG 11:24 Wheel cylinder removal

11:7 Rear drum brakes

This section covers models having rear drum units for both service brake and handbrake, the auxiliary drum brakes fitted to models having rear disc brakes being covered in **Section 11:11**.

Removing brake shoes:

Chock the front wheels against rotation, then raise the rear of the car and remove the road wheels. Fully release the handbrake.

Remove the brake drum as shown in **FIG 11:20**, slackening the adjusters as described in **Section 11:2** if the brake shoes bind against the drum and make removal difficult. Use a screwdriver to lever one shoe out of the lower mounting as shown in **FIG 11:21**, then pull the shoe away from the backplate and disconnect the return spring. Pull the upper ends of the shoes from the wheel cylinder as shown in **FIG 11:22**, then detach the thrust rod, upper return spring and handbrake cable. Note that the rear shoe is serviced complete with handbrake operating lever.

Clean all dirt and grease from the inside of the brake assembly. Clean the inside surfaces of the brake drum, using a suitable solvent to remove all traces of grease.

Refitting:

This is a reversal of the removal procedure, making sure that the return springs are properly fitted to the shoe webs. Note that the longer hooked end of the upper return spring locates in the hole in the handbrake lever on the rear shoe. Check that the shoe webs engage correctly in the slots provided in the wheel cylinder pistons. On completion, adjust the brake shoes as described in **Section 11:2**.

Relining brake shoes:

It is not recommended that owners attempt to reline brake shoes themselves. It is important that the linings should be properly bedded to the shoes and ground for concentricity. For this reason it is best to obtain sets of replacement shoes, or have the relining carried out by a service station. **Do not allow grease, oil or brake fluid to contact brake linings.** If the linings become contaminated in any way they must be renewed as they cannot be successfully cleaned. **If any one lining is** worn or contaminated all four linings for the rear brakes must be renewed. Do not renew linings singly or on one side only.

Servicing a wheel cylinder:

Remove the brake drum and plug the fluid reservoir outlets, all as described previously. Slacken the brake adjusters fully as described in **Section 11 : 2**. Refer to **FIG 11 : 23** and disconnect the brake pipe from the wheel cylinder, plugging the end of the pipe to prevent the entry of dirt. Remove the two screws indicated by the lower arrows. Remove the wheel cylinder by pressing it to the right and simultaneously pulling forward as shown in **FIG 11 : 24**.

Refer to **FIG 11 : 25**. Remove dust covers 5, then remove pistons 4 and spring 2 from wheel cylinder 1. If necessary, remove bleed screw 6 with dust cover 7. Remove and discard seals 3 as new ones must always be used when reassembling. Also renew the dust covers 5 unless in perfect condition. Wash all remaining metal parts in commercial alcohol, methylated spirits or approved brake fluid only. Inspect all parts for wear or damage and renew any found to be unserviceable.

Smear all internal parts with ATE brake cylinder paste or dip them in clean approved brake fluid during reassembly. Use the fingers only to fit the seals to the pistons to avoid damage.

Refit the wheel cylinder in the reverse order of removal, correctly engaging brake shoe webs in the piston slots. Bleed the brake on completion as described in **Section 11 : 12**.

11 : 8 The master cylinder

Removal:

Plug the fluid outlets in the reservoir and pull the flexible hoses from the sealing plugs in the master cylinder, all as described previously. As an additional precaution against loss of fluid, raise the free ends of the flexible hoses above the level of fluid in the reservoir and tie the hoses in this position. Refer to **FIG 11 : 26** and disconnect the brake pipes from the master cylinder. Pipe connections are as follows:

1 front righthand and 2 front lefthand (second brake circuit), 3 front righthand, 4 front lefthand and 5 both rear brakes (first brake circuit). Plug the open ends of the pipes to prevent the entry of dirt. Unscrew the mounting nuts and detach the master cylinder, collecting the sealing ring fitted between the mounting flange and the brake servo unit.

Dismantling:

Refer to **FIG 11 : 27**. Press secondary piston 1 down the bore slightly to relieve spring pressure then remove stop screw 2. Remove circlip 3 and extract the secondary piston assembly. Pull off stop washer 4, seal 5, intermediate ring 6, seal 7 and stop washer 8. To dismantle the piston assembly, refer to **FIG 11 : 28** and remove special screw 9. Remove spring cap 10, spring 11, spring cup 12, pressure plate 13, seal 8 and spacing washer 14.

Apply low pressure compressed air to the front feed pipe union to eject the primary piston 15 (see **FIG 11 : 29**). Pull off spring 16, spring cup 17, pressure plate 18, seal 19 and spacing washer 20. Remove seals 21 and 22.

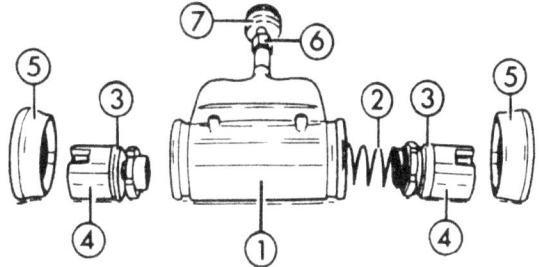
FIG 11 : 25   Wheel cylinder components

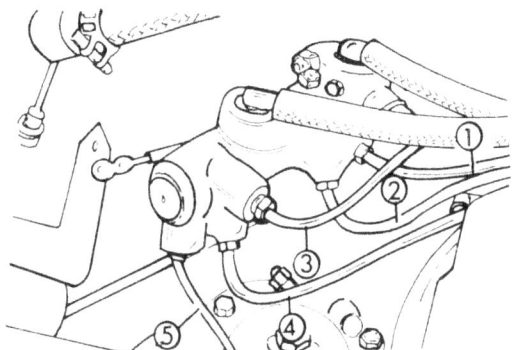
FIG 11 : 26   Master cylinder removal

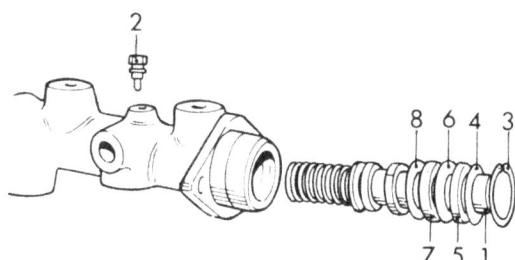
FIG 11 : 27   Removing secondary piston

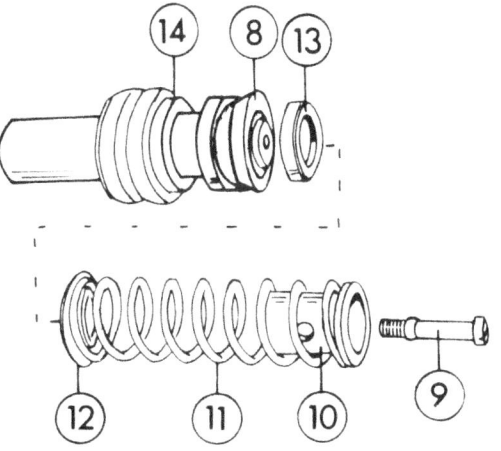
FIG 11 : 28   Dismantling secondary piston

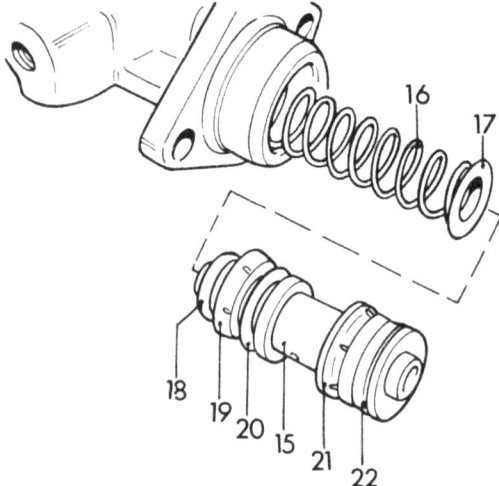

FIG 11:29   Removing primary piston

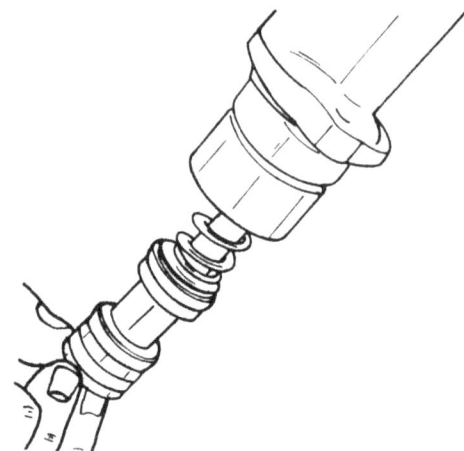

FIG 11:30   Refitting pistons to master cylinder

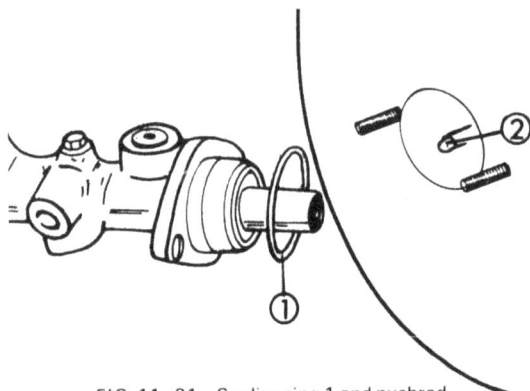

FIG 11:31   Sealing ring 1 and pushrod

Servicing:

Wash all parts in commercial alcohol, methylated spirits or approved brake fluid. Use no other cleaner or solvent on brake hydraulic system components. Inspect the pistons and cylinder bore for score marks and inspect all parts for wear or damage. Renew any faulty parts. Always use new rubber seals and a new copper gasket for the stop screw. Check the feed pipe plugs and renew if not in perfect condition.

Reassembly:

Observe absolute cleanliness to prevent the entry of dirt or any trace of oil or grease. Coat all internal components with ATE brake cylinder paste or dip them in clean approved brake fluid during reassembly. Clamp the master cylinder vertically in a vice with the open end down, so that internal components will not be displaced when refitted. Use tool 6063 if available to ensure that the seals are correctly entered into the bore (see **FIG 11 :30**). If this tool is not available, carefully enter the seals into the bore using the fingers, making sure that the seal lips are not turned back.

Reassemble in the reverse order of dismantling. When the primary piston assembly has been installed, carefully push it down the bore against spring pressure and insert the stop screw. The stop screw must retain the piston assembly in position.

Refitting:

Before installing the master cylinder assembly, check the sealing ring shown at 1 in **FIG 11 :31** and renew if not in perfect condition. A faulty sealing ring will prevent the vacuum servo unit from operating correctly. Install the master cylinder assembly temporarily, placing a piece of Plastigage between the piston and the servo pushrod. Tighten the nuts to the specified torque then remove the master cylinder again and check the resulting thickness of Plastigage with the scale provided with the material. This will give the clearance between the piston and pushrod, which should be 0.5mm (0.02in). Adjust to the correct clearance, if necessary, by adding a shim 2 of suitable thickness. Finally install the master cylinder assembly in the reverse order of removal, then bleed the braking system as described in **Section 11 :12**.

11 :9 Vacuum servo unit

The vacuum servo unit operates to assist the pressure applied at the brake pedal and so reduce braking effort. The vacuum cylinder in the servo is connected to the engine inlet manifold by a hose. The servo unit is a sealed assembly and, if it is faulty or inoperative, a new unit must be fitted.

Testing:

To test the servo unit, switch off the engine and pump the brake pedal several times to exhaust all vacuum from the unit. Hold a steady light pressure on the brake pedal and start the engine. If the servo is working properly, the brake pedal will move further down without further foot pressure, due to the build-up of vacuum in the system.

With the brakes off, run the engine to medium speed and turn off the ignition, immediately closing the throttle.

This builds up a vacuum in the system. Wait one to two minutes, then try the brake action again with the engine still switched off. If not vacuum assisted for two or three operations, the servo check valve is faulty. Poor overall performance of the vacuum servo unit can be caused by a clogged air filter, or a faulty master cylinder sealing ring shown at 1 in **FIG 11 : 31**.

Check valve renewal:

Remove and discard the old check valve, which is fitted in the hose between the servo unit and the inlet manifold (see **FIG 11 : 32**). Make sure that the hose is clear, then fit a new check valve with the arrow or the black coloured end facing towards the inlet manifold.

Servo unit removal:

Refer to **Chapter 2** and remove the air cleaner assembly. Disconnect and remove the battery. On models with power assisted steering, carefully detach the fluid reservoir and move to one side. Disconnect the expansion tank to radiator hose at the tank and secure to one side. Plug the brake fluid reservoir outlets and disconnect the fluid feed hoses from the master cylinder sealing plugs, all as described previously.

Remove the lower instrument panel housing for access to the pedal connections and secure the housing to one side. Refer to **FIG 11 : 33** and remove pin 6 at the brake pedal. Detach the vacuum hose from the inlet manifold, then detach the brake pipes from the master cylinder connection 1, 2, 3, 4 and 5, as described previously. Remove the nuts securing the servo unit to the support bracket and pull out the servo and master cylinder assembly towards the front of the car.

Refitting:

This is a reversal of the removal procedure, carrying out the following adjustment procedures to ensure the

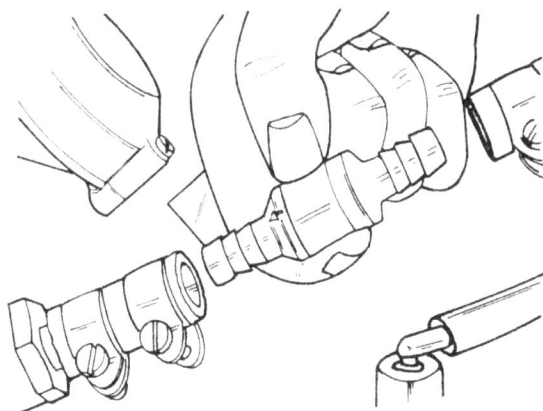

FIG 11 : 32 Servo check valve installation

correct dimensions **A**, **B** and **C** shown in **FIG 11 : 33**. Adjust length of piston rod (**A**) to 367 ÷ 1mm (14.45 ÷ 0.04in) by slackening both locknuts and rotating the pushrod as necessary. Tighten the nuts securely on completion. Check distance **B** between brake pedal pad and bulkhead. This should be 245mm (9.65in). Adjust position of stop light switch by slackening locknut and turning the switch assembly, until dimension **C** is 6.0 to 7.0mm (0.24 to 0.28in).

Filter and silencer renewal:

Refer to **FIG 11 : 34**. Pull off rubber boot 1, retaining ring 2, silencer 3 and filter 4. Discard the filter and silencer. Reassemble in the reverse order of removal, using a new filter and silencer.

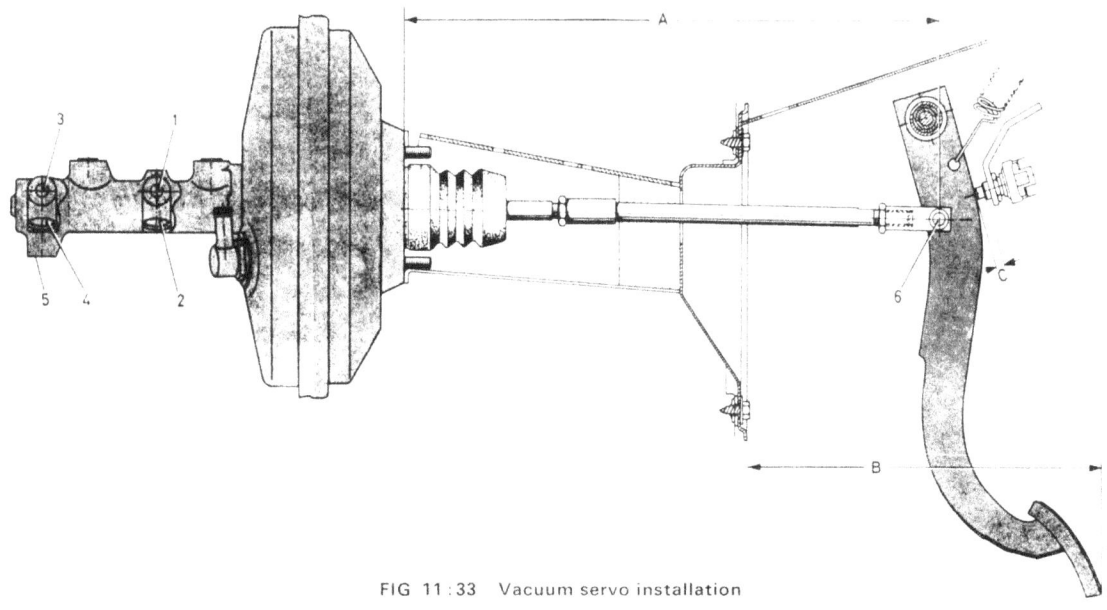

FIG 11 : 33 Vacuum servo installation

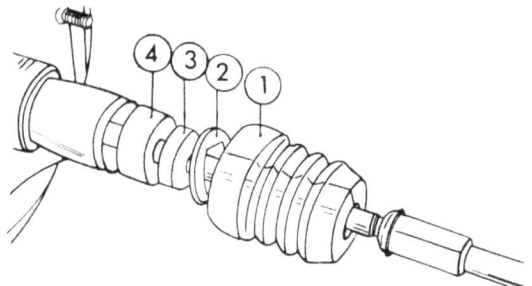

FIG 11:34   Removing servo filter and silencer

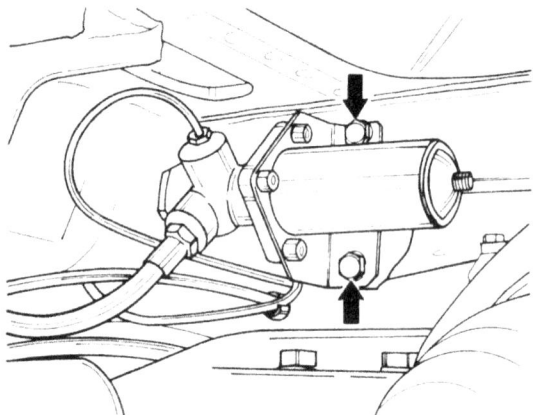

FIG 11:35   Pressure regulating valve mounting bolts

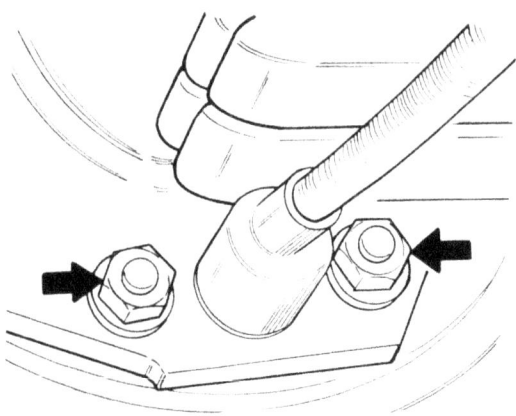

FIG 11:36   Handbrake cable support

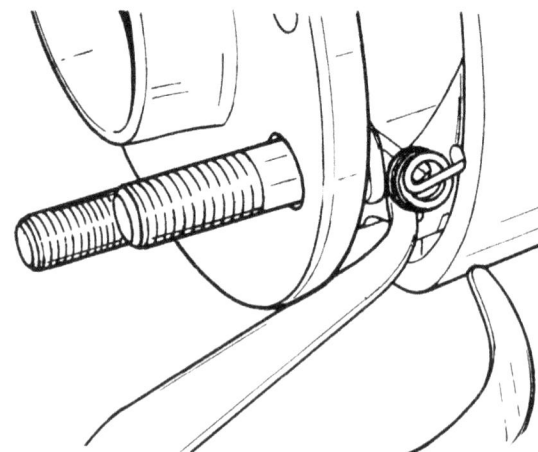

FIG 11:37   Disconnecting lower return spring

11:10 Pressure regulating valve

The pressure regulating valve operates to progressively reduce the pressure supplied to the rear brake hydraulic circuit under increasing brake pedal pressure. This reduces the tendency for the rear wheels to lock under heavy braking. The unit is a sealed assembly and must be renewed complete if defective.

Removal:

Plug the brake fluid reservoir outlets with two dowels and remove the rear lefthand brake hose, all as described previously. Disconnect the brake pipes from the pressure regulating valve and plug the ends of the pipes to prevent the entry of dirt. Remove the two bolts arrowed in **FIG 11:35** and remove the regulating valve.

Refitting is a reversal of the removal procedure, bleeding the braking system on completion as described in **Section 11:12.**

11:11 The handbrake

Handbrake adjustment procedures for all models are described in **Section 11:2.**

Cable removal:

Refer to **Section 11:2** and remove the cable lock-nuts and adjusting nuts at the handbrake lever. Pull the front ends of the cable through the floor panel from beneath the car. Disconnect the handbrake cables from the rear suspension arms and pull the cables from the protective sleeves. Note that the rubber caps must be perfectly tight on the seals to seal effectively when the cables are refitted.

On models with drum rear brakes, refer to **Section 11:7** and disconnect the lower brake shoe return spring and detach the handbrake cable from the lever on the rear shoe. Pull the cable outer sleeve from the location at the brake backplate.

On models fitted with disc rear brakes, remove the handbrake shoe expander as described later, then loosen the handbrake cable support as shown in **FIG 11:36** and pull the cable assembly from the backplate. Note that the collar on the outer sleeve must fit securely in the location when the cable is refitted.

Refit handbrake cables in the reverse order of removal, carrying out the adjustment procedures described in **Section 11:2** on completion.

Handbrake shoe removal:

To remove the handbrake shoes on models equipped with rear disc brakes, the disc must first be removed as described in **Section 11:6**. Use a suitable hooked tool to disconnect the lower return spring as shown in **FIG 11:37**. Use tool 7014 or other suitable Allen key to detach the shoe retaining springs, as shown in **FIG 11:38**. Pull the shoes apart at the bottom and lift away upwards, then disconnect the upper return spring.

To remove the handbrake expander mechanism, refer to **FIG 11:39** Pull component **A** to the right and press out pin **B**, then pull component **C** to the left. Install in the reverse order of removal, coating the sliding surface with a thin layer of Molykote paste.

Install the handbrake shoes in the reverse order of removal, then slacken the brake adjuster completely as described in **Section 11:2** before installing the brake disc. On completion, adjust the handbrake shoes and cables as described in **Section 11:2**.

11:12 Bleeding the system

This is not routine maintenance and is only necessary if air has entered the hydraulic system due to parts being dismantled, or because the level in the master cylinder supply reservoir has been allowed to drop too low. The need for bleeding is indicated by a spongy feeling at the brake pedal accompanied by poor braking performance. Each brake must be bled in turn, starting with the one furthest from the master cylinder and finishing with the one nearest the master cylinder. **Vacuum must be exhausted from the servo by depressing the brake pedal several times with the engine switched off before starting the work and the engine must not be run whilst bleeding is carried out. Do not attempt to bleed the brakes with any drum or caliper removed.**

Top up the fluid reservoir to the correct level with approved brake fluid. Clean dirt from around the first bleed screw and remove the rubber dust cap. Fit a length of rubber or plastic tube to the screw and lead the free end of the tube into a clean glass jar containing a small amount of approved brake fluid. The end of the tube must remain immersed in the fluid during the bleeding operation.

Unscrew the bleed screw about half-a-turn and have an assistant depress the brake pedal fully. With the pedal held down tighten the bleed screw. Allow the pedal to return fully and wait a few seconds for the master cylinder to refill with fluid before repeating the operation. Continue operating the pedal in this manner until no air bubbles can be seen in the fluid flowing into the jar, then hold the pedal against the floor on a down stroke while the bleed valve is tightened. **Do not overtighten.**

On rear brake units, bleeding is carried out at the single bleed screw on each brake caliper or wheel cylinder. On front disc brakes, bleeding must be carried out at the three screws shown in **FIG 11:40** It is essential to bleed

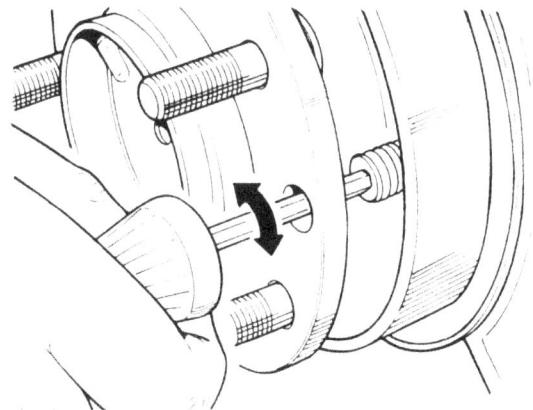

FIG 11:38   Detaching retaining spring

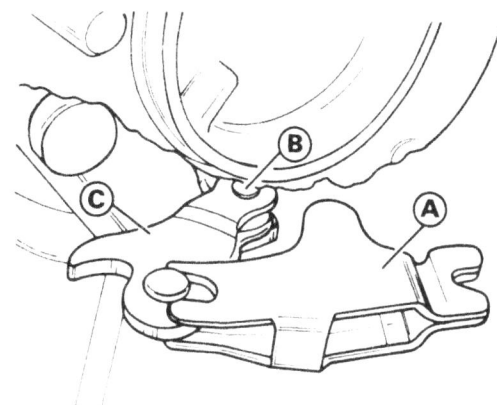

FIG 11:39   Shoe expander mechanism

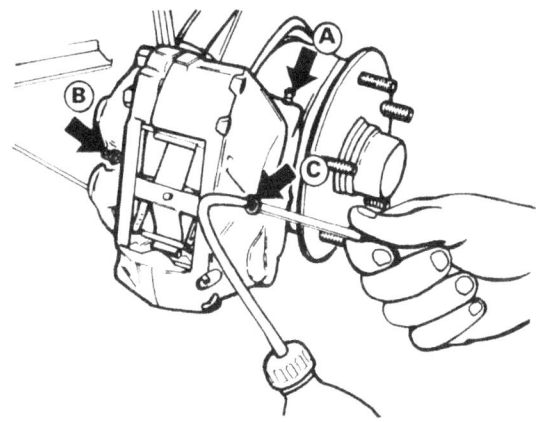

FIG 11:40   Front brake caliper bleed screws

at each screw separately, in the order **B**, **C** and **A**. If this is not carried out correctly, air bubbles may be trapped in the caliper.

At frequent intervals during the operation, check the level of fluid in the reservoir, topping up as needed. If the level drops too low air will enter the system and the operation will have to be restarted.

Remove the bleed tube, refit the dust cap and repeat the operation on each other brake unit in turn.

On completion top up the fluid to the correct level. Discard all used fluid. Always store brake fluid in clean, sealed containers to avoid air or moisture contamination.

11:13 Fault diagnosis

(a) Spongy pedal

1 Leak in the system
2 Worn master cylinder
3 Leaking wheel or caliper cylinders
4 Air in the fluid system
5 Gaps between brake shoes and underside of linings

(b) Excessive pedal movement

1 Check 1 and 4 in (a)
2 Excessive lining or pad wear
3 Drum brakes require adjustment
4 Very low fluid level in supply reservoir

(c) Brakes grab or pull to one side

1 Distorted discs or drums
2 Wet or oily pads or linings
3 Loose backplate or caliper
4 Disc or hub loose

5 Worn suspension or steering connections
6 Mixed linings of different grades
7 Uneven tyre pressures
8 Broken shoe return springs
9 Seized handbrake cable
10 Seized wheel cylinder or caliper piston

(d) Brakes partly or fully locked on

1 Swollen pads or linings
2 Damaged brake pipes preventing fluid return
3 Master cylinder compensating hole blocked
4 Master cylinder piston seized
5 Brake or pedal return spring broken
6 Dirt in the hydraulic system
7 Seized wheel cylinder or caliper piston
8 Seized drum brake adjusters
9 Seized handbrake mechanism or cable

(e) Brake failure

1 Empty fluid reservoir
2 Broken hydraulic pipeline
3 Ruptured master cylinder seal
4 Ruptured wheel cylinder or caliper seal

(f) Reservoir empties too quickly

1 Leaks in pipelines
2 Deteriorated cylinder seals

(g) Pedal yields under continuous pressure

1 Faulty master cylinder seals
2 Faulty wheel cylinder or caliper seals
3 Leak in brake pipe or hose

CHAPTER 12

THE ELECTRICAL SYSTEM

12:1 Description

All models covered by this manual have 12-volt electrical systems in which the negative terminal of the battery is earthed to the car bodywork.

There are wiring diagrams in **Technical Data** at the end of this manual which will enable those with electrical experience to trace and correct faults.

Instructions for servicing the items of electrical equipment are given in this chapter, but it must be pointed out that it is not sensible to try to repair units which are seriously defective, electrically or mechanically. Such faulty equipment should be replaced by new or reconditioned units.

12:2 The battery

To maintain the performance of the battery, it is essential to carry out the following operations, particularly in winter when heavy current demands must be met.

Keep the top and surrounding parts of the battery clean and dry, as dampness can cause current leakage. Clean off corrosion from the metal parts of the battery mounting with diluted ammonia and coat them with anti-sulphuric paint. Clean the terminal posts and smear them with petroleum jelly, tightening the terminal clamps securely. Check the battery earth lead connection to the car body for looseness or corrosion. High electrical resistance due to corrosion at the battery terminals can be responsible for a lack of sufficient current to operate the starter motor.

Regularly remove the screw caps from the battery and check the electrolyte level in each cell, topping up with distilled water if necessary to just cover the separator plates.

If a battery fault is suspected, test the condition of the cells with a hydrometer. **Never add neat acid to the battery. If it is necessary to prepare new electrolyte due to loss or spillage, add sulphuric acid to distilled water. It is highly dangerous to add water to acid.** It is safest to have the battery refilled with electrolyte if it is necessary by a service station.

The indications from the hydrometer readings of the specific gravity are as follows.

For climates below 27 C or 80 F	Specific gravity
Cell fully charged	1.270 to 1.290
Cell half discharged	1.190 to 1.210
Cell discharged	1.110 to 1.130

For climates above 27 C or 80 F	
Cell fully charged	1.210 to 1.230
Cell half discharged	1.130 to 1.150
Cell discharged	1.050 to 1.070

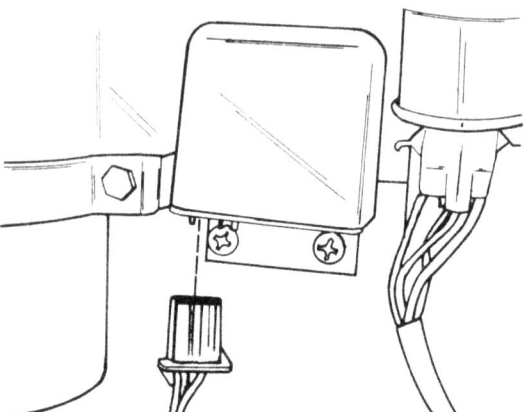

FIG 12:1 Regulator plug connection and mounting screws

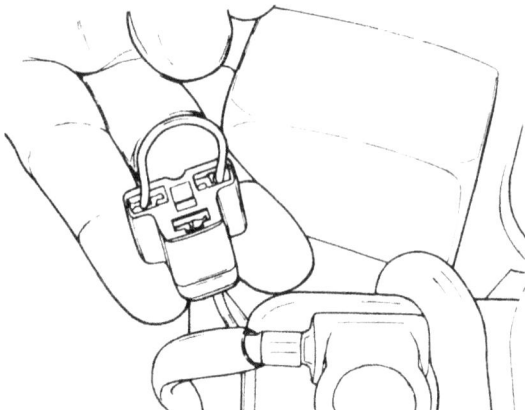

FIG 12:2 Shorting plug connectors for test purposes

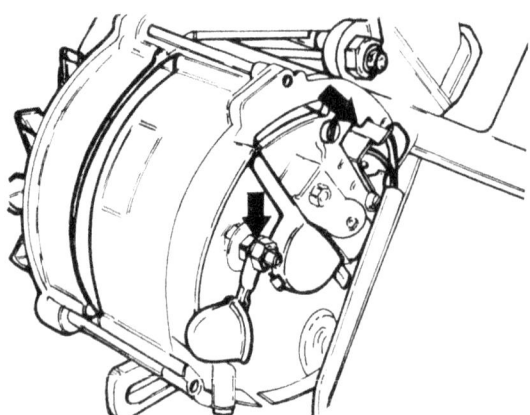

FIG 12:3 Alternator wiring connections

These figures assume electrolyte temperature of 60°F or 16°C. If the temperature of the electrolyte exceeds this, add 0.002 to the readings for each 5°F or 3°C rise. Subtract 0.002 for any corresponding drop below 60°F or 16°C.

If the battery is in a low state of charge, take the car for a long daylight run or put the battery on a charger at 5amps, with the vents in place, until it gases freely. Do not use a naked light near the battery as the gas is inflammable. If the battery is to stand unused for long periods give a refreshing charge every month. It will be ruined if it is left uncharged.

12:3 The alternator

The alternator provides current for the various items of electrical equipment and to charge the battery, the unit operating at all engine speeds. The current produced is alternate, this being rectified to direct current supply by diodes mounted in the alternator casing. Alternator drive is by belt from the crankshaft pulley. Very little maintenance is needed, apart from the occasional check on belt tension as described in **Chapter 4, Section 4:4**, and on the condition and tightness of the wiring connections. Keep the outside of the unit free from dirt, particularly around the ventilation holes in the cover.

The alternator must never be run with the battery disconnected, nor must the battery cables be reversed at any time. Test connections must be carefully made, and the battery and alternator must be completely disconnected before any electric welding is carried out on any part of the car. The engine must never be started with a battery charger still connected to the battery. These warnings must be observed, otherwise extensive damage to the alternator components, particularly the diodes, will result.

The alternator is designed and constructed to give many years of trouble-free service. If, however, a fault should develop in the unit, it should be checked and serviced by a fully equipped service station or a reconditioned unit obtained and fitted.

Alternator testing:

A simple check on alternator charging can be carried out after dark by switching on the headlamps and starting the engine. If the alternator is charging, the headlamps will brighten considerably as the system voltage rises from the nominal battery voltage to the higher figure produced by the alternator.

If the alternator is not charging, check the wiring and connections in the charging circuit. If these are in order, the alternator should be checked and repaired by a service station.

If the ignition warning light stays on when the engine is running, a simple electrical test is possible. Switch off the engine and pull the multiple plug from the regulator unit as shown in **FIG 12:1**. Use a suitable piece of wire to join the connectors for the blue wire and black wire as shown in **FIG 12:2**. Start the engine and run it at approximately 1000rev/min. If the ignition warning light goes out immediately, the regulator is defective and a new regulator should be fitted. If the ignition warning light glows or continues to burn brightly, there is a fault in the alternator, which should be checked and repaired by a service station.

Alternator removal:

Disconnect the battery negative cable, then refer to **FIG 12 : 3** and disconnect the multiple plug and the single cable from the rear of the alternator. Note that the brown wire goes to earth and the red wire to the B+ terminal. Slacken the alternator mounting bolts, swing the unit towards the engine to slacken the drive belt, then remove the belt. Unbolt and remove the alternator.

Refitting is a reversal of the removal procedure, adjusting the belt tension as described in **Chapter 4, Section 4 : 4**.

12 : 4 The starter motor

The starter is a brush type series wound motor equipped with an overrunning clutch and operated by a solenoid. The armature shaft is supported in metal bushes which require no routine servicing.

When the starter is operated from the switch, the engagement lever moves the pinion into mesh with the engine ring gear. When the pinion meshes with the ring gear teeth, the solenoid contact closes the circuit and the starter motor operates to turn the engine. When the engine starts, the speed of the rotating ring gear causes the pinion to overrun the clutch and armature. The pinion continues in engagement until the switch is released when the engagement lever returns it to the rest position under spring pressure.

Tests for a starter which does not operate:

Check that the battery is in good condition and fully charged and that its connections are clean and tight. Switch on the headlamps and operate the starter switch. Current is reaching the starter if the lights dim when the starter is operated, in which case it will be necessary to remove the starter for servicing. If the lights do not dim significantly, switch them off and operate the starter switch while listening for a clicking sound at the starter motor, which will indicate that the starter solenoid is operating.

If no sound can be heard at the starter when the switch is operated, check the wiring and connections between the battery and the starter switch and between the switch and the solenoid. If the solenoid can be heard operating when the starter switch is operated, check the wiring and connections between the battery and the main starter motor terminal, taking care not to accidentally earth the main battery to starter motor lead which is live at all times. If the wiring is not the cause of the trouble, the fault is internal and the starter motor must be removed and serviced.

Removing the starter:

Disconnect the battery earth cable, then disconnect the wiring from the starter motor as indicated by the arrows in **FIG 12 : 4**. Remove the fixing bolts then lift the starter motor from the engine.

Starter dismantling:

Disconnect the cable from the solenoid connection. Remove the fixing screws and detach the solenoid, unhooking the plunger from the engagement lever as shown in **FIG 12 : 5** Refer to **FIG 12 : 6** and detach the

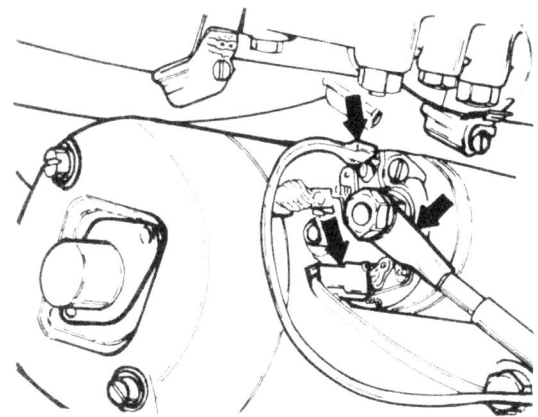

FIG 12 : 4   Starter motor wiring connections

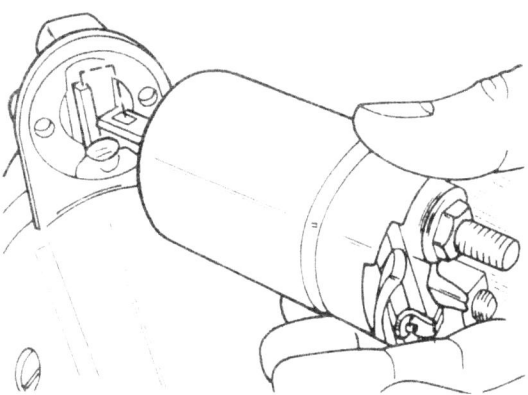

FIG 12 : 5   Solenoid removal

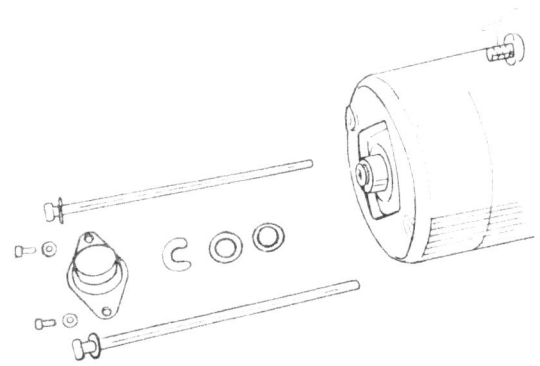

FIG 12 : 6   Removing end cap and through bolts

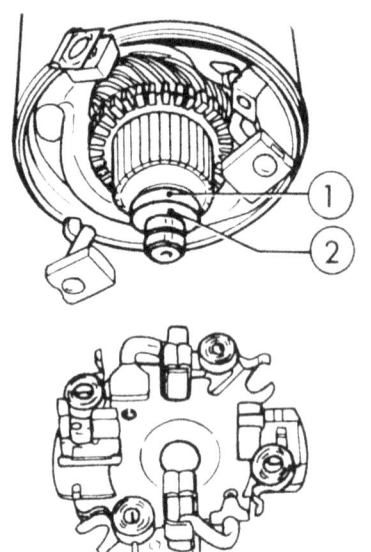

FIG 12:7   Removing brush holder assembly

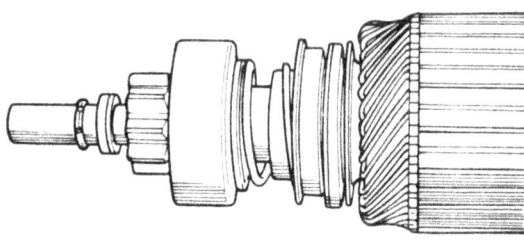

FIG 12:8   Drive pinion removal

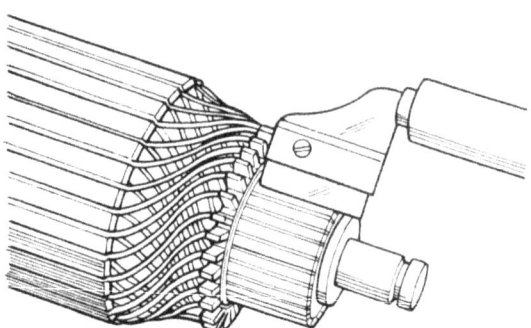

FIG 12:9   Undercutting commutator insulation

end cap. Remove the securing plate, shim and seal. Note that shim thickness should be modified if necessary during reassembly, to ensure an armature end play of 0.1 to 0.15mm (0.0039 to 0.0059in). Remove the two through bolts.

Pull back the springs and lift out the positive brushes, then detach the brush holder assembly as shown in **FIG 12:7**, noting washer 1 and insulating washer 2. Detach the starter body from the armature and drive end bracket assembly. Remove the engagement lever pivot bolt, then pull the armature and engagement lever from the drive end bracket.

To remove the drive pinion, refer to **FIG 12:8** and use a suitable piece of tube to drive the stop collar towards the gear, then remove the stop ring from the groove and pull off the collar and pinion assembly.

Starter motor servicing:

Cleaning:

Blow away all loose dust and dirt with an air line. Use a small brush to clean out crevices. Petrol or methylated spirits may be used to help in cleaning the metal parts, but the field coils, armature and drive pinion assembly must under no circumstances be soaked with solvent.

Brush gear:

Check the brushes for wear or contamination and renew if necessary. The old brushes should be unsoldered one at a time, then the new brushes soldered carefully into place. Grip the end of the flexible lead near to the joint when soldering to prevent solder from running down the lead.

Clean the brushes and brush holder assembly with a petrol moistened cloth and check that the brushes move freely in their holders. If a brush sticks in position, remove it and carefully ease the sides against a fine file. When installing the brushes to their holders, lift each brush and retain in the top of the holder by engaging the spring against the side of the brush. When the holder assembly has been refitted, push the brushes down into place and locate the springs correctly on top of each brush.

The commutator:

The commutator on which the carbon brushes operate should have a smooth polished surface which is dark in appearance. Wiping over with a piece of cloth moistened with methylated spirits or petrol is usually sufficient to clean the surface. Light burn marks or scores can be polished off with fine grade glasspaper (do not use emerycloth as this leaves particles embedded in the copper). Deeper damage may be skimmed off in a lathe, at high speed and using a very sharp tool. A diamond-tipped tool should be used for a light final cut. Note that the commutator must not be reduced below the minimum diameter of 33mm (1.3in). On completion, undercut the insulation between commutator segments as shown in **FIG 12:9**, using a special tool as illustrated or a suitable hacksaw blade ground to the thickness of the insulation. Undercut the insulation to a depth of 0.5mm (0.0197in) below the level of the segments. Finally, clean away all dust from the commutator.

The armature:

Check the armature for charred insulation, loose segments or laminations and for scored laminations. Shortcircuited windings may be suspected if individual commutator segments are badly burnt. If the armature is damaged in any way it should be renewed. If an electrical fault in the armature is suspected, have it tested on special equipment at a service station.

Field coils:

Test for insulation breakdown by connecting a 12-volt supply and test lamp between the terminal and starter body as shown in **FIG 12:10**. If the lamp lights it indicates a shortcircuit between the field coils and earth. Use the test lamp to check continuity by connecting the leads so that the coil windings are in series. If the lamp does not light there is a break in the field coil windings. Renewal of field coils should be carried out at a service station.

Drive pinion assembly:

The starter drive pinion and clutch assembly must not be washed in solvents as this would wash away the internal lubricant. Cleaning should be confined to wiping away dirt with a cloth. Light damage to the pinion teeth which engage the engine ring gear can be cleaned off with a fine file or oilstone, but deeper damage necessitates the renewal of the complete drive assembly. Check that the clutch takes up the drive instantaneously but slips freely in the opposite direction. The complete pinion and clutch assembly must be renewed if the clutch is defective.

Bearings:

The bearings in the drive end and commutator end brackets should be renewed if worn or damaged. If suitable mandrels and press equipment are not available, have the work carried out at a service station. Before installing a new bush, soak it for at least half-an-hour in engine oil, then shake off excess oil and press into position until flush with the housing. If the original bushes are in serviceable condition, lubricate them lightly with engine oil when reassembling the starter.

Solenoid:

No attempt should be made to service a faulty solenoid unit. Any mechanical or electrical faults will dictate renewal of the assembly. Check the engagement lever which moves the pinion into mesh with the engine ring gear and renew if worn or damaged.

Reassembly:

This is a reversal of the dismantling procedure. Lightly lubricate the engagement lever pivot bolt using an approved grade of grease. When reassembling the drive pinion assembly, tap the stop collar down the shaft past the groove, install the stop ring firmly in the groove, then force the stop collar over the stop ring to secure.

12:5 Fuses

The fuses which protect the main electrical circuits are mounted in a fuse box provided with a snap-on cover as shown in **FIG 12:11**.

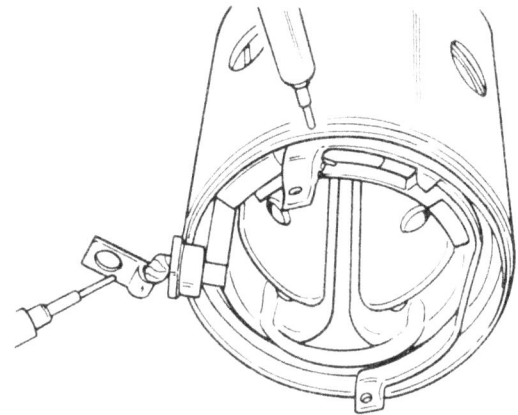

FIG 12:10   Field coil insulation test

FIG 12:11   The fuse box

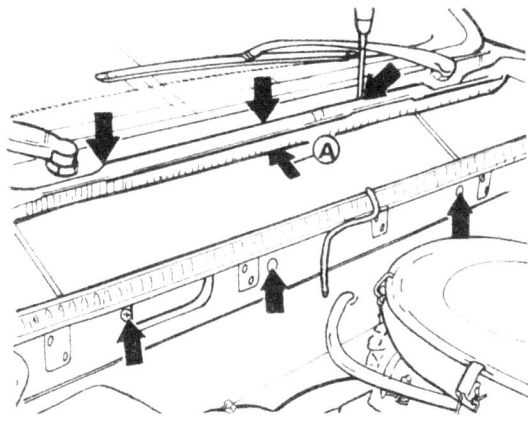

FIG 12:12   Heater coverplate removal

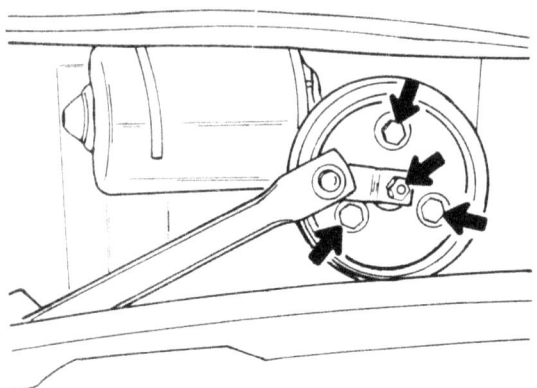

FIG 12:13 Wiper motor removal

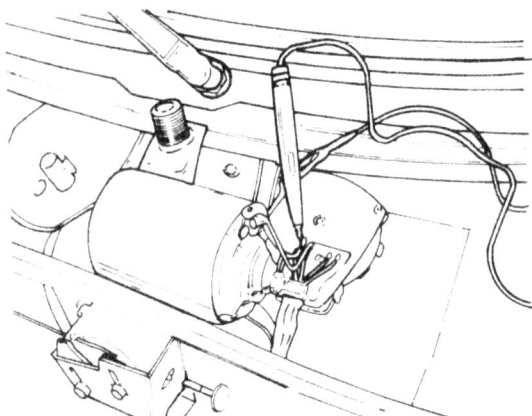

FIG 12:14 Checking current supply to wiper motor

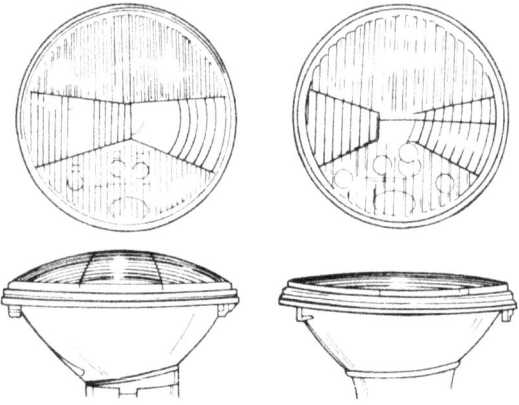

FIG 12:15 Early (left) and later (right) headlamp units

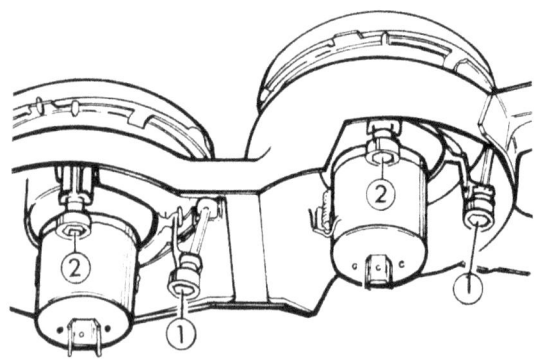

FIG 12:16 Headlamp beam setting screws

If a fuse blows, briefly check the circuit that it protects and install a new fuse. Check each circuit in turn and if the new fuse does not blow, it is possible that the old one had weakened with age. If the new fuse blows, carefully check the circuit that was live at the time and do not fit another fuse until the fault has been found and repaired. A fuse that blows intermittently will make it more difficult to correct the fault, but try shaking the wiring loom as the fault is likely to be caused by chafed insulation making intermittent contact.

Never fit a fuse of higher rating than that specified, and never use anything as a substitute for a fuse of the correct type. The fuse is designed to be the weak link in the circuit and if a higher rated fuse or an incorrect substitute is installed the wiring may fail instead, possibly causing a fire.

12:6 Windscreen wipers

Wiper motor removal:

Refer to **FIG 12:12** and remove the heater unit cover plate, noting the position of the special sealing strip **A** between cover plate and water drain gutter. Make sure that the wiper linkage is in the parked position. If the motor has failed with the wipers in any other position, move to the parked position by turning the motor crank. Refer to **FIG 12:13**. Remove the nut to detach the crank and remove the three screws to release the wiper motor from its mountings. Pull off the multiple plug and remove the wiper by tilting downwards.

If the motor is inoperative, check the current supply as shown in **FIG 12:14**. Reconnect the multiple plug to the motor, then switch on the ignition and wiper switches. Use a test lamp or voltmeter at terminal 53 (black/yellow and green cables) or 53b (black/white and red cables) to check if current is reaching the wiper motor. If the cables are live, the wiper motor must be internally defective.

Refit the wiper motor in the reverse order of removal. To ensure that the motor is in the parked position, temporarily connect the multiple plug then switch on the ignition and wiper switches. Allow the motor to run for a few seconds, then switch off at the wiper switch. The motor will then stop automatically in the parked position.

Wiper linkage removal:

To remove the wiper linkage and motor complete, first remove the heater unit cover plate as described previously. Remove the wiper arms by pulling the bosses from the splined shafts. If removal proves difficult, carefully lever the arms from the shafts by twisting the blade of a large screwdriver between the boss and the nut. Remove the nuts and washers securing the wiper arm shafts in position, then push the shafts through the mounting holes and detach the linkage assembly complete. Pull the multiple plug from the plug board and remove complete with rubber grommet. If necessary, press off the connecting link and drive rod and unscrew the wiper pivot bearings.

Refitting is a reversal of the removal procedure. Make sure that the motor and linkage are in the parked position, as described previously. Push the wiper arms on to the shafts so that the blades are approximately 1 to 2cm (0.4 to 0.8in) from the edge of the screen in the parked position.

12:7 Headlamps

Lamp unit removal:

The lamp units are of the sealed beam type and must be renewed complete if either of the filaments should fail. Remove the fixing screws and detach the ornamental grill from the front of the car. Remove the fixing screws and lift the headlamp unit from the housing, then disconnect the multiple plug from the rear of the unit. When installing, make sure that the headlamp unit is correctly located in the recesses provided in the housing frame.

Modifications:

Later models are fitted with an improved type of headlamp unit, having a flat lens instead of the earlier type of rounded lens, as shown in **FIG 12:15**. It is recommended that earlier models be fitted with this later type of headlamp unit, as it provides a beam of greater intensity and range.

Headlamp beam setting:

The headlamp main beams should be set so that, when the car is loaded with a weight of 70kg (155lb), or the weight of one person, in the centre of the rear seat, the main beams are parallel to each other and to the road. The dipped beams should provide a good spread of light to the front and nearside of the car without dazzling oncoming drivers. The tyres must be correctly inflated when checking beam settings.

The knurled headlamp beam adjustment screws are shown in **FIG 12:16**, horizontal adjustment being carried out at screws 1 and vertical adjustment at screws 2. The screws are accessible from the inside of the engine compartment. It is recommended that headlamp beam setting be carried out at a service station having special optical equipment, this method giving the most accurate results.

12:8 Fault diagnosis

(a) Battery discharged

1 Terminal connections loose or dirty
2 Shorts in lighting circuits
3 Alternator not charging
4 Regulator faulty
5 Battery internally defective

(b) Insufficient charge rate

1 Check 1 and 4 in (a)
2 Drive belt slipping
3 Alternator defective

(c) Battery will not hold charge

1 Low electrolyte level
2 Battery plates sulphated
3 Electrolyte leakage from cracked case
4 Battery internally defective

(d) Battery overcharged

1 Regulator faulty

(e) Alternator output low or nil

1 Drive belt broken or slipping
2 Regulator faulty
3 Brushes sticking, springs weak or broken
4 Faulty internal windings
5 Defective diode(s)

(f) Starter motor lacks power or will not turn

1 Battery discharged, loose cable connections
2 Starter switch or solenoid faulty
3 Brushes worn or sticking, leads detached or shorting
4 Commutator dirty or worn
5 Starter shaft bent
6 Engine abnormally stiff

(g) Starter runs but does not turn engine

1 Pinion engagement mechanism faulty
2 Broken teeth on pinion or engine ring gear

(h) Starter motor rough or noisy

1 Mounting bolts loose
2 Pinion engagement mechanism faulty
3 Damaged pinion or engine ring gear teeth

(j) Noisy starter when engine is running

1 Pinion return mechanism faulty
2 Mounting bolts loose

(k) Starter motor inoperative

1 Check 1 and 3 in (f)
2 Armature or field coils faulty

(l) Lamps inoperative or erratic

1 Battery low, bulbs burned out
2 Faulty earthing of lamps or battery
3 Lighting switch faulty, loose or broken connections

(m) Wiper motor sluggish, taking high current

1 Wiper motor internally defective
2 Wiper motor fixings loose
3 Linkage worn or binding

NOTES

CHAPTER 13

THE BODYWORK

13:1 Bodywork finish

Large scale repairs to body panels are best left to expert panel beaters. Even small dents can be tricky, as too much hammering will stretch the metal and make things worse instead of better. If panel beating is to be attempted, use a dolly on the opposite side of the panel. The head of a large hammer will suffice for small dents, but for large dents a heavy block of metal will be necessary. Use light hammer blows to reshape the panel, pressing the dolly against the opposite side of the panel to absorb the blows. If this method is used to reduce the depth of dents, final smoothing with a suitable filler will be easier, although it may be better to avoid hammering minor dents and just use the filler.

Clean the area to be filled, making sure that it is free from paint, rust and grease, then roughen the area with emerycloth or a file to ensure a good bond. Use a proprietary fibre glass filler paste mixed according to the instructions and press it into the dent with a putty knife. Allow the filler to stand proud of the surrounding area to allow for rubbing down after hardening. Use a file and emerycloth or a disc sander to blend the repaired area to the surrounding bodywork, using finer grade abrasives as the work nears completion. Apply a coat of primer surfacer and, when it is dry, rub down with 'Wet-or-Dry' paper lubricated with soapy water, finishing with 400 grade. Apply more primer and repeat the operation until the surface is perfectly smooth. Take time in achieving the best finish possible at this stage as it will control the final effect.

The touching-up of paintwork can be carried out with self-spraying cans of paint, these being available in a wide range of colours. Use a piece of newspaper or board as a test panel to practice on first, so that the action of the spray will be familiar when it is used on the panel. Before spraying the panel, remove all traces of wax polish. Mask off large areas such as windows with newspaper and masking tape. Small areas such as trim strips or door handles can be wrapped with masking tape or carefully coated with grease or petroleum jelly. Apply the touching-up paint, spraying with short bursts and keeping the spray moving. Do not attempt to cover the area in one coat, applying several successive coats with a few minutes drying time between each. If too much paint is applied at one time, runs will develop. If so, do not try to remove the run by wiping but wait until it is dry and rub down as before.

After the final coat has been applied, allow a few hours of drying time before blending the new finish to the old with fine cutting compound and a cloth, buffing

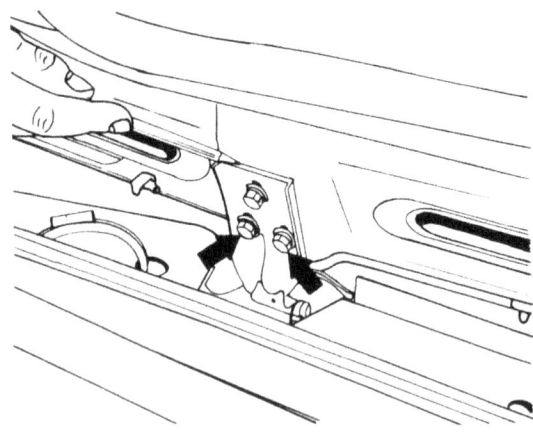

FIG 13:1   Bonnet hinge details

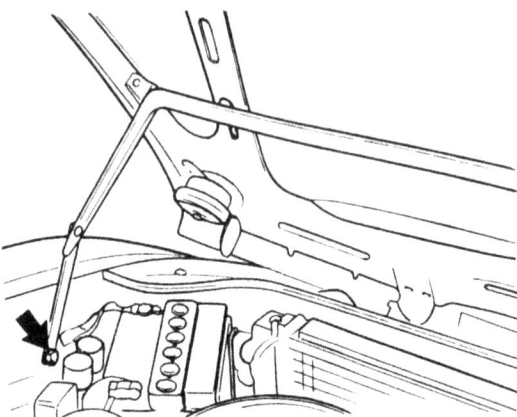

FIG 13:2   Bonnet support arm fixing

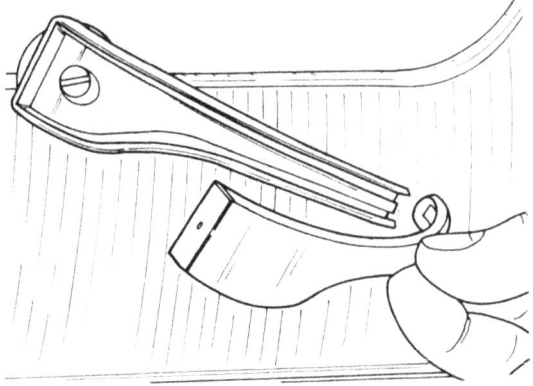

FIG 13:3   Removing inside door handle

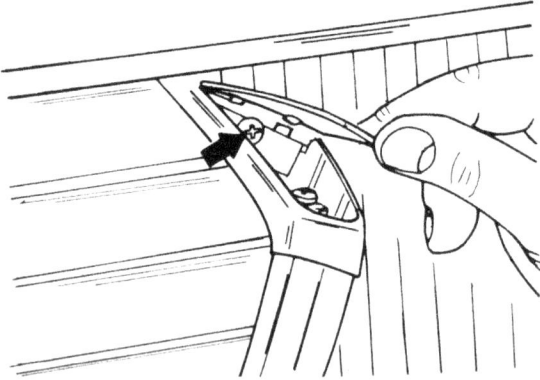

FIG 13:4   Removing front door armrest

with a light circular motion. Leave the paint to harden for a period of weeks rather than days before applying wax polish.

13:2 The bonnet
Bonnet removal:

Open the bonnet fully, then detach the horn wiring from the clips on the bonnet panel and detach the wiring connector from the horn. Refer to **FIG 13:1** and scribe round the outline of the hinge plates so that the bonnet panel can be refitted in its original position. Remove the two lower bolts which are arrowed and slacken the third upper bolt. Have an assistant steady the bonnet panel, then remove the bolts securing the support arms on each side as shown in **FIG 13:2**. Remove the remaining hinge mounting bolt and carefully lift off the bonnet panel.

Refitting is a reversal of the removal procedure, carefully aligning the hinges with the scribe marks on the panel.

Bonnet alignment:

If the bonnet panel does not fit correctly in the body aperture, scribe round the hinge plates as shown in **FIG 13:1** so that the amount of adjustment can be assessed, then slacken the hinge mounting bolts and move the panel within the limits allowed by the slotted mounting holes. Tighten the bolts and recheck alignment.

13:3 Door components
Removing trim panel:

Remove the lock knob, which is threaded on to the lock rod. Press the inside door handle trim down at the rear and lift out at the front, as shown in **FIG 13:3**. Remove the single screw and detach the handle. Remove the armrest on front doors by lifting the cover plate as shown in **FIG 13:4**, then removing the single screw arrowed and the remaining three lower screws. On rear doors, remove the armrest by pressing together the upper and lower ends of the trim pad as shown in **FIG 13:5**, then removing the two lower fixing screws. Remove the regulator handle by pulling out the trim, then removing the single screw. Collect the thrust washer.

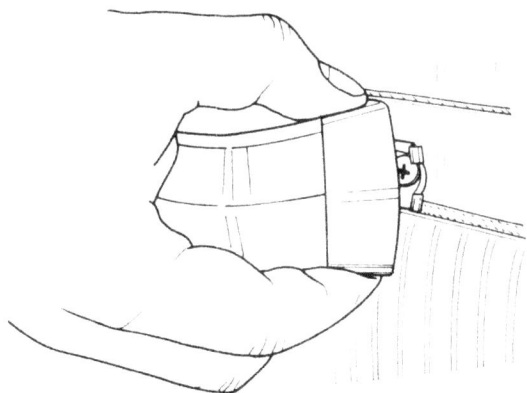

FIG 13:5 Removing rear door armrest

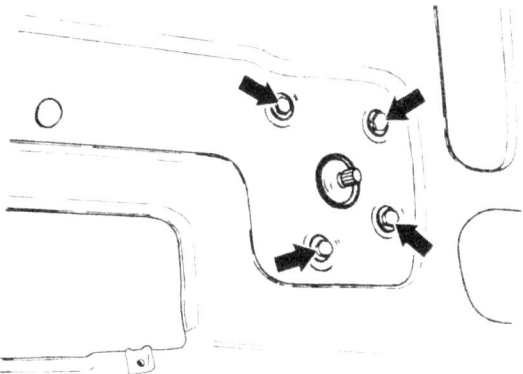

FIG 13:6 Regulator fixing screws, front door shown

Lift out the front and rear window aperture corner seals, then remove the two fixing screws which secure the upper part of the trim panel to the door frame. Carefully pull the trim panel away from the door to release the spring clips. If access to door internal components is required, carefully pull the plastic sealing sheet from the door panel. Always renew the sealing sheet if it is damaged in any way.

Refitting:

This is a reversal of the removal procedure. The plastic sealing sheet should be attached to the door panel using Terokal 2012 adhesive or similar, carefully smoothing the sheet into place to ensure an effective seal against water leakage. When installing the trim panel, note that the larger diameter of conical spring for regulator handle must face the trim panel.

Removing regulator mechanism:

Remove the trim panel as described previously. Make sure that the window is fully closed, then refer to **FIG 13:6** and remove the four screws on front door or three screws on rear door to detach regulator mechanism.

Use a wedge or other suitable means to hold the glass firmly in the closed position, then move the regulator arm to the open end of the slot to detach from the lift rail, as shown in **FIG 13:7**. Note that the plastic washers 1 must locate on each side of the lift rail when the regulator mechanism is installed.

Refitting is a reversal of the removal procedure. Lubricate toothed segment on regulator mechanism using multi-purpose grease.

Front door glass removal:

Remove the trim panel as described previously. Refer to **FIG 13:8** and lift out the cover clips at front and rear of window frame. Beginning at the rear, loosen the window aperture trim strip by light blows against a suitable hardwood wedge, then remove the trim strip. Refer to **FIG 13:9** and remove the window lift rail holder. Lower the glass by approximately 17cm (7in), then tilt forwards and detach the lift arm from the lift rail as shown in **FIG 13:7**. Carefully remove the glass from the door panel.

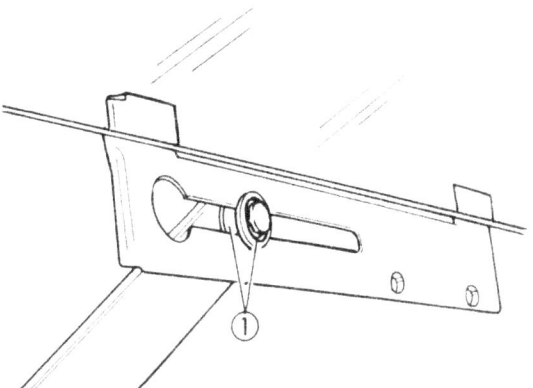

FIG 13:7 Window lift rail, front door shown

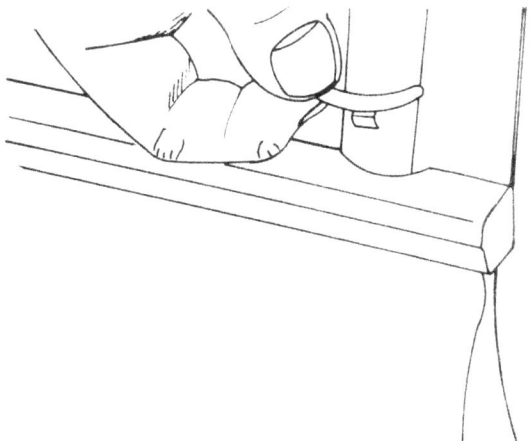

FIG 13:8 Window aperture trim clip

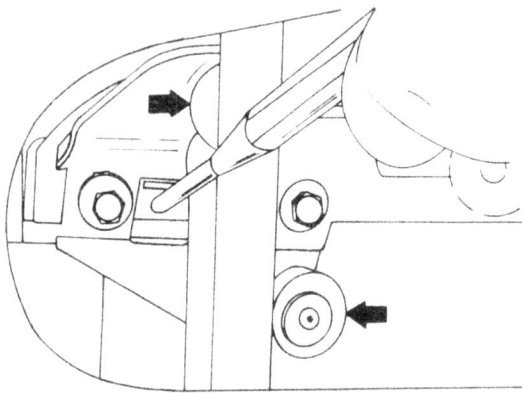

FIG 13:9   Window lift rail holder

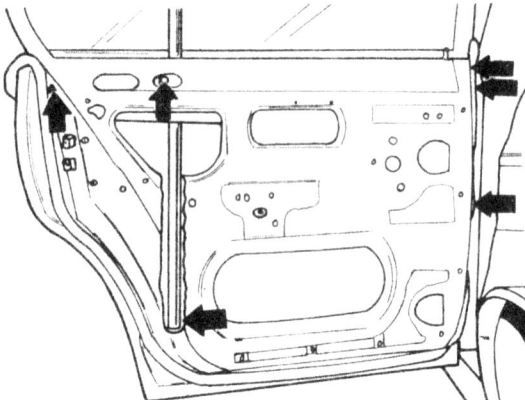

FIG 13:10   Rear door window frame securing screws

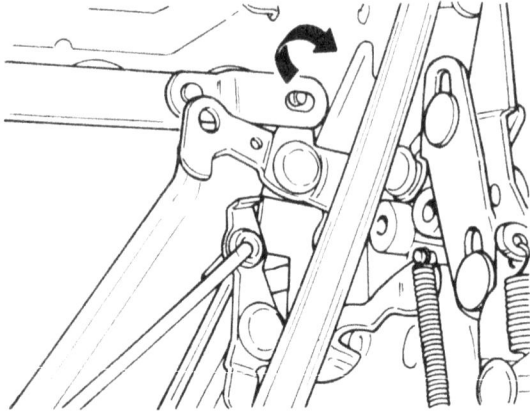

FIG 13:11   Rear door lock connecting rod

Refitting:

This is a reversal of the removal procedure. Before tightening the lift rail holder attachments, move the guide rail to align the door window with the frame. When tightening the lift rail holder fixings, press the holder upwards as shown in **FIG 13:9** so that the guide rollers are pressed against the guide rail as indicated by the arrows. Note that the plastic washers shown at 1 in **FIG 13:7** must run on each side of the lift rail.

Rear door glass removal:

Remove the trim panel as described previously. Remove the outer window aperture trim strip in the manner previously described for front door components. Lift out the short inner window aperture seal, then pull the door sealing rubber away from the window frame. Remove the fixing screws arrowed in **FIG 13:10**, then lower the window glass fully and pull out the complete window frame. Detach the lift arm from the lift rail in the manner shown in **FIG 13:7**, then carefully lift out the glass.

Refitting:

This is a reversal of the removal procedure. Note that the plastic washers shown at 1 in **FIG 13:7** must run on each side of the lift rail. Before fully tightening the window frame securing screws shown in **FIG 13:10**, check that the window can be raised and lowered smoothly. If necessary, lower the glass and adjust the position of the window frame then tighten the screws and raise the glass to recheck. Always adjust window frame position with the glass lowered.

Front door lock removal:

Remove the door trim panel as described previously, then lower the window fully. Remove the fixing screws and detach the inner window aperture trim strip. Partly pull away the rubber seal from the window frame and door then remove the Allen screw securing the upper front of the window frame, working through the access hole provided. Pull the rubber seal away from the door at the rear, then take out the upper and lower sealing plugs and remove the bolts exposed. Remove the upper and lower door window frame retaining screws through the apertures in the door panel, then lift out the window frame trim clips as shown in **FIG 13:8**. Pull out the window frame assembly.

Remove the three fixing bolts located around the inner door handle shaft to release the remote control mechanism from the panel. Remove the guide buffer from the edge of the door, collecting the spacing rollers. Remove the four cross-headed screws securing the lock mechanism to the door panel, then remove the lock in the closed position complete with remote operating mechanism.

Refitting is a reversal of the removal procedure. Make sure that the spacing rollers are inserted into the guide buffer. Install the window frame assembly loosely at first, then check that the window glass raises and lowers fully and fits accurately in the frame. If necessary, lower the glass and adjust the frame position, then raise the glass and recheck. Always carry out adjustments with the glass lowered. Fully tighten the frame fixings on completion.

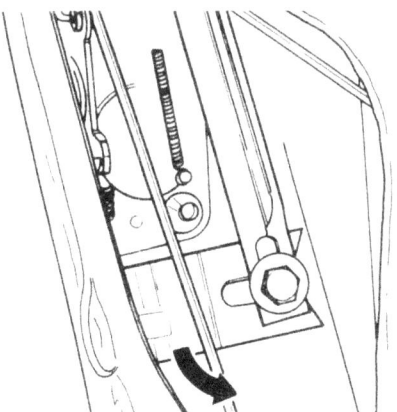

FIG 13:12 Rear door window frame front support bracket

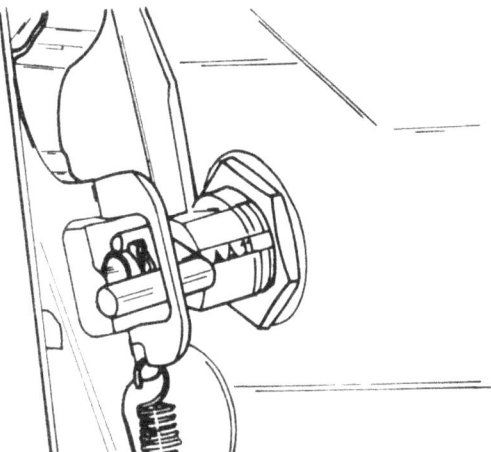

FIG 13:13 Front door lock barrel removal

Rear door lock removal:

Remove the trim panel as described previously. Remove the three screws located around the inner door handle shaft to release the remote control mechanism. Refer to **FIG 13:11** and detach the connecting rod at the door lock. Unscrew the front support bracket for the window frame as shown in **FIG 13:12**, then swing the bracket inwards. Remove the guide buffer from the edge of the door, collecting the spacing rollers. Remove the three cross-headed screws securing the lock to the door panel, then remove the lock complete with remote operating mechanism in the closed position.

Refitting is a reversal of the removal procedure. Note that the child-proof locking mechanism lever on the door lock assembly must be in the upper (open) position when installing the assembly. Make sure that the spacing rollers are correctly inserted into the guide buffer.

Outside door handle removal:

To remove the outside handle on front or rear door, pull the handle outwards and take out the two screws to release the handle from the operating levers. To remove the inner mechanism, detach the trim panel as described previously then remove the two fixing screws securing the assembly to the door panel.

Refitting is a reversal of the removal procedure, making sure that the outer handle rests against the rubber buffers provided when it is in the closed position.

Front door lock barrel removal:

Remove the trim panel as described previously. Refer to **FIG 13:13** and remove the nut from the inside of the lock barrel. Extract the lock barrel towards the outside. Do not attempt to dismantle the lock barrel. The key number is stamped on the side of the barrel.

Refitting is a reversal of the removal procedure.

13:4 Heating and air conditioning

Heater blower motor removal:

Remove the heater motor cover plate as described in **Chapter 12, Section 12:6** Lift out the mesh grid fitted over the heater blower assembly, then pull off the cable connectors. Remove the screws securing the

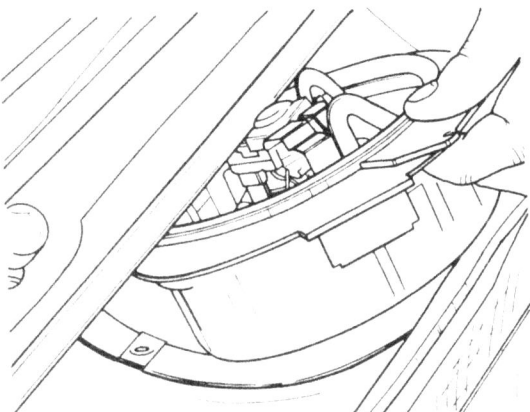

FIG 13:14 Removing heater blower motor assembly

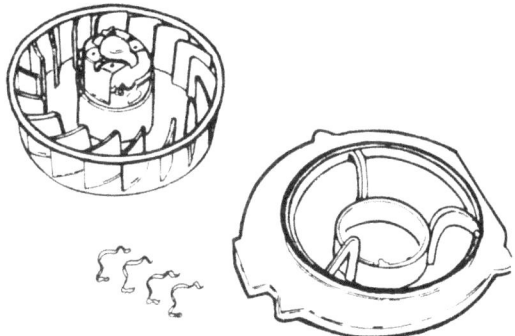

FIG 13:15 Blower unit and mounting

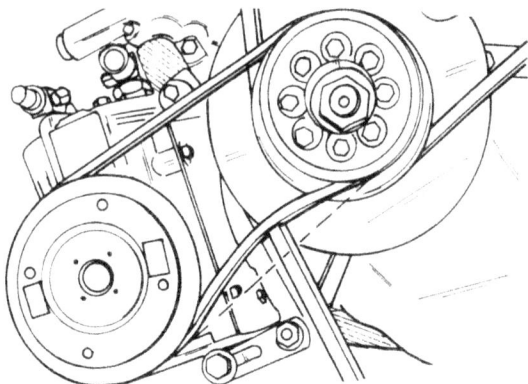

FIG 13:16   Checking compressor drive belt tension

motor mounting to the housing and pull the unit out diagonally upwards, as shown in **FIG 13:14**. Release the retaining clips, then pull the motor from its mounting as shown in **FIG 13:15**.

Do not attempt to separate the blower from the motor shaft as these components are balanced as a matched assembly. If the motor unit is faulty the motor and blower unit must be renewed complete.

Refitting:

This is a reversal of the removal procedure. When installing the motor assembly to the mounting, the shorter ends of the clips should be pressed over the motor mounting.

Air conditioning system:

Owners of vehicles fitted with air conditioning (refrigeration) systems should not attempt to remove or dismantle any of the related components due to the possibility of refrigerant leakage. If the pressurised system is opened, liquid refrigerant will escape, immediately evaporating and instantly freezing anything it contacts. Uncontrolled release of the refrigerant will cause frostbite or possibly more serious injury if it contacts any part of the body. For this reason, all work involving removal of air conditioning system components or opening of the pressurised system should be entrusted only to a BMW service station having the necessary special equipment and trained personnel.

Compressor drive belt tensioning:

The tension is correct when the belt can be deflected by 5 to 10mm (0.2 to 0.4in) when firmly pressed at the centre points between the pulleys as shown in **FIG 13:16**. To adjust the tension, slacken the upper bolt on the compressor swivel plate and the lower bolt in the slotted mounting link. Pull the compressor unit away from the engine until the tension is correct, then hold in position while tightening the mounting bolts. Recheck the tension. To remove the belt, slacken the bolts as described previously, then push the compressor towards the engine until the belt can be removed over the pulleys. Refit in the reverse order, correctly tensioning the belt as described previously.

APPENDIX

TECHNICAL DATA

Engine   Fuel system   Ignition system   Cooling system
Clutch   Manual transmission   Automatic transmission
Rear suspension   Front suspension   Steering   Brakes
Electrical equipment   Capacities   Torque wrench settings
Wiring diagrams

HINTS ON MAINTENANCE AND OVERHAUL

GLOSSARY OF TERMS

INDEX

Inches	Decimals	Milli metres	Inches to Millimetres Inches	mm	Millimetres to Inches mm	Inches
1/64	.015625	.3969	.001	.0254	.01	.00039
1/32	.03125	.7937	.002	.0508	.02	.00079
3/64	.046875	1.1906	.003	.0762	.03	.00118
1/16	.0625	1.5875	.004	.1016	.04	.00157
5/64	.078125	1.9844	.005	.1270	.05	.00197
3/32	.09375	2.3812	.006	.1524	.06	.00236
7/64	.109375	2.7781	.007	.1778	.07	.00276
1/8	.125	3.1750	.008	.2032	.08	.00315
9/64	.140625	3.5719	.009	.2286	.09	.00354
5/32	.15625	3.9687	.01	.254	.1	.00394
11/64	.171875	4.3656	.02	.508	.2	.00787
3/16	.1875	4.7625	.03	.762	.3	.01181
13/64	.203125	5.1594	.04	1.016	.4	.01575
7/32	.21875	5.5562	.05	1.270	.5	.01969
15/64	.234375	5.9531	.06	1.524	.6	.02362
1/4	.25	6.3500	.07	1.778	.7	.02756
17/64	.265625	6.7469	.08	2.032	.8	.03150
9/32	.28125	7.1437	.09	2.286	.9	.03543
19/64	.296875	7.5406	1	2.54	1	.03937
5/16	.3125	7.9375	2	5.08	2	.07874
21/64	.328125	8.3344	3	7.62	3	.11811
11/32	.34375	8.7312	4	10.16	4	.15748
23/64	.359375	9.1281	5	12.70	5	.19685
3/8	.375	9.5250	6	15.24	6	.23622
25/64	.390625	9.9219	7	17.78	7	.27559
13/32	.40625	10.3187	8	20.32	8	.31496
27/64	.421875	10.7156	9	22.86	9	.35433
7/16	.4375	11.1125	1	25.4	10	.39370
29/64	.453125	11.5094	2	50.8	11	.43307
15/32	.46875	11.9062	3	76.2	12	.47244
31/64	.484375	12.3031	4	101.6	13	.51181
1/2	.5	12.7000	5	127.0	14	.55118
33/64	.515625	13.0969	6	152.4	15	.59055
17/32	.53125	13.4937	7	177.8	16	.62992
35/64	.546875	13.8906	8	203.2	17	.66929
9/16	.5625	14.2875	9	228.6	18	.70866
37/64	.578125	14.6844	10	254.0	19	.74803
19/32	.59375	15.0812	11	279.4	20	.78740
39/64	.609375	15.4781	12	304.8	21	.82677
5/8	.625	15.8750	13	330.2	22	.86614
41/64	.640625	16.2719	14	355.6	23	.90551
21/32	.65625	16.6687	15	381.0	24	.94488
43/64	.671875	17.0656	16	406.4	25	.98425
11/16	.6875	17.4625	17	431.8	26	1.02362
45/64	.703125	17.8594	18	457.2	27	1.06299
23/32	.71875	18.2562	19	482.6	28	1.10236
47/64	.734375	18.6531	20	508.0	29	1.14173
3/4	.75	19.0500	21	533.4	30	1.18110
49/64	.765625	19.4469	22	558.8	31	1.22047
25/32	.78125	19.8437	23	584.2	32	1.25984
51/64	.796875	20.2406	24	609.6	33	1.29921
13/16	.8125	20.6375	25	635.0	34	1.33858
53/64	.828125	21.0344	26	660.4	35	1.37795
27/32	.84375	21.4312	27	685.8	36	1.41732
55/64	.859375	21.8281	28	711.2	37	1.4567
7/8	.875	22.2250	29	736.6	38	1.4961
57/64	.890625	22.6219	30	762.0	39	1.5354
29/32	.90625	23.0187	31	787.4	40	1.5748
59/64	.921875	23.4156	32	812.8	41	1.6142
15/16	.9375	23.8125	33	838.2	42	1.6535
61/64	.953125	24.2094	34	863.6	43	1.6929
31/32	.96875	24.6062	35	889.0	44	1.7323
63/64	.984375	25.0031	36	914.4	45	1.7717

UNITS	Pints to Litres	Gallons to Litres	Litres to Pints	Litres to Gallons	Miles to Kilometres	Kilometres to Miles	Lbs per sq In to Kg per sq Cm	Kg per sq Cm to Lbs per sq In
1	.57	4.55	1.76	.22	1.61	.62	.07	14.22
2	1.14	9.09	3.52	.44	3.22	1.24	.14	28.50
3	1.70	13.64	5.28	.66	4.83	1.86	.21	42.67
4	2.27	18.18	7.04	.88	6.44	2.49	.28	56.89
5	2.84	22.73	8.80	1.10	8.05	3.11	.35	71.12
6	3.41	27.28	10.56	1.32	9.66	3.73	.42	85.34
7	3.98	31.82	12.32	1.54	11.27	4.35	.49	99.56
8	4.55	36.37	14.08	1.76	12.88	4.97	.56	113.79
9		40.91	15.84	1.98	14.48	5.59	.63	128.00
10		45.46	17.60	2.20	16.09	6.21	.70	142.23
20				4.40	32.19	12.43	1.41	284.47
30				6.60	48.28	18.64	2.11	426.70
40				8.80	64.37	24.85		
50					80.47	31.07		
60					96.56	37.28		
70					112.65	43.50		
80					128.75	49.71		
90					144.84	55.92		
100					160.93	62.14		

UNITS	Lb ft to kgm	Kgm to lb ft	UNITS	Lb ft to kgm	Kgm to lb ft
1	.138	7.233	7	.967	50.631
2	.276	14.466	8	1.106	57.864
3	.414	21.699	9	1.244	65.097
4	.553	28.932	10	1.382	72.330
5	.691	36.165	20	2.765	144.660
6	.829	43.398	30	4.147	216.990

TECHNICAL DATA

Dimensions are in millimetres with inches equivalents in brackets unless otherwise stated

ENGINE

Bore and stroke:

2500	86 (3.386) × 71.6 (2.819)
2800	86 (3.386) × 80 (3.150)
3.0	89 (3.504) × 80 (3.150)
3.0 CSL	89.25 (3.514) × 80 (3.150)
3.0 CSL (3.15 litres)	89.25 (3.514) × 84 (3.307)
3.3 to late 1975	89 (3.504) × 88.4 (3.480)
3.3 from late 1975	89 (3.504) × 86 (3.386)

Capacity:

2500	2495cc (152.25cu in)
2800	2788cc (170.13cu in)
3.0	2985cc (182.16cu in)
3.0 CSL	3003cc (183.25cu in)
3.0 CSL (3.15 litres)	3153cc (192.41cu in)
3.3 to late 1975	3299cc (201.32cu in)
3.3 from late 1975	3210cc (195.88cu in)

Compression ratio:

SI models and 3.15 litres	9.5:1
Remainder	9:1

Crankshaft:

Main journal diameter:	
Red	59.990 to 59.970 (2.3618 to 2.3610)
Blue	59.970 to 59.971 (2.3610 to 2.3611)
Regrind stages	0.25 (0.0098), 0.50 (0.0197), 0.75 (0.0295)
Main bearing clearance	0.030 to 0.070 (0.0012 to 0.0028)
Crankpin diameter	47.991 to 47.996 (1.8894 to 1.8884)
Regrind stages	0.25 (0.0098), 0.50 (0.0197), 0.75 (0.0295)
End float	0.085 to 0.174 (0.0035 to 0.0068)
Maximum run-out at centre main journal	0.10 (0.004)

Connecting rods:

Length	135 ± 0.10 (5.315 ± 0.004)
Maximum weight variation	± 4gr (± 0.141oz)
Big-end clearance	0.023 to 0.069 (0.0009 to 0.0027)

Cylinder bore:

Maximum ovality	0.01 (0.0004)
Maximum taper	0.01 (0.0004)

Pistons:

Clearance in bore	0.045 (0.0018)
Maximum weight variation	10gr (0.35oz)

Piston rings:

Top:	
Thickness	1.740 to 1.728 (0.0685 to 0.0680)
Gap	0.30 to 0.50 (0.012 to 0.020)
Groove clearance	0.060 to 0.082 (0.0024 to 0.0032)
Middle:	
Thickness	1.990 to 1.978 (0.0783 to 0.0778)
Gap:	
2500 and 2800	0.30 to 0.45 (0.012 to 0.018)
Remainder	0.20 to 0.40 (0.008 to 0.016)
Groove clearance	0.030 to 0.062 (0.0012 to 0.0024)

Bottom:
    Thickness .. .. 3.990 to 3.978 (0.1571 to 0.1566)
    Gap .. .. 0.25 to 0.40 (0.010 to 0.016)
    Groove clearance .. .. 0.030 to 0.062 (0.0012 to 0.0024)

Gudgeon pins:
Diameter:
    White 21.998 (0.8661)
    Black .. .. 21.997 to 21.994 (0.8660 to 0.8659)
Small-end bush internal diameter:
    Pin stamped 'W' .. .. .. 22.003 to 22.005 (0.8663 to 0.8664)
    Pin stamped 'S' .. .. .. 22.001 to 22.003 (0.8662 to 0.8663)
    Clearance in piston .. .. .. 0.001 to 0.005 (0.00004 to 0.0002)
Clearance in small-end:
    White .. .. 0.005 to 0.013 (0.0002 to 0.0005)
    Black .. .. 0.008 to 0.016 (0.00032 to 0.00063)

Valves:
Inlet:
    Length .. .. 106.5 ± 0.2 (4.193 ± 0.008)
    Head diameter .. .. 46.00 to 45.84 (1.811 to 1.805)
    Stem diameter .. .. .. 7.975 to 7.960 (0.3140 to 0.3134)
    Minimum rim thickness 1.2 (0.047)
    Seat angle .. .. .. 45° ± 20'
    Maximum head run-out 0.02 (0.0008)
Exhaust:
    Length .. .. 107.2 ± 0.2 (4.221 ± 0.008)
    Head diameter .. .. 38.00 to 37.98 (1.4960 to 1.4952)
    Stem diameter .. .. 7.960 to 7.945 (0.3133 to 0.3130)
    Minimum rim thickness 1.9 (0.075)
    Seat angle .. .. .. 45° ± 20'
    Maximum head run-out 0.02 (0.0008)

Valve clearance:
Below 35°C .. .. .. 0.25 to 0.30 (0.010 to 0.012)
Normal operating temperature .. .. 0.30 to 0.35 (0.012 to 0.014)

Valve guides:
Length 52 (2.047)
Internal diameter .. .. 8.000 to 8.015 (0.3150 to 0.3156)
Projection in cylinder head .. .. 15.0 to 14.5 (0.591 to 0.571)

Valve clearance in guide:
Inlet .. .. 0.025 to 0.055 (0.001 to 0.002)
Exhaust .. .. 0.040 to 0.070 (0.0016 to 0.0028)
Maximum wear 0.15 (0.006)

Valve springs:
Free length 43.5 (1.713)

Rockers and shafts:
Shaft clearance in head .. .. .. 0.016 to 0.061 (0.0006 to 0.0024)
Rocker clearance on shaft .. .. 0.016 to 0.052 (0.0006 to 0.0021)

Camshaft:
Clearance in bearings .. .. .. 0.034 to 0.075 (0.0014 to 0.0030)
End float .. .. 0.03 to 0.18 (0.0012 to 0.0071)

Chain tensioner:
Free length of spring 155.5 (6.122)

Flywheel:
Maximum run-out at 92mm (3.62in) diameter .. 0.03 (0.0012)
Clutch contact face maximum machining .. 0.4 to 0.5 (0.016 to 0.020)
Contact face minimum thickness 13.5 (0.53)

Vibration damper:
Maximum radial run-out 0.2 (0.008)

Maximum axial run-out at 210mm (8.27in)
  diameter 0.4 (0.016)
Lubrication:
  Oil pressure at idle .. .. 1.8 to 2.0 bar (25.6 to 28.5lb/sq in)
  Oil pressure at maximum speed .. .. .. Approximately 5 bar (71lb/sq in)
  Pressure relief valve opens .. .. .. 4 to 5 bar (57 to 71lb/sq in)
  Relief valve spring free length 68 (2.68)
  Oil pressure warning light .. .. .. 0.05 to 0.15 bar (0.7 to 2.1lb/sq in)
Oil pump clearances:
  Rotor to housing .. .. 0.1 ± 0.025 (0.004 ± 0.001)
  Rotor end float .. .. 0.050 to 0.091 (0.0010 to 0.0036)
  Internal to external rotor .. .. .. 0.12 to 0.30 (0.005 to 0.012)

FUEL SYSTEM

Fuel pump:
  Pressure at 4000rev/min .. .. 0.21 to 0.25 bar (3.0 to 3.5lb/sq in)
  Pump plunger length .. .. 107.2 ± 0.1 (4.220 ± 0.004)
  Flange with gasket 20 (0.79)
Carburetters:

Zenith 32/40 INAT:

	Primary	*Secondary*
Air venturi	24	30
Main jet	115	130
Air correction jet	80	120
Diffuser	4S	11N
Idle jet	47.5	
Idle air jet	120	
Additional fuel jet	40	
Additional fuel air jet	80	
Additional fuel mixture jet	40	
Needle valve	2.0	
Needle valve sealing ring	1.0 (0.04)	
Float weight	8.5gr (0.3oz)	
Injection quantity per stroke	0.6 to 0.9cc	
Thermostart:		
Fuel jet	45	
Air jet	80	
Idle speed	850 to 950rev/min	
CO content at idle	1.5 to 2.0%	

Zenith 35/40 INAT: As Zenith 32/40 INAT except

	Primary	*Secondary*
Main jet	117.5	145
Air correction jet	100	100
Diffuser	6S	4N
Idle jet, 2800 models	45	
3.3 models	42.5	
Additional fuel mixture jet, 3.0 and 3.3 models	45	
Choke plate opening, 2500 and 2500A	2.8 ± 0.1 (0.11 ± 0.004)	
other models	3.0 ± 0.1 (0.12 ± 0.004)	
CO content at idle, 2800 and 3.0 models	3 to 4%	

Zenith 35/40 INAT (USA versions):
          As Zenith 35/40 INAT except:

	Primary	*Secondary*
Main jet:		
2500 and 2800 models	×115	×140
3.0 models	×117.5	×145

Air corrector jet:
   3.0 models, manual   80   80
                        automatic   100   100
Idle jet:
   2500 and 2800 models 42.5
Diffuser:
   3.0 models 10S

IGNITION SYSTEM

Coil:
   Type   ..   ..   Bosch KW 12V
Spark plugs:
   Type   ..   ..   Bosch W175 T 30
                                                Beru 175/14/3A
                                              Champion N 9 Y
   Gap   ..   ..   0.6 to 0.7 (0.024 to 0.028)
Firing order   1–5–3–6–2–4
Distributor:
   Governor operation, engine speed:
      3.3 LA   ..   ..   6350 ± 150rev/min
      All other models   ..   ..   ..   6600 ± 150rev/min
   Static timing   ..   ..   TDC
   Stroboscopic timing, vacuum disconnected:
      Distributor 0231 306 001   ..   ..   22° BTDC at 2500rev/min
      Other models   ..   ..   ..   22° BTDC at 1700rev/min
   Contact breaker points gap   ..   ..   0.35 to 0.40 (0.014 to 0.016)
   Spring pressure   ..   ..   ..   450 to 500gr (15.9 to 17.6oz)
   Dwell angle:
      Degrees   ..   ..   35 to 41
      Per cent   ..   ..   58 to 60

COOLING SYSTEM

Radiator:
   Filler cap:
      Pressure   ..   ..   1.15 to 0.90 (16.33 to 12.78lb/sq in)
      Suction   ..   ..   0.1 bar (1.42lb/sq in)
   Test pressure   ..   ..   1.5 bar (21.3lb/sq in)
Water pump:
   Impeller to housing clearance   ..   ..   0.9 ± 0.2 (0.0354 ± 0.008)
Thermostat:
   Opening commences:
      Manual transmission   ..   ..   84°C
      Automatic transmission   ..   ..   80°C
Fan coupling:
   Cut-in temperature   ..   ..   ..   55° ± 2.5°C

CLUTCH

Clutch disc:
   Minimum thickness 7.8 (0.307)
   Maximum run-out 0.6 (0.024)
Clutch pedal:
   Free play 5 (0.2)
   Travel   ..   ..   158 to 165 (6.22 to 6.50)

MANUAL TRANSMISSION

ZF gearbox:
  Ratios:

First	3.85:1
Second	2.08:1
Third	1.375:1
Top	1.0:1
Reverse	4.13:1
Speedometer drive	2.5:1

  Mainshaft:

End play	1.5 (0.059) maximum

  Layshaft:

End play	0.1 to 0.2 (0.004 to 0.008)

  Output flange:
    Run-out:

Radial	0.07 (0.0028)
Face	0.07 (0.0028)

Getrag gearbox:
  Ratios:

First	3.855:1
Second	2.202:1
Third	1.401:1
Top	1.0:1
Reverse	4.3:1
Speedometer drive	2.5:1

  Mainshaft:

End play	0.17 to 0.40 (0.0067 to 0.0157)

  Layshaft:

End play	0.1 to 0.2 (0.004 to 0.008)

  Output flange:
    Run-out:

Radial	0.07 (0.0028)
Face	0.07 (0.0028)

AUTOMATIC TRANSMISSION

Ratios up to 1976:

First	2.5:1
Second	1.5:1
Third	1.0:1
Reverse	2.0:1

Ratios from 1976:

First	2.478:1
Second	1.478:1
Third	1.0:1
Reverse	2.09:1

Stall speed:

2500	2010 ± 50rev/min
Remainder, pre-1976	2020 ± 50rev/min
1976 models	2100 ± 50rev/min

Towing:
  With propeller shaft attached:

Maximum distance	50km (30 miles)
Maximum speed	50km/hr (30 miles/hr)

REAR SUSPENSION

Coil springs:
  Free length:

CS models	364.5 (14.350)
Remainder	306.2 (12.055)

Cellrulcollan spring:
Length	85 (3.3465)
Rubber disc thickness	15 (0.5906)

Final drive ratio:
2500 models and USA	3.64:1
2800 and 3.0 S, SI, CS	3.45:1
Remainder	3.25:1

Wheel bearing:
End play	0.02 to 0.06 (0.0008 to 0.0024)

FRONT SUSPENSION

Coil springs:
Free length:
CS models	306.3 (12.059)
Remainder	322.6 (12.700)

Auxiliary springs:
Free length	85 ± 1 (3.3465 ± 0.03937)

Wheel bearing:
End play	0.02 to 0.06 (0.0008 to 0.0024)

Wheel alignment:
Normal load:
Front seats	2 × 65kg (2 × 143lb)
Rear seat	1 × 65kg (1 × 143lb)
Luggage compartment	30kg (66lb) left side
Fuel tank	Full
Toe-in	0° 10′ ± 10′
	1 ± 1 (0.04 ± 0.04)
Camber	0° ± 30′
Castor	9° 30′ ± 30′
Kingpin inclination	6° 20′ ± 30′

STEERING

Segment or roller spindle:
End play	0.05 (0.002)

ZF-Gemmer:
Ratio	16.4:1
Wheel turns	4.4

ZF hydraulic:
Ratio	15.7:1
Wheel turns	4.1

Power steering:
Pump speed:
Minimum	500rev/min
Maximum	6000rev/min
Pressure	82 ± 7 atmos (1165 ± 100lb/sq in)

BRAKES

Discs:
Diameter	272 ± 0.2 (10.709 ± 0.008)

Maximum run-out:
Measured on car	0.2 (0.008)
Measured on bench	0.05 (0.002)
Maximum variation in thickness in contact area ..	0.02 (0.0008)

Minimum thickness:
Front:
2500 and 2800 models	11.7 (0.461)
Remainder	21 (0.827)

Rear, where fitted:
    2500 and 2800 models 8.5 (0.335)
    Remainder 18 (0.709)

Brake pads:
    Blocks, minimum thickness 7 (0.276)
    Lining, minimum thickness 2 (0.079)

Brake drums:
    Diameter 250 (9.8425)
    Regrind stages 0.5 (0.020), 1.0 (0.040)
    Maximum ovality 0.1 (0.004)

Brake shoes
    Lining, minimum thickness 3.0 (0.118)

Handbrake:
    Diameter of drum 160 (6.30)

ELECTRICAL EQUIPMENT

Starter:
    Operating voltage   ..   ..   ..   6 to 12
    Test voltage   13
    Test temperature ..   ..   ..   20°C
    Type   ..   ..   ..   Bosch GF – 12V 1 PS (hp)
        Maximum output   ..   ..   1.03kW (1.38hp) at 210amp, 9.8 volts
        Maximum torque   ..   ..   17.5Nm (1.75kgm, 12.66lb ft) at 380amp, 8-volts
        Maximum speed 13,000rev/min
    Type   ..   ..   ..   Bosch GF – 12V 1.2 PS (hp)
        Maximum output   ..   ..   1.34kW (1.8hp) at 270amp, 9.1 volts
        Maximum torque   ..   ..   21Nm (2.1kgm, 15.2lb ft)
        Maximum speed   ..   ..   10,000rev/min at 540amp, 6.8 volts

Alternator:
    Type   ..   ..   ..   Bosch 14V 45A
        Nominal voltage   12
        Output voltage   14
        Maximum current 45amp
        Maximum output   ..   ..   630 watts
        Maximum speed 14,000rev/min
        Charging begins   ..   ..   1150rev/min approximately
        Maximum current at 6000rev/min
    Type   ..   ..   ..   Bosch 14V 55A
        Maximum current 55amp
        Maximum output   ..   ..   770 watts
        Maximum speed 12,000rev/min
        Charging begins   ..   ..   1000rev/min approximately

Voltage regulator:
    Nominal voltage   12
    Operating voltage   ..   ..   9 to 15
    Regulated voltage   ..   ..   13.5 to 14.2 at 20°C

Battery:
    Voltage   12
    Capacity 55amp/hr
    Earth   ..   ..   ..   Negative

CAPACITIES

	Litres	Pints	US pints
Engine	5	8.8	10.6
With filter	5.75	10.1	12.2

	Litres	Pints	US pints
Coolant with heater	12	21	25.4
Gearbox:			
ZF S4–18/3	1.2	2.1	2.5
Getrag 262/8	1.1	1.9	2.3
Automatic gearbox:			
Initial filling, ZF 3HP–20:			
2500	8	14	17
2800	8.3	14.6	17.5
Initial filling, ZF 3HP–22:			
All models	6	10.6	12.7
Rear axle	1.6	2.8 ·	3.4
Fuel tank:	Litres	Gallons	US gallons
Saloon, up to 1974	75	16.5	19.8
Coupé, up to 1974	70	15.4	18.5
Saloon, from 1974	78	17.2	20.6
Coupé, from 1974	72	15.8	19

TORQUE WRENCH SETTINGS

Engine:	Nm	kgm	lb ft
Cylinder head studs:			
1st stage	40	4	29
2nd stage	62.5	6.25	45
3rd stage at maximum 35 C ..	70	7	50
Main bearing caps	60	6	43
Big-end bolts	54	5.4	39
Flywheel to crankshaft	107	10.7	77
Chain tensioner plug	35	3.5	25
Rocker clamp screw	10	1	7
Pressure relief valve plug ..	27.5	2.75	20
Oil drain plug	62.5	6.25	45
Oil sump	10	1	7
Hollow screw, camshaft oil line ..	12	1.2	9
Vibration damper:			
Flat nut	250	25	180
Shouldered nut	450	45	325
Timing case covers	10	1	7
Crankshaft pulley	145	14.5	105
Timing sprocket	40	4	29
Fuel system:			
Carburetter to manifold	17	1.7	12
Heat sensitive switch	30	3	22
Fuel pump	12	1.2	9
Idle shut-off valve	2.75	0.275	2
Fuel tank attachments	45	4.5	33
Coolant system:			
Radiator:			
Cap	10	1	7
Drain plug	10	1	7
Mounting	8	0.8	6
Headertank:			
M6 bolts	9	0.9	6.5
M8 bolts	26	2.6	19
Oil cooler pipes	13	1.3	10
Heat sensitive switch	18	1.8	13

	Nm	kgm	lb ft
Exhaust system:			
Exhaust pipe:			
To manifold	31.5	3.15	23
To triangular flange	23	2.3	17
Retainer plate	9.5	0.95	6.9
Clip	16	1.6	12
Rear retaining bracket	45	4.5	33
Exhaust manifold:			
To cylinder head	31.5	3.15	23
M8 × 1mm plug	11	1.1	8
Collar nut, EGR pipe	10	1	7
Clutch:			
Clutch to flywheel	23	2.3	17
Thrust rod at pedal	33	3.3	24
Master cylinder bolts	23	2.3	17
Pipe and hose unions	14	1.4	10
Pivot bolt stop nut	34	3.4	25
Clutch housing to engine:			
M8	23	2.3	17
M10	45	4.5	33
Gearbox, manual:			
Gearbox to bellhousing:			
M8	23	2.3	17
M10	45	4.5	33
Output flange:			
ZF gearbox	150	15	108
Getrag gearbox	100	10	72
Sealing flange, Getrag	10	1	7
Support bracket mounting	23	2.3	17
Oil drain plug	60	6	43
Gearbox cover, Getrag	25	2.5	18
Rubber mounting, Getrag	25	2.5	18
Bracket on body, Getrag	25	2.5	18
Centring flange	23	2.3	17
Gearbox casing	23	2.3	17
Gearbox, automatic:			
Gearbox to engine:			
M8	25	2.5	18
M10	47	4.7	34
Shoulder nut, output flange	110	11	20
Oil drain plug	35	3.5	25
End cap:			
M24 × 1.5	60	6	43
M18 × 1.5	35	3.5	25
Allen screws	15	1.5	11
Throttle cable	15	1.5	11
Extension	15	1.5	11
Propeller shaft:			
Jurid joint, automatic:			
M12 bolts	118	11.8	85
Giubo joint:			
M10 bolts	67	6.7	48
M12 bolts	118	11.8	85
Centre bearing	23	2.3	17
Threaded bush	40	4	29
Final drive	67	6.7	48

	Nm	kgm	lb ft
Rear axle:			
Cover on housing	22.5	2.25	16
Drive shaft on drive flange	63	6.3	45
Support to body	150	15	108
Radius rod to body	27	2.7	20
Rubber bush in body	45	4.5	32
Final drive on rubber bush	85	8.5	61
Semi-trailing arm on axle support with normal load	70	7	50
Damper:			
Bottom	140	14	101
Top	26	2.6	19
Front axle:			
Damper:			
Bottom	76	7.6	55
Top	23	2.3	17
Threaded ring	130	13	94
Track rod on steering knuckle	46	4.6	33
Guide joint on track rod arm	60	6	43
Track control arm on axle support with normal load	160	16	116
Axle support on body	75	7.5	54
Tie bars with normal load	61	6.1	44
Steering:			
Steering wheel	57	5.7	41
Joint disc	22	2.2	16
Universal joint	26	2.6	19
Pitman arm	130	13	94
Pump bearing block to engine	23	2.3	17
Pump to bearing block	23	2.3	17
Adjustment bolt locknut	30	3	22
High pressure hoses	47	4.7	34
Steering box	45	4.5	33
Idler arm to support	90	9	65
Idler arm castellated nut	80	8	58
Trackrod arm:			
Castellated nut	38	3.8	27
Clamping bolt	14	1.4	10
Brakes:			
Caliper on steering knuckle	90	9	65
Caliper on rear axle	63	6.3	45
Disc on hub	63	6.3	45
Hose on caliper	14	1.4	10
Cap nut on brake pipe	15	1.5	11
Clamp on rear brake servo	23	2.3	17
Servo clamp on wheel arch	23	2.3	17
Caliper halves:			
Front	40	4	29
Rear	22	2.2	16
Wheel nuts	85	8.5	61
Brake light switch locknut	4	0.4	3
Electrical:			
Alternator pulley	40	4	29
Starter bolts	47	4.7	34
Spark plugs	27	2.7	34
Oil pressure switch	32	3.2	23

WIRING DIAGRAMS

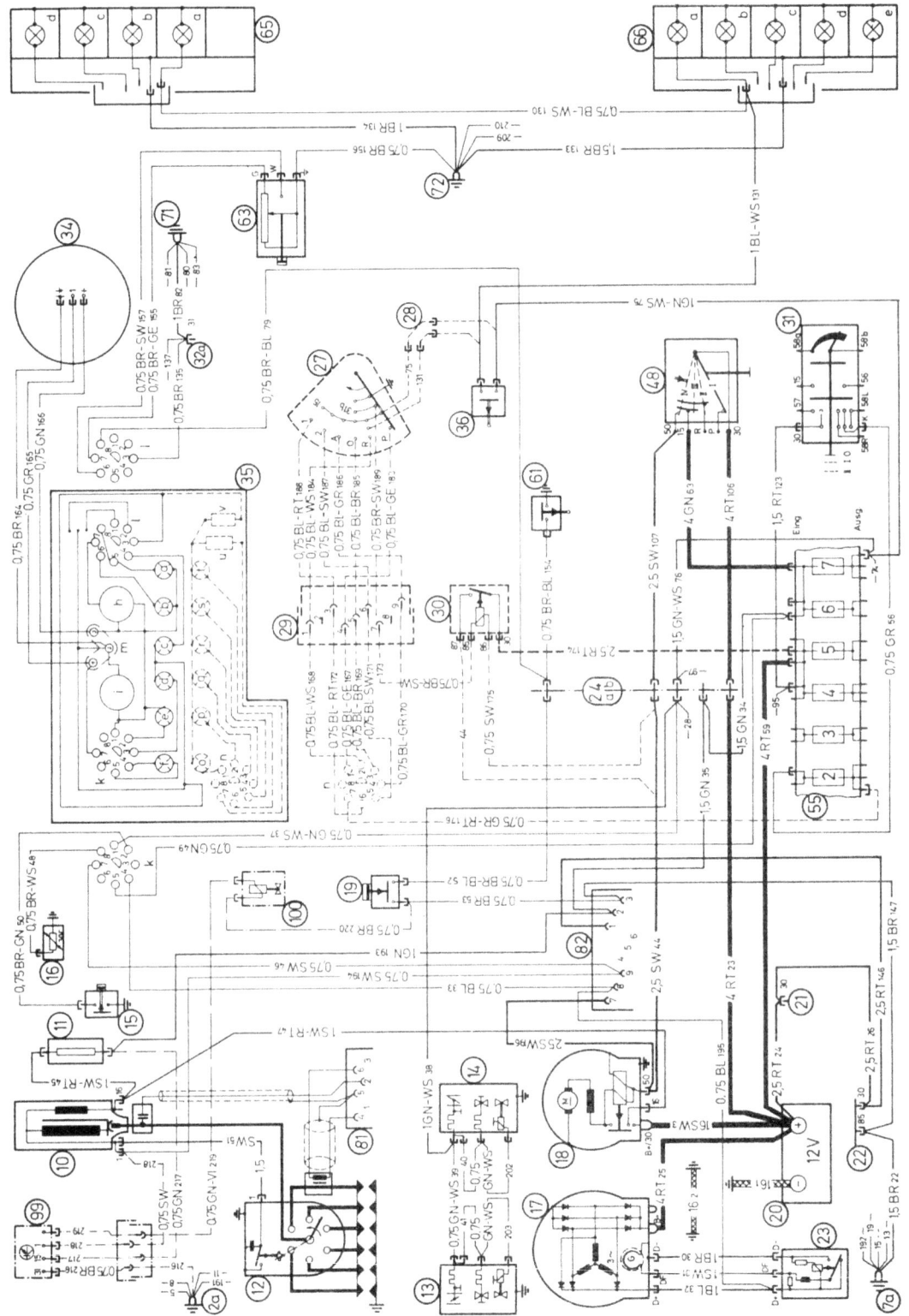

FIG 14:1 Wiring diagram. typical engine electrical system and controls

154

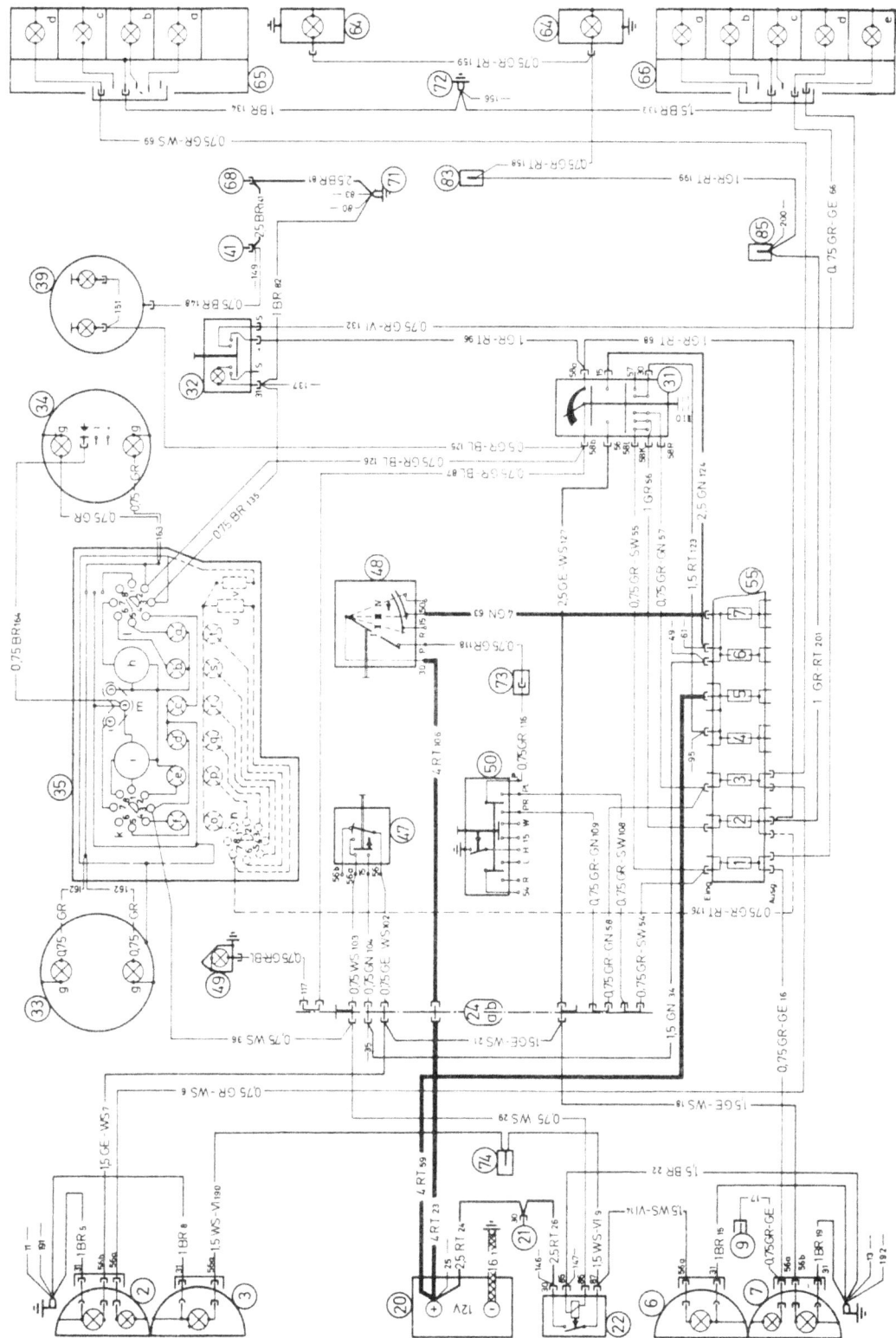

FIG 14·2 Wiring diagram, typical lighting system (Europe)

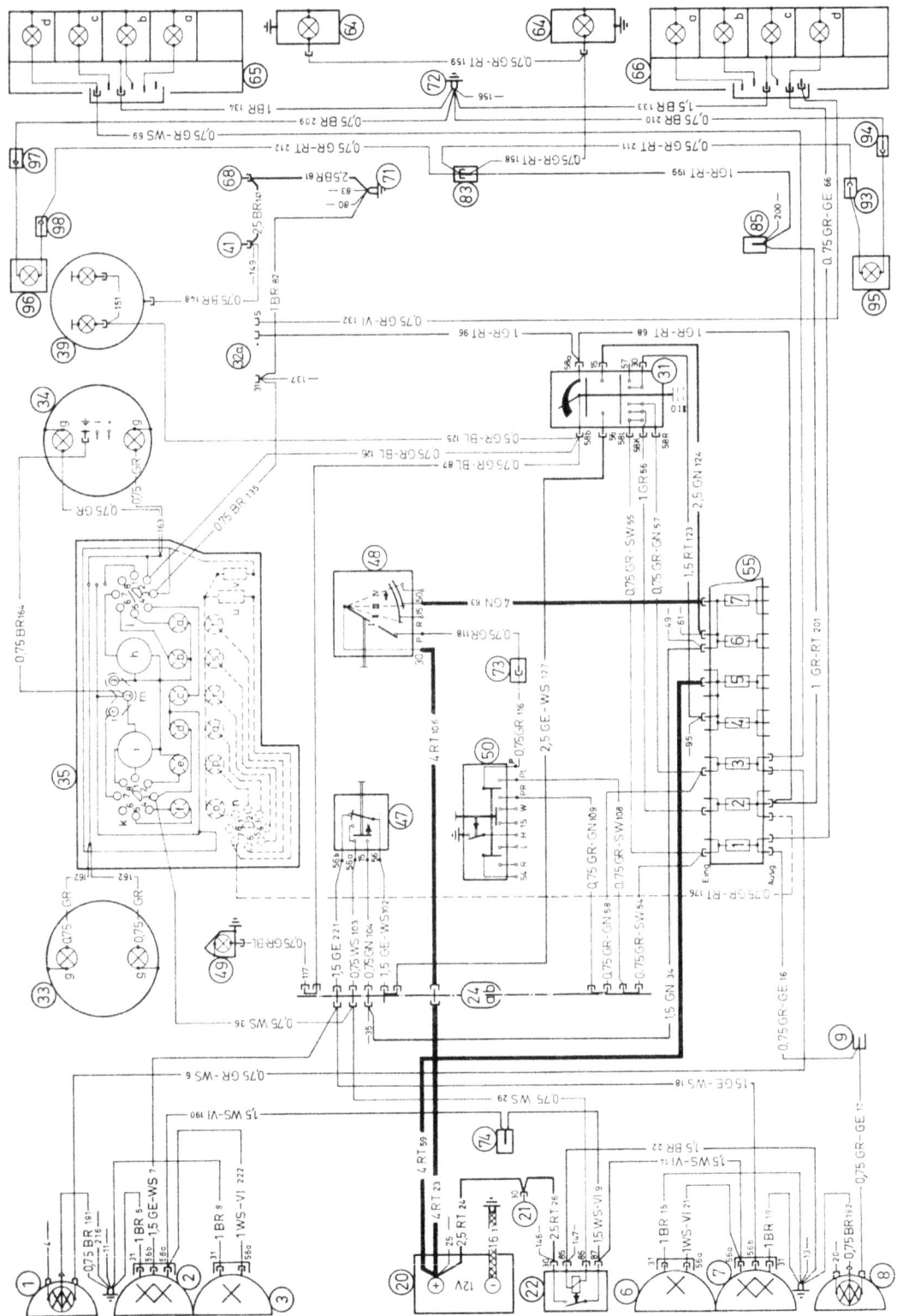

FIG 14:3 Wiring diagram, typical lighting system (USA)

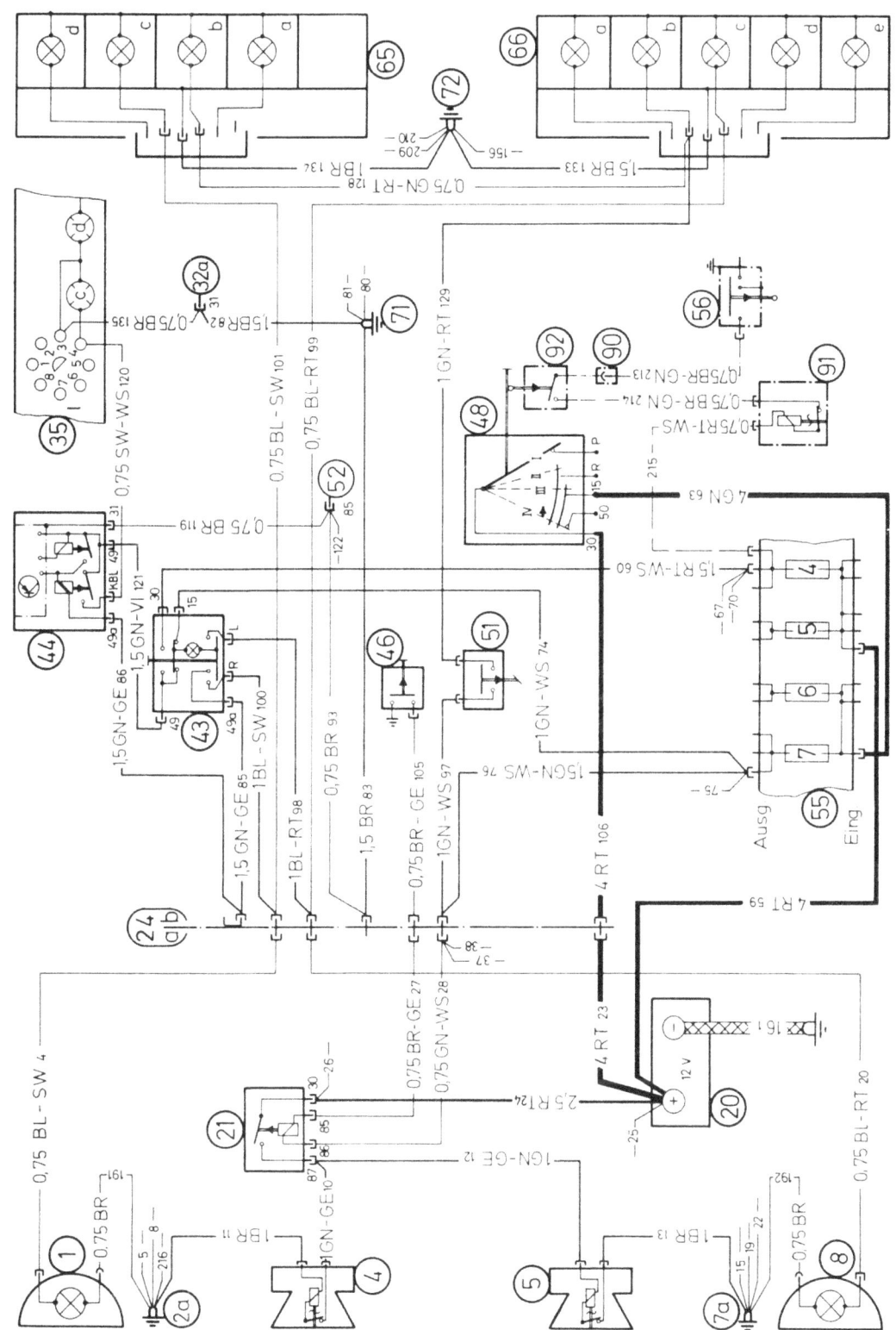

FIG 14:4 Wiring diagram, typical signalling system

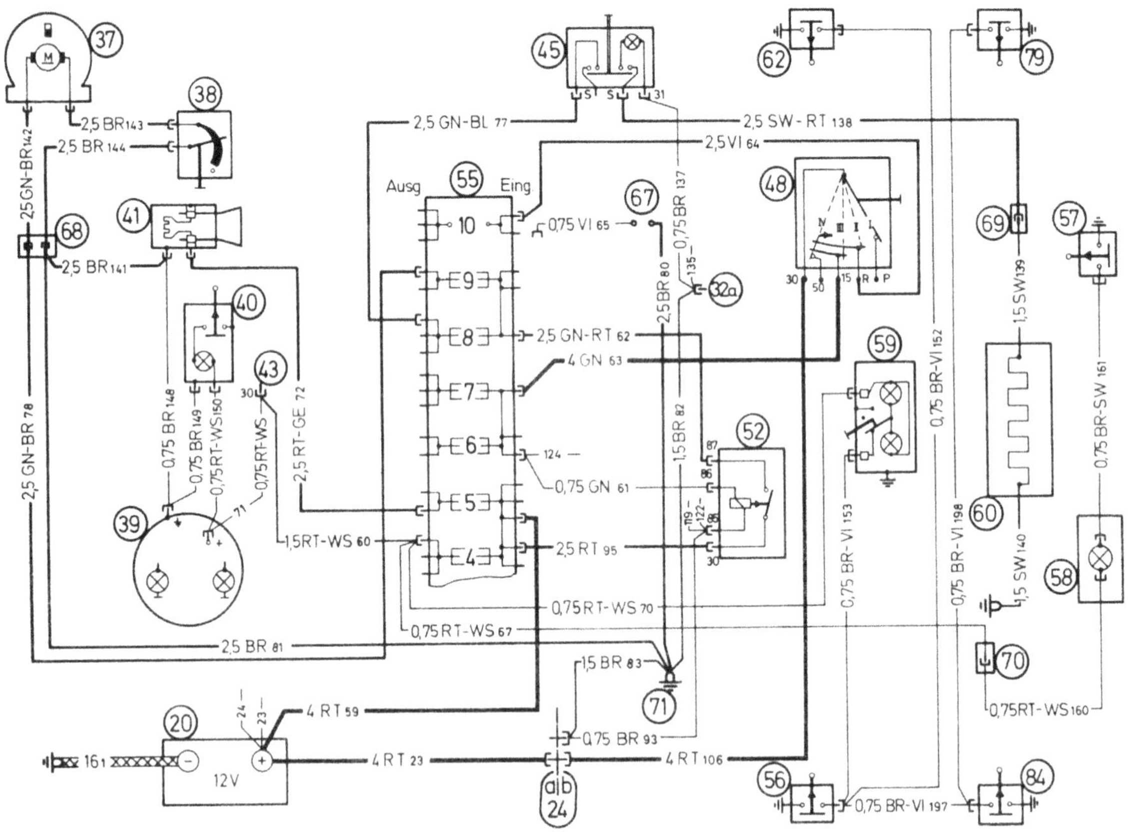

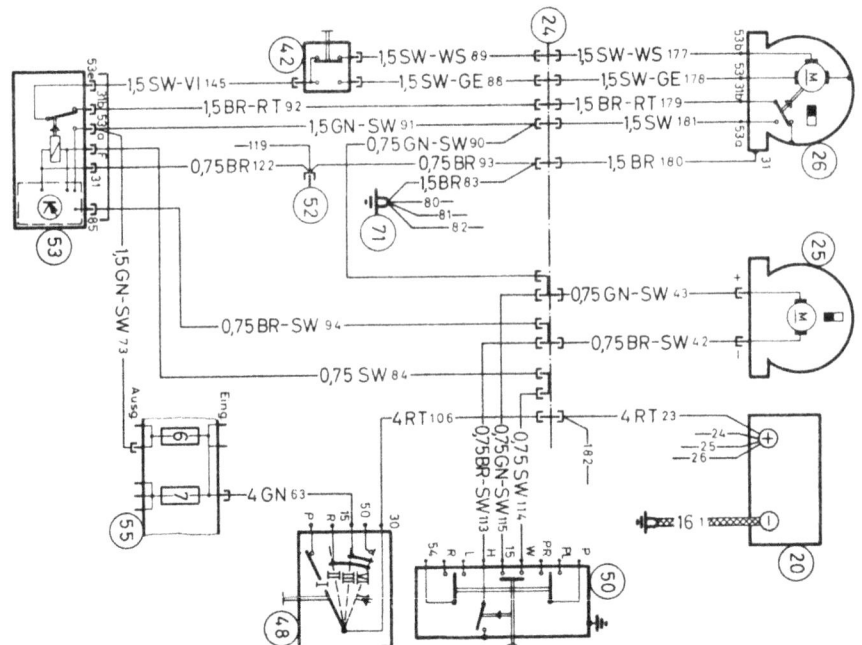

FIG 14:5 Wiring diagram, typical body electrical system

FIG 14:6 Wiring diagram, typical wiper and washer system

Key to wiring diagrams: 1 Turn indicator, front right 2 Low beam headlight with sidelight, right 2a Earth for headlight, right 3 High beam headlight, right 4 Horn right 5 Horn, left 6 High beam headlight, left 7 Low beam headlight with sidelight, left 7a Earth for headlight, left 8 Turn indicator, front left 9 Connection for engine compartment light 10 Coil 11 Primary resistance 12 Distributor 13 Electrical connection to automatic choke, front carburetter 14 Electrical connection to automatic choke, rear carburetter 15 Oil pressure switch 16 Remote coolant thermometer contact 17 Alternator 18 Starter 19 Brake fluid level control switch 20 Battery 21 Horn relay 22 Headlight high beam relay 23 Regulator 24a Plug board, engine side 24b Plug board, passenger side 25 Screenwasher pump 26 Screenwiper motor 27 Gearbox switch (automatic only) 28 Plug for gearbox switch (automatic only) 29 Plug for gearbox switch (automatic only) 30 Starter relay (automatic only) 31 Light switch 32 Switch for rear fog light 32a Connection for fog lamp switch

Instrument panel: 22 Speedometer 34 Revolution counter 35 Printed circuit panel a Brake fluid and handbrake telltale (red) b Fuel level telltale (white) c Turn indicator telltale (green) d Headlight main beam (blue) e Oil pressure telltale (orange) f Battery charge (red) g Dial illumination h Fuel gauge i Coolant thermometer k Plug for instrument panel l Plug for instrument panel m Plug for instrument panel

Automatic transmission only: n Plug for instrument panel o Selector lever position indicator P (white) p Selector lever position indicator R (red) q Selector lever position indicator O (white) r Selector lever position indicator A (green) s Selector lever position indicator 2 (green) t Selector lever position indicator 1 (green) u Primary resistance v Primary resistance

36 Reversing light switch (not automatic transmission) 37 Heater blower motor 38 Heater controls 39 Clock 40 Glove box illumination 41 Cigar lighter and socket 42 Wiper speed control 43 Hazard warning flasher switch 44 Hazard warning flasher unit 45 Switch for heated rear window 46 Horn push ring 47 Dip and flasher switch 48 Ignition/starter switch. I Halt II O III Fahrt (Drive) IV Start 49 Switch illumination 50 Turn indicator switch 51 Stoplight switch 52 Load shedding relay 53 Changeover relay 54 Delay relay 55 Fuse box 56 Door operated switch, left 57 Switch for luggage compartment light 58 Luggage compartment light 59 Interior light 60 Heated rear window 61 Handbrake contact 62 Door operated switch right 63 Fuel gauge contact 64 Licence plate lighting 65 Rear light cluster right a Reversing light b Stoplight c Turn indicator d Rear light 66 Rear light cluster left a Reversing light b Stoplight c Turn indicator d Rear light e Rear fog light 67 Connection for radio 68 Plug connector for heater 69 Plug connector for heated rear window 70 Plug connector for luggage compartment light 71 Earth 72 Earth 73 Plug connector for ignition/starter switch 74 Connection for fog light relay 75 Connection for electric sliding roof 76 Connection for electric fuel pump 77 Connection for motor operated radio aerial 78 Connection for trailer turn indicators 79 Door operated switch, rear right 81 Diagnostic plug: ignition system 82 Diagnostic plug 83 Connection for sidelight 84 Door-operated switch, rear left 85 Connection for reading light 90 Plug for warning buzzer (USA) 91 Warning buzzer (USA) 92 Warning buzzer contact (USA) 93 Plug for side marker light, rear left 94 Plug for side marker light, rear right 95 Side marker light, rear left 96 Side marker light, rear right 97 Plug for side marker light, rear right 98 Plug for side marker light, rear right 99 Engine speed governor switch (USA) 100 Magnetic valve (USA)

Wiring colour code: BL Blue BR Brown GE Yellow GN Green GR Grey RT Red SW Black WS White

Where a cable has two colour codes, the first denotes the main colour, the second the colour of the tracer stripe. The figure preceding the colour code indicates the cross sectional area of the wire in sq mm. The figure following the colour code is the individual cable number

Key to fuel injection circuit: 151 Electronic control unit 152 Multiple plug 153 Temperature sensor, air 154 Soldered joint 155 Soldered joint 156 Earth 157 Injection valves 158 Temperature sensor, coolant 159 Starting valve 160 Thermo-switch, coolant 161 Throttle valve switch 162 Main relay 163 Vacuum sensor 164 Triggering device 165 Fuel pump relay 166 Earth 167 Fuel pump 168 Plug connector 169 Cold starting relay 17 Battery 22 Primary resistor 23 Ignition coil 27 Starter 36 Fuse box 62 Ignition/starter switch 100 Connection for electric fuel pump

Wiring colour code: As for preceding wiring diagrams. Cables without code are black.

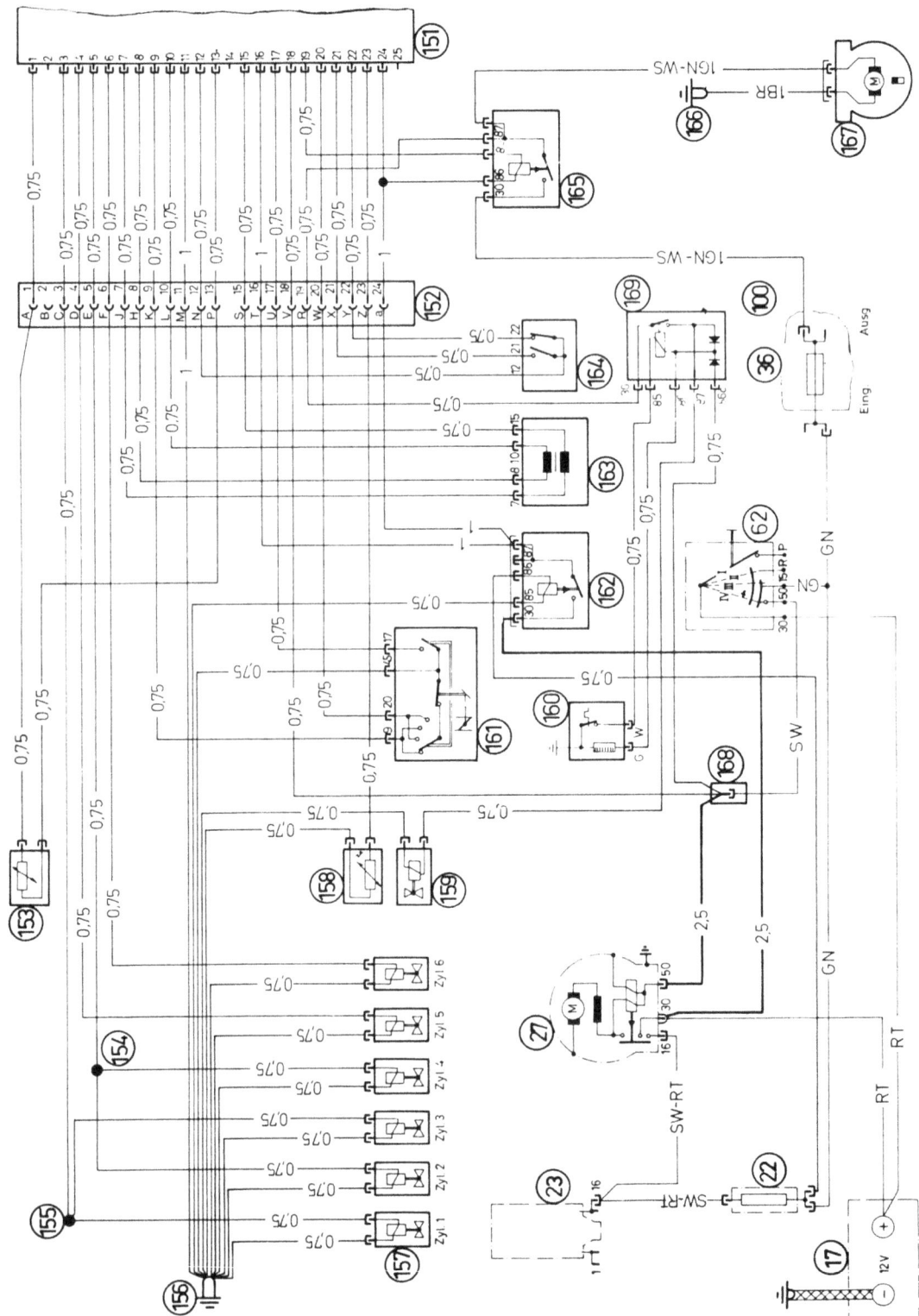

FIG 14:7   Electronically controlled fuel injection system circuit

HINTS ON MAINTENANCE AND OVERHAUL

There are few things more rewarding than the restoration of a vehicle's original peak of efficiency and smooth performance.

The following notes are intended to help the owner to reach that state of perfection. Providing that he possesses the basic manual skills he should have no difficulty in performing most of the operations detailed in this manual. It must be stressed, however, that where recommended in the manual, highly-skilled operations ought to be entrusted to experts, who have the necessary equipment, to carry out the work satisfactorily.

Quality of workmanship:

The hazardous driving conditions on the roads to-day demand that vehicles should be as nearly perfect, mechanically, as possible. It is therefore most important that amateur work be carried out with care, bearing in mind the often inadequate working conditions, and also the inferior tools which may have to be used. It is easy to counsel perfection in all things, and we recognise that it may be setting an impossibly high standard. We do, however, suggest that every care should be taken to ensure that a vehicle is as safe to take on the road as it is humanly possible to make it.

Safe working conditions:

Even though a vehicle may be stationary, it is still potentially dangerous if certain sensible precautions are not taken when working on it while it is supported on jacks or blocks. It is indeed preferable not to use jacks alone, but to supplement them with carefully placed blocks, so that there will be plenty of support if the car rolls off the jacks during a strenuous manoeuvre. Axle stands are an excellent way of providing a rigid base which is not readily disturbed. Piles of bricks are a dangerous substitute. Be careful not to get under heavy loads on lifting tackle, the load could fall. It is preferable not to work alone when lifting an engine, or when working underneath a vehicle which is supported well off the ground. To be trapped, particularly under the vehicle, may have unpleasant results if help is not quickly forthcoming. Make some provision, however humble, to deal with fires. Always disconnect a battery if there is a likelihood of electrical shorts. These may start a fire if there is leaking fuel about. This applies particularly to leads which can carry a heavy current, like those in the starter circuit. While on the subject of electricity, we must also stress the danger of using equipment which is run off the mains and which has no earth or has faulty wiring or connections. So many workshops have damp floors, and electrical shocks are of such a nature that it is sometimes impossible to let go of a live lead or piece of equipment due to the muscular spasms which take place.

Work demanding special care:

This involves the servicing of braking, steering and suspension systems. On the road, failure of the braking system may be disastrous. Make quite sure that there can be no possibility of failure through the bursting of rusty brake pipes or rotten hoses, nor to a sudden loss of pressure due to defective seals or valves.

Problems:

The chief problems which may face an operator are
1 External dirt.
2 Difficulty in undoing tight fixings.
3 Dismantling unfamiliar mechanisms.
4 Deciding in what respect parts are defective.
5 Confusion about the correct order for reassembly.
6 Adjusting running clearance.
7 Road testing.
8 Final tuning.

Practical suggestions to solve the problems:

1 Preliminary cleaning of large parts – engines, transmissions, steering, suspensions, etc. – should be carried out before removal from the car. Where road dirt and mud alone are present, wash clean with a high-pressure water jet, brushing to remove stubborn adhesions, and allow to drain and dry. Where oil or grease is also present, wash down with a proprietary compound (Gunk, Teepol etc.) applying with a stiff brush – an old paint brush is suitable – into all crevices. Cover the distributor and ignition coils with a polythene bag and then apply a strong water jet to clear the loosened deposits. Allow to drain and dry. The assemblies will then be sufficiently clean to remove and transfer to the bench for the next stage.

On the bench, further cleaning can be carried out, first wiping the parts as free as possible from grease with old newspaper. Avoid using rag or cotton waste which can leave clogging fibres behind. Any remaining grease can be removed with a brush dipped in paraffin. If necessary, traces of paraffin can be removed by carbon tetrachloride. Avoid using paraffin or petrol in large quantities for cleaning in enclosed areas, such as garages, on account of the high fire risk.

When all exteriors have been cleaned, and not before, dismantling can be commenced. This ensures that dirt will not enter into interiors and orifices revealed by dismantling. In the next phases, where components have to be cleaned, use carbon tetrachloride in preference to petrol and keep the containers covered except when in use. After the components have been cleaned, plug small holes with tapered hard wood plugs cut to size and blank off larger orifices with greaseproof paper and masking tape. Do not use soft wood plugs or matchsticks as they may break.

2 It is not advisable to hammer on the end of a screw thread, but if it must be done, first screw on a nut to protect the thread, and use a lead hammer. This applies particularly to the removal of tapered cotters. Nuts and bolts seem to 'grow' together, especially in exhaust systems. If penetrating oil does not work, try the judicious application of heat, but be careful of starting a fire. Asbestos sheet or cloth is useful to isolate heat.

Tight bushes or pieces of tail-pipe rusted into a silencer can be removed by splitting them with an open-ended hacksaw. Tight screws can sometimes be started by a tap from a hammer on the end of a suitable screwdriver. Many tight fittings will yield to the judicious use of a hammer, but it must be a soft-faced hammer if damage is to be avoided, use a heavy block on the opposite side to absorb shock. Any parts of the steering system which have been damaged should be renewed, as attempts to repair them may lead to cracking and subsequent failure, and steering ball joints should be disconnected using a recommended tool to prevent damage.

3   It often happens that an owner is baffled when trying to dismantle an unfamiliar piece of equipment. So many modern devices are pressed together or assembled by spinning-over flanges, that they must be sawn apart. The intention is that the whole assembly must be renewed. However, parts which appear to be in one piece to the naked eye, may reveal close-fitting joint lines when inspected with a magnifying glass, and, this may provide the necessary clue to dismantling. Lefthanded screw threads are used where rotational forces would tend to unscrew a righthanded screw thread.

Be very careful when dismantling mechanisms which may come apart suddenly. Work in an enclosed space where the parts will be contained, and drape a piece of cloth over the device if springs are likely to fly in all directions. Mark everything which might be reassembled in the wrong position, scratched symbols may be used on unstressed parts, or a sequence of tiny dots from a centre punch can be useful. Stressed parts should never be scratched or centre-popped as this may lead to cracking under working conditions. Store parts which look alike in the correct order for reassembly. Never rely upon memory to assist in the assembly of complicated mechanisms, especially when they will be dismantled for a long time, but make notes, and drawings to supplement the diagrams in the manual, and put labels on detached wires. Rust stains may indicate unlubricated wear. This can sometimes be seen round the outside edge of a bearing cup in a universal joint. Look for bright rubbing marks on parts which normally should not make heavy contact. These might prove that something is bent or running out of truth. For example, there might be bright marks on one side of a piston, at the top near the ring grooves, and others at the bottom of the skirt on the other side. This could well be the clue to a bent connecting rod. Suspected cracks can be proved by heating the component in a light oil to approximately 100°C, removing, drying off, and dusting with french chalk, if a crack is present the oil retained in the crack will stain the french chalk.

4   In determining wear, and the degree, against the permissible limits set in the manual, accurate measurement can only be achieved by the use of a micrometer. In many cases, the wear is given to the fourth place of decimals; that is in ten-thousandths of an inch. This can be read by the vernier scale on the barrel of a good micrometer. Bore diameters are more difficult to determine. If, however, the matching shaft is accurately measured, the degree of play in the bore can be felt as a guide to its suitability. In other cases, the shank of a twist drill of known diameter is a handy check.

Many methods have been devised for determining the clearance between bearing surfaces. To-day the best and simplest is by the use of Plastigage, obtainable from most garages. A thin plastic thread is laid between the two surfaces and the bearing is tightened, flattening

the thread. On removal, the width of the thread is compared with a scale supplied with the thread and the clearance is read off directly. Sometimes joint faces leak persistently, even after gasket renewal. The fault will then be traceable to distortion, dirt or burrs. Studs which are screwed into soft metal frequently raise burrs at the point of entry. A quick cure for this is to chamfer the edge of the hole in the part which fits over the stud.

5   **Always check a replacement part with the original one before it is fitted.**

If parts are not marked, and the order for reassembly is not known, a little detective work will help. Look for marks which are due to wear to see if they can be mated. Joint faces may not be identical due to manufacturing errors, and parts which overlap may be stained, giving a clue to the correct position. Most fixings leave identifying marks especially if they were painted over on assembly. It is then easier to decide whether a nut, for instance, has a plain, a spring, or a shakeproof washer under it. All running surfaces become 'bedded' together after long spells of work and tiny imperfections on one part will be found to have left corresponding marks on the other. This is particularly true of shafts and bearings and even a score on a cylinder wall will show on the piston.

6   Checking end float or rocker clearances by feeler gauge may not always give accurate results because of wear. For instance, the rocker tip which bears on a valve stem may be deeply pitted, in which case the feeler will simply be bridging a depression. Thrust washers may also wear depressions in opposing faces to make accurate measurement difficult. End float is then easier to check by using a dial gauge. It is common practice to adjust end play in bearing assemblies, like front hubs with taper rollers, by doing up the axle nut until the hub becomes stiff to turn and then backing it off a little. Do not use this method with ballbearing hubs as the assembly is often preloaded by tightening the axle nut to its fullest extent. If the splitpin hole will not line up, file the base of the nut a little.

Steering assemblies often wear in the straight-ahead position. If any part is adjusted, make sure that it remains free when moved from lock to lock. Do not be surprised if an assembly like a steering gearbox, which is known to be carefully adjusted outside the car, becomes stiff when it is bolted in place. This will be due to distortion of the case by the pull of the mounting bolts, particularly if the mounting points are not all touching together. This problem may be met in other equipment and is cured by careful attention to the alignment of mounting points.

When a spanner is stamped with a size and A/F it means that the dimension is the width between the jaws and has no connection with ANF, which is the designation for the American National Fine thread. Coarse threads like Whitworth are rarely used on cars to-day except for studs which screw into soft aluminium or cast iron. For this reason it might be found that the top end of a cylinder head stud has a fine thread and the lower end a coarse thread to screw into the cylinder block. If the car has mainly UNF threads then it is likely that any coarse threads will be UNC, which are not the same as Whitworth. Small sizes have the same number of threads in Whitworth and UNC, but in the ½ inch size for example, there are twelve threads to the inch in the former and thirteen in the latter.

7 After a major overhaul, particularly if a great deal of work has been done on the braking, steering and suspension systems, it is advisable to approach the problem of testing with care. If the braking system has been overhauled, apply heavy pressure to the brake pedal and get a second operator to check every possible source of leakage. The brakes may work extremely well, but a leak could cause complete failure after a few miles.

Do not fit the hub caps until every wheel nut has been checked for tightness, and make sure the tyre pressures are correct. Check the levels of coolant, lubricants and hydraulic fluids. Being satisfied that all is well, take the car on the road and test the brakes at once. Check the steering and the action of the handbrake. Do all this at moderate speeds on quiet roads, and make sure there is no other vehicle behind you when you try a rapid stop.

Finally, remember that many parts settle down after a time, so check for tightness of all fixings after the car has been on the road for a hundred miles or so.

8 It is useless to tune an engine which has not reached its normal running temperature. In the same way, the tune of an engine which is stiff after a rebore will be different when the engine is again running free. Remember too, that rocker clearances on pushrod operated valve gear will change when the cylinder head nuts are tightened after an initial period of running with a new head gasket.

Trouble may not always be due to what seems the obvious cause. Ignition, carburation and mechanical condition are interdependent and spitting back through the carburetter, which might be attributed to a weak mixture, can be caused by a sticking inlet valve.

For one final hint on tuning, never adjust more than one thing at a time or it will be impossible to tell which adjustment produced the desired result.

NOTES

GLOSSARY OF TERMS

Allen key Cranked wrench of hexagonal section for use with socket head screws.

Alternator Electrical generator producing alternating current. Rectified to direct current for battery charging.

Ambient temperature Surrounding atmospheric temperature.

Annulus Used in engineering to indicate the outer ring gear of an epicyclic gear train.

Armature The shaft carrying the windings, which rotates in the magnetic field of a generator or starter motor. That part of a solenoid or relay which is activated by the magnetic field.

Axial In line with, or pertaining to, an axis.

Backlash Play in meshing gears.

Balance lever A bar where force applied at the centre is equally divided between connections at the ends.

Banjo axle Axle casing with large diameter housing for the crownwheel and differential.

Bendix pinion A self-engaging and self-disengaging drive on a starter motor shaft.

Bevel pinion A conical shaped gearwheel, designed to mesh with a similar gear with an axis usually at 90 deg. to its own.

bhp Brake horse power, measured on a dynamometer.

bmep Brake mean effective pressure. Average pressure on a piston during the working stroke.

Brake cylinder Cylinder with hydraulically operated piston(s) acting on brake shoes or pad(s).

Brake regulator Control valve fitted in hydraulic braking system which limits brake pressure to rear brakes during heavy braking to prevent rear wheel locking.

Camber Angle at which a wheel is tilted from the vertical.

Capacitor Modern term for an electrical condenser. Part of distributor assembly, connected across contact breaker points, acts as an interference suppressor.

Castellated Top face of a nut, slotted across the flats, to take a locking splitpin.

Castor Angle at which the kingpin or swivel pin is tilted when viewed from the side.

cc Cubic centimetres. Engine capacity is arrived at by multiplying the area of the bore in sq cm by the stroke in cm by the number of cylinders.

Clevis U-shaped forked connector used with a clevis pin, usually at handbrake connections.

Collet A type of collar, usually split and located in a groove in a shaft, and held in place by a retainer. The arrangement used to retain the spring(s) on a valve stem in most cases.

Commutator Rotating segmented current distributor between armature windings and brushes in generator or motor.

Compression ratio The ratio, or quantitative relation, of the total volume (piston at bottom of stroke) to the unswept volume (piston at top of stroke) in an engine cylinder.

Condenser See capacitor.

Core plug Plug for blanking off a manufacturing hole in a casting.

Crownwheel Large bevel gear in rear axle, driven by a bevel pinion attached to the propeller shaft. Sometimes called a 'ring gear'.

'C'-spanner Like a 'C' with a handle. For use on screwed collars without flats, but with slots or holes.

Damper Modern term for shock-absorber, used in vehicle suspension systems to damp out spring oscillations.

Depression The lowering of atmospheric pressure as in the inlet manifold and carburetter.

Dowel Close tolerance pin, peg, tube, or bolt, which accurately locates mating parts.

Drag link Rod connecting steering box drop arm (pitman arm) to nearest front wheel steering arm in certain types of steering systems.

Dry liner Thinwall tube pressed into cylinder bore

Dry sump Lubrication system where all oil is scavenged from the sump, and returned to a separate tank.

Dynamo See Generator.

Electrode Terminal, part of an electrical component, such as the points or 'Electrodes' of a sparking plug.

Electrolyte In lead-acid car batteries a solution of sulphuric acid and distilled water.

End float The axial movement between associated parts, end play.

EP Extreme pressure. In lubricants, special grades for heavily loaded bearing surfaces, such as gear teeth in a gearbox, or crownwheel and pinion in a rear axle.

Fade	Of brakes. Reduced efficiency due to overheating.	**Journals**	Those parts of a shaft that are in contact with the bearings.
Field coils	Windings on the polepieces of motors and generators.	**Kingpin**	The main vertical pin which carries the front wheel spindle, and permits steering movement. May be called 'steering pin' or 'swivel pin'.
Fillets	Narrow finishing strips usually applied to interior bodywork.		
First motion shaft	Input shaft from clutch to gearbox.	**Layshaft**	The shaft which carries the laygear in the gearbox. The laygear is driven by the first motion shaft and drives the third motion shaft according to the gear selected. Sometimes called the 'countershaft' or 'second motion shaft.'
Fullflow filter	Filters in which all the oil is pumped to the engine. If the element becomes clogged, a bypass valve operates to pass unfiltered oil to the engine.		
FWD	Front wheel drive.	**lb ft**	A measure of twist or torque. A pull of 10 lb at a radius of 1 ft is a torque of 10 lb ft.
Gear pump	Two meshing gears in a close fitting casing. Oil is carried from the inlet round the outside of both gears in the spaces between the gear teeth and casing to the outlet, the meshing gear teeth prevent oil passing back to the inlet, and the oil is forced through the outlet port.		
		lb/sq in	Pounds per square inch.
		Little-end	The small, or piston end of a connecting rod. Sometimes called the 'small-end'.
		LT	Low Tension. The current output from the battery.
Generator	Modern term for 'Dynamo'. When rotated produces electrical current.	**Mandrel**	Accurately manufactured bar or rod used for test or centring purposes.
Grommet	A ring of protective or sealing material. Can be used to protect pipes or leads passing through bulkheads.	**Manifold**	A pipe, duct, or chamber, with several branches.
		Needle rollers	Bearing rollers with a length many times their diameter.
Grubscrew	Fully threaded headless screw with screwdriver slot. Used for locking, or alignment purposes.	**Oil bath**	Reservoir which lubricates parts by immersion. In air filters, a separate oil supply for wetting a wire mesh element to hold the dust.
Gudgeon pin	Shaft which connects a piston to its connecting rod. Sometimes called 'wrist pin', or 'piston pin'.		
Halfshaft	One of a pair transmitting drive from the differential.	**Oil wetted**	In air filters, a wire mesh element lightly oiled to trap and hold airborne dust.
Helical	In spiral form. The teeth of helical gears are cut at a spiral angle to the side faces of the gearwheel.	**Overlap**	Period during which inlet and exhaust valves are open together.
		Panhard rod	Bar connected between fixed point on chassis and another on axle to control sideways movement.
Hot spot	Hot area that assists vapourisation of fuel on its way to cylinders. Often provided by close contact between inlet and exhaust manifolds.		
		Pawl	Pivoted catch which engages in the teeth of a ratchet to permit movement in one direction only.
HT	High Tension. Applied to electrical current produced by the ignition coil for the sparking plugs.	**Peg spanner**	Tool with pegs, or pins, to engage in holes or slots in the part to be turned.
Hydrometer	A device for checking specific gravity of liquids. Used to check specific gravity of electrolyte.	**Pendant pedals**	Pedals with levers that are pivoted at the top end.
Hypoid bevel gears	A form of bevel gear used in the rear axle drive gears. The bevel pinion meshes below the centre line of the crownwheel, giving a lower propeller shaft line.	**Phillips screwdriver**	A cross-point screwdriver for use with the cross-slotted heads of Phillips screws.
		Pinion	A small gear, usually in relation to another gear.
Idler	A device for passing on movement: A free running gear between driving and driven gears. A lever transmitting track rod movement to a side rod in steering gear.	**Piston-type damper**	Shock absorber in which damping is controlled by a piston working in a closed oil-filled cylinder.
		Preloading	Preset static pressure on ball or roller bearings not due to working loads.
Impeller	A centrifugal pumping element. Used in water pumps to stimulate flow.	**Radial**	Radiating from a centre, like the spokes of a wheel.

Radius rod	Pivoted arm confining movement of a part to an arc of fixed radius.
Ratchet	Toothed wheel or rack which can move in one direction only, movement in the other being prevented by a pawl.
Ring gear	A gear tooth ring attached to outer periphery of flywheel. Starter pinion engages with it during starting.
Runout	Amount by which rotating part is out of true.
Semi-floating axle	Outer end of rear axle halfshaft is carried on bearing inside axle casing. Wheel hub is secured to end of shaft.
Servo	A hydraulic or pneumatic system for assisting, or, augmenting a physical effort. See 'Vacuum Servo'.
Setscrew	One which is threaded for the full length of the shank.
Shackle	A coupling link, used in the form of two parallel pins connected by side plates to secure the end of the master suspension spring and absorb the effects of deflection.
Shell bearing	Thinwalled steel shell lined with anti-friction metal. Usually semi-circular and used in pairs for main and big-end bearings.
Shock absorber	See 'Damper'.
Silentbloc	Rubber bush bonded to inner and outer metal sleeves.
Socket-head screw	Screw with hexagonal socket for an Allen key.
Solenoid	A coil of wire creating a magnetic field when electric current passes through it. Used with a soft iron core to operate contacts or a mechanical device.
Spur gear	A gear with teeth cut axially across the periphery.
Stub axle	Short axle fixed at one end only.
Tachometer	An instrument for accurate measurement of rotating speed. Usually indicates in revolutions per minute.

TDC	Top Dead Centre. The highest point reached by a piston in a cylinder, with the crank and connecting rod in line.
Thermostat	Automatic device for regulating temperature. Used in vehicle coolant systems to open a valve which restricts circulation at low temperature.
Third motion shaft	Output shaft of gearbox.
Threequarter floating axle	Outer end of rear axle halfshaft flanged and bolted to wheel hub, which runs on bearing mounted on outside of axle casing. Vehicle weight is not carried by the axle shaft.
Thrust bearing or washer	Used to reduce friction in rotating parts subject to axial loads.
Torque	Turning or twisting effort. See 'lb ft'.
Track rod	The bar(s) across the vehicle which connect the steering arms and maintain the front wheels in their correct alignment.
UJ	Universal joint. A coupling between shafts which permits angular movement.
UNF	Unified National Fine screw thread.
Vacuum servo	Device used in brake system, using difference between atmospheric pressure and inlet manifold depression to operate a piston which acts to augment brake pressure as required. See 'Servo'.
Venturi	A restriction or 'choke' in a tube, as in a carburetter, used to increase velocity to obtain a reduction in pressure.
Vernier	A sliding scale for obtaining fractional readings of the graduations of an adjacent scale.
Welch plug	A domed thin metal disc which is partially flattened to lock in a recess. Used to plug core holes in castings.
Wet liner	Removable cylinder barrel, sealed against coolant leakage, where the coolant is in direct contact with the outer surface.
Wet sump	A reservoir attached to the crankcase to hold the lubricating oil.

NOTES

INDEX